THE POLITICAL
OLYMPICS

THE POLITICAL OLYMPICS

Moscow,
Afghanistan,
and the
1980 U.S. Boycott

Derick L. Hulme, Jr.

PRAEGER

New York
Westport, Connecticut
London

Copyright Acknowledgments

The author and publisher are grateful to the following for allowing the use of their material:

From "Political Problems in the Olympic Games" by J. M. Leiper. In *Olympism* (pp. 106–13) by J. Segrave and D. Chu (Eds.), 1981, Champaign, IL: Human Kinetics. Copyright 1981 by J. Segrave and D. Chu. Reprinted by permission.

From "Nationalism: Inevitable and Incurable?" by D. P. Toohey and K. Warning. In *Olympism* (pp. 120–24) by J. Segrave and D. Chu (Eds.), 1981, Champaign, IL: Human Kinetics. Copyright 1981 by J. Segrave and D. Chu. Reprinted by permission.

Excerpts from pp. 10–12, 71, 144–45, 151, 172–73, 175–85, 187–88, 192, 194–96, 202, 205, 208–15, 222 from MY OLYMPIC YEARS by Lord Killanin. Copyright © 1983 by Lord Killanin. Reprinted by permission of William Morrow & Co., Inc.

Excerpts from pp. 10–12, 71, 151, 175–85, 187–88, 192, 194, 196, 202, 205, 208, 209, 212–14 from *My Olympic Years* by Lord Killanin. Copyright © 1983 by Lord Killanin. Reprinted by permission of Martin Secker & Warburg.

Library of Congress Cataloging-in-Publication Data

Hulme, Derick L., Jr.
   The political olympics : Moscow, Afghanistan, and the 1980 U.S.
boycott / Derick L. Hulme, Jr.
      p.   cm.
   Includes bibliographical references.
   ISBN 0–275–93466–7 (alk. paper)
   1. Sports and state—United States. 2. Olympic Games (22nd : 1980 :
Moscow, R.S.F.S.R.) 3. Boycott—United States. 4. United States—
Foreign relations.   I. Title.
GV706.35.H85   1990
796.98—dc20   89–78402

British Library Cataloging-in-Publication Data is available.

Library of Congress Catalog Card Number: 89–78402
ISBN: 0–275–93466–7

First published in 1990

Praeger Publishers, One Madison Avenue, New York, NY 10010
An imprint of Greenwood Publishing Group, Inc.

Printed in the United States of America

The paper used in this book complies with the
Permanent Paper Standard issued by the National
Information Standards Organization (Z39.48-1984).

10 9 8 7 6 5 4 3 2 1

For Olivia Lane Hulme,
with all my love

Contents

Preface   ix

Acknowledgments   xiii

1. **Introduction**   1

2. **The Boycott Decision**   17

3. **The Domestic Campaign**   21

4. **The International Campaign**   43

5. **Consequences of the Boycott**   75

6. **Endemic Obstacles to the Boycott**   89

7. **U.S. Shortcomings**   105

8. **Evaluation of the Use of the Boycott**   123

Notes   129

Selected Bibliography   169

Index   171

Preface

AFGHAN PRESIDENT IS OUSTED
AND EXECUTED IN KABUL COUP
REPORTEDLY WITH SOVIET HELP
New York Times, 28 December 1979

The movement of Soviet troops into Afghanistan on December 27, 1979, precipitated a chain of events that was ultimately to lead to the largest Olympic
boycott in the history of the Games.[1] Never before had the tool of sport been
wielded on such a massive scale in order to punish politically an "offending"
nation. While the politicizing of sport may be thought to be a recent phenomenon, sport and politics have been integrally related from ancient times.[2] The
1980 Olympic boycott was unprecedented in scope, however, and as such served
to draw attention to a dimension of sport not normally reflected upon: politics.

When Dr. Rolf Pauls, the West German ambassador to an emergency meeting in Brussels of the North Atlantic Treaty Organization (NATO), broached
the idea of a boycott of the upcoming Moscow Olympics as a retaliatory measure for Soviet actions in Afghanistan, little did he realize just what he had
begun.[3] Although Pauls's suggestion, put forth without the authorization of his
government and much to its dismay, elicited a degree of interest, no firm commitments were either sought or received. However, within official U.S. governmental circles, the idea of a boycott quickly gained supporters, the most
important of whom was President Jimmy Carter. Concluding that "direct military action on our part was not advisable," Carter proceeded to review his

possible avenues of action. He stressed that during his meetings with the National Security Council "we inventoried every conceivable alternative. World-wide condemnation, continuing publicity about the Soviet crime, economic sanctions that would hit the Soviets where they were most vulnerable, and indirect military assistance to the Afghan freedom fighters were all available options." [4]

The president, barely one week after the invasion, focused on the Summer Games as his primary weapon to seek "worldwide condemnation." Used in conjunction with an embargo on U.S. grain shipments and certain high technology items, a boycott would be one crucial element in a multifaceted U.S., and, it was hoped, Western response. As one senior government official realistically surmised, "Short of war, short of bombing people, what can we do in the modern world to express outrage? . . . We have to take the options that are there." [5] Carter thus took to the American people, and to a worldwide audience as well, his threat to boycott the 1980 Moscow Olympics: "Although the United States would prefer not to withdraw from the Olympic games scheduled in Moscow this summer, the Soviet Union must realize that its continued aggressive actions will endanger both the participation of athletes and the travel to Moscow by spectators who would normally wish to attend the Olympic games." [6]

With this pronouncement began what would become a complex, difficult, and, at best, only partially successful, boycott movement. This work will address the general question of the degree to which political leaders can hope to utilize sport in a punitive fashion in the international arena. The U.S. boycott will be examined as a means through which we can hope to make a number of far-reaching conclusions. The scope of U.S. actions, coupled with the enormous effort undertaken by the Carter administration, allows one to construct a credible case for the U.S. initiative being in many ways a paradigm for similar endeavors in the future.

There are a number of specific questions with which this study will be concerned. The first of these issues is how government leaders come to the use of international sport as a means of achieving political goals. Are actions in the arena of international sport indeed appropriate in terms of the political issues at hand? What other options are considered, and why are these rejected in favor of what many perceive as a rather unorthodox use of sports? If we are to achieve any understanding as to how sport can be employed in at least some political fashion (a conclusion which should not be embraced too readily), we must address these questions. After all, it is imperative to determine why sport has been used for political purposes in the past if we are to posit any conclusions as to its future efficacy.

The second issue that demands attention is the question of how sport is used as a political weapon. Through an examination of the process by which the U.S. boycott was realized, the obstacles which are likely to confront such efforts in the future are suggested. The United States-sponsored boycott had several difficulties particular to itself: an ignorance of the nature of the international sporting establishment by those involved in the boycott's implementation; the poor political judgment in general of the Carter administration; and President Carter's ill-advised tendency to project moralistic visions of interpersonal relations onto the area of global politics.[7] Among the many problems endemic to any large-scale political use of sport are the necessity of soliciting support from the broadest spectrum of states in an extremely limited time and the need to comprehend thoroughly the highly complex and differentiated organizational structure of the international sporting establishment. There is also the difficulty of overcoming the heartfelt belief of many that the politicizing of one of the few remaining symbols of man's hopes for increased cooperation and human understanding—international sport—must be stopped.

The implementation of the boycott campaign thus revealed that any such effort must surmount numerous obstacles. Difficulties particular to each action will likely manifest themselves in conjunction with problems of a more general nature. An awareness of the magnitude and probability of implementational barriers is essential for any statesman contemplating the political use of sport.

The third and final issue which will be addressed by this work concerns the actual results of the U.S. boycott effort. Did the boycott succeed in inflicting the amount of political damage on the Soviet Union originally anticipated by the White House? What costs were borne by the Carter administration for its action? How will the ramifications of the boycott affect the likelihood of other leaders engaging in similar actions in the future?

Through an examination of how and why the boycott instrument was selected, the manner in which it was implemented, and the dividends it did or did not produce, we should be able to answer the central question of this study, the extent to which statesmen can hope to wield the weapon of international sport for politically punitive purposes. The nature of the 1980 U.S. Olympic boycott imbues it with a significance extending beyond itself. That the United States chose to punish the Soviet Union for aggression vis-à-vis the Olympic Games, that the United States acted on a global scale and effected an unprecedented withdrawal of states from the paramount sporting event in the world, and that the United States succeeded in making the mere act of *participation* in a sports contest, as opposed to the results of such a contest, into a political issue makes the 1980 boycott perhaps the tantamount example of the integration of sports and politics in a consciously directed, focused fashion. Thus, the U.S. boycott will permit us to generalize about the use of sport as an alternative political tool to an extent otherwise ill-advised.

While sport may be viewed by some as simply frivolous leisure time activity, it is hardly perceived as such by the leaders and statesmen in whose hands political power resides. However, if sport is sought to be employed as a policy tool by those who function in the international arena, they must understand the parameters within which such efforts may succeed, as well as the potential costs and liabilities. It is this need for a realistic approach to the application of politics to sports that inspires this book.

Acknowledgments

The completion of this book was made possible through the generous contributions of many individuals and several institutions. I wish to thank the Eisenhower World Affairs Institute for fellowship assistance that enabled me to devote an entire year to my work. The Fletcher School of Law and Diplomacy also provided substantial financial support over several years.

The early drafts of this work benefited from the careful editing and constructive criticism of my mother, Eleanor Hulme, who often labored under intense pressure from her overly demanding "boss." My father, Derick Hulme, Sr., my brother, Robin Hulme, Bob Patten, Bob Smith, and John Kosbuth all "came through" during some rather trying times, and indeed enabled the book to reach its final stages.

Helen Strovers exercised great care in supervising the physical preparation of the completed text, notes, and index, while Darlene Day, Melissa Schmied, Karen Palmer, John Baldridge, and LeAnn Dahm did much of the "dirty work." My wife, Diana Hulme, provided invaluable assistance in smoothing out the many awkward passages and in forcing me to clarify my arguments. My dear wife also joyfully sacrificed her new husband to the task at hand and made its completion all the more rewarding. Finally, I wish to thank my editors at Praeger, Mary Glenn and Bert Yaeger, for having confidence in this project and seeing it through to its completion.

THE POLITICAL
OLYMPICS

1

Introduction

HISTORICAL USES OF SPORT

Before proceeding to the events comprising the 1980 Olympic boycott, a brief summary of the political component of past Olympics, both of the ancient and of the modern eras, will be undertaken. This will provide a historical perspective in order better to assess recent events.

The ancient Games, far from being innocent sporting contests, were political affairs of the highest magnitude. The virtual deification of the victorious by their respective city-states, and the corresponding castigation of the defeated, reflected the symbolic significance attached to the Games by the political units sponsoring the contests.[1] Monetary rewards were offered by leaders in order to spur their subjects to greater achievements. One historian observed, "Solon, the archon of Athens in the early sixth century BC, legislated a reward of 500 drachmas for every Athenian who won at the ancient Olympics in an effort to increase Athens' image."[2] The exclusion of all non-Greeks from participation at the height of the Games further attests to their political character.[3]

If Baron de Coubertin, the founder of the modern Games in 1896, either mistakenly idealized the ancient Greek Games or believed he could drastically alter the nature of such an international event, his vision would be shattered by the evolution of the modern Olympics. Political considerations dictated the exclusion of Germany from participation in 1920 and 1924, as they did for Soviet Russia beginning in 1920.[4] The movement to boycott the Berlin Olympics of 1936, although unsuccessful, once again brought to the fore the significance of politics in international sports in general, and in the Olympics in particular.

Two separate boycotts occurred in 1956, both as a result of governmental decisions to utilize the Olympic forum to further national policy. Spain, Switzerland, and the Netherlands initiated one boycott,[5] while Egypt, Lebanon, and Iraq conducted the other. The first group sought to protest the Soviet invasion of Hungary, while the second acted to show hostility to the Anglo-French seizure of Suez.[6] In 1972, the Games were used by a nonstate actor, the Palestinian Liberation Organization, to promote its political objectives. This violent event added a new dimension to the political manipulation of the Olympics.[7] Four years later, in 1976, a bloc of black African states utilized a boycott to protest the presence of New Zealand's Olympic team in the Montreal Games because of that country's sporting ties to South Africa. That same year, the United States, in a none-too-veiled threat, hinted that it too would boycott Montreal, but for a quite different reason: it was concerned that Taiwan would be barred from competing.[8]

It is a mistake, however, to conceive of states as being solely responsible for the politicizing of the Games. From the inception of the modern Olympic movement at the Congress of Sorbonne in 1894 to the first Olympiad two years later, from the post-World War I to the post-World War II Games, and from the first participation of the Soviet Union in the Olympic Games in 1952 to the events of 1980, the leaders of the International Olympic Committee (IOC) and of its various component organizations have revealed an ambivalence and inconsistency regarding the role of politics in the Olympic movement. The supposedly idealistic founder of the modern Games, Baron Pierre de Coubertin, himself reflected both the compelling desire to transform the Olympics from a contest among individuals to a fight for national glory and the yearning to use international sport to nurture the seeds of a more peaceful world. Evaluating the 1896 Olympic games, the first of the modern era, Coubertin observed:

One may be filled with a desire to see the colors of one's club or college triumph in a national meeting, but how much stronger is the feeling when the the [*sic*] colors of one's own country are at stake . . . ! It was with these thoughts in mind that I sought to revive the Olympic Games. I have succeeded after many efforts . . . [I hope] it may be a potent, if indirect, factor in securing international peace.[9]

That Coubertin was not overly concerned with the ostensibly pacific aspects of sports, nor averse to its direct political potential, may be surmised from a letter he sent to all IOC members after World War I:

A completely new situation has arisen. Sports now stands at the forefront of the architects of victory. Thanks to sports, the dramatic improvisations of England and the United States thrust unexpected armies into the theatres of war. Thanks to sports, Sokol's valiant soldiers gathered victory laurels for their native countries even before their borders had been staked out and their freedoms ensured. Thanks to it, France, just as bravely but with incomparably greater strength than in 1870, was able to oppose the invasion with a rampart of hardened muscle. After France had generated such incomparable soldiers, sport was able to maintain their zeal and to quiet their cries of pain. In close proximity to the front, and in the distant sadness of prisoner-of-war camps they played football, fenced and boxed. The public conscience is aware of these things and appreciates them. A deserved enthusiasm, inspiration will sanctify the value of physical conditioning and proclaim the victory of sports.[10]

That the IOC was cognizant of what "victory" Coubertin exalted was apparent when it delegated the task of issuing invitations to compete in the 1920 Antwerp Games to the host nation, Belgium.[11] Although it was unlikely that the defeated powers would receive invitations from their erstwhile adversary, the IOC effectively foreclosed such a possibility by stating that "only those countries represented on the IOC were allowed to compete," and, since "no one had any information about the previous members from the 'Central Powers,' those countries were not listed as eligible."[12] Similar reasoning prevailed after World War II when the Axis powers were excluded from competition by the IOC on the grounds that since only those "countries with NOCs could compete, the countries occupied by the Allied forces (Germany, Italy, and Japan) did not fit this category; the occupied countries had no internal governments and therefore no legal institutions such as NOCs."[13]

While the IOC thus acted effectively to bar the defeated powers of World War II from the ensuing Olympiad strictly on the basis of political considerations, prior to the war it went to great lengths to deny the relevance of political concerns to Olympic matters. During the controversy over the 1936 Berlin Olympiad, IOC President Baillet-Latour remarked, "The Olympic Games are not held in Berlin, in Los Angeles or in Amsterdam. When the 5-circled Olympic flag is raised over the Stadium it becomes sacred Olympic territory and theoretically, and for all practical purposes, the Games are held in ancient Olympia. There, I am the master."[14] Reflecting a similar desire to have a clear delineation between political and sporting affairs, future IOC president Avery Brundage echoed Baillet-Latour's sentiments about the 1936 Games:

Frankly, . . . I don't think we have any business to meddle in this question [Nazism]. We are a sports group, organized and pledged to promote clean competition and sportsmanship. When we let politics, racial questions or social disputes creep into our actions, we're in for trouble. . . . Certain Jews must now [after a boycott of the Berlin Games was defeated] understand that they cannot use these games as a weapon in their boycott against the Nazis.[15]

Twenty years later, Brundage revealed a view diametrically opposed to Coubertin's when he opened the fifty-second session of the IOC prior to the 1956 Melbourne Olympics:

In the Golden Age there was an Olympic truce and all warfare stopped during the period of the Games, [but now] after two thousand years of civilization, we stop the Games and continue our wars. One of the objectives of the Games is to develop international goodwill. Alas, the Olympic Movement has no soldiers and no money. It, therefore, cannot stop warfare, but it can and does set a good example, and only when politicians of the world adopt those principles of fair play and good sportsmanship which prevail on the fields of amateur sport will there no longer be necessity for wars.[16]

Such a characterization of sport as a vehicle imbued with the potential to mitigate, if not eradicate, man's proclivity toward warfare stands in stark contrast to Coubertin's triumphant exaltation of sport as an essential factor in the Allied victory in World War I. Although in subsequent years Brundage repeatedly stated that the Games could survive only if participation in sporting contests was not made dependent upon prevailing political conditions,[17] and if "the strength of a great ideal" was maintained,[18] even his ostensibly unambiguous position becomes suspect upon closer examination. Most significantly, Brundage referred to the essence of the Olympic spirit as "the lofty ideals laid down by the Baron de Coubertin."[19] Assuming that a man of Brundage's past was acquainted reasonably well with the views of "the founder of the modern Olympics," one must question precisely what "lofty ideals" Brundage was extolling.

Perhaps in no other individual did the contradictory positions of the IOC on such questions as politics, nationalism, and the role of sport in international relations manifest themselves so clearly as in Lord Killanin, president of the IOC during the 1980 boycott. Killanin's discussion of the awarding of the Games to Moscow is particularly illuminating. Relating that the final vote in favor of Moscow "was almost unanimous" and that "most of the West voted for Moscow,"[20] Killanin next proceeded to assess the factors behind the decision. Attempting to dispel the impression that the IOC was out of touch with reality, he observed, "Few among us were naive enough not to realise that in putting on the Games Moscow would present the Soviet way of life, which meant propounding communism. But every city that has staged the Games has wanted to mirror the country and lifestyle that surround it. . . . No doubt people thought in casting their vote for Moscow they were supporting the mood of detente."[21] From this statement it is reasonable to conclude that IOC members were fully aware both of Moscow's political/propaganda goals relative to the Games and of the potential effects of the Games on the world political climate; Killanin made explicit the link between supporting Moscow and furthering detente among the IOC member countries. However, in another statement he attempted to refute the influence of political considerations on the IOC, yet did so in a manner that revealed the political nature of the decision. He stated, "Had it become a political vote the IOC, which is basically conservative, might have voted differently. But this was the height of East-West détente and, in any case, the voting was based purely on sporting grounds."[22] If indeed the vote was "based purely on sporting grounds," why mention détente at all? Despite his subsequent observation that "the Games were the Games of the IOC being held in Moscow and therefore had no connection with the politics of the country in which the Games were to take place," [23] the issue of political infringement on the Olympic Games hardly appeared resolved in Killanin's mind. In one breath the IOC president admitted to a significant place for political concerns in the Olympic movement; in the next he reverted to a highly idealistic position in which all political matters were relegated beyond the pale of the sacrosanct Games.

Killanin's ambiguity concerning the relationship between international sports and politics mirrored his uncertainty over the place of nationalism in the Olympic movement. While lamenting his "complete defeat in . . . attempts to make the spirit of the Games less nationalistic," Killanin nonetheless appeared unwilling to challenge the premise that international sport derives much of its appeal from nationalistic aspirations. He thus attacked "overt nationalism," such as national flags and anthems,[24] while failing to realize that such nationalistic manifestations were only symptomatic of the underlying belief that international sport is a nonviolent expression of intense national rivalries. Far from seeking to reduce the nationalistic roots of international sport, Killanin sought to reinforce such influences. He remarked, "We [the IOC] are against the domination or the use of sport for national aggrandisement, but not for the development of a natural national pride, which is a fundamental basis for true competition." [25]

While the leaders of the Olympic movement manifested a personal ambivalence toward the issues of politics, nationalism, and the character of international sport, the very nature of the Games as implemented by the IOC reflected the failure to resolve adequately these questions. One observer captured the essence of this situation when he wrote:

The inherent paradox between nationalism and internationalism is evidenct [sic] in the Olympic Rules and Regulations. The IOC has stated that Games are contests between individuals and not between countries, that athletes will represent their respective countries at the Olympic Games, and that individuals cannot enter the Olympics unless under the aegis of a National Olympic Committee.[26]

A brief analysis of the policy positions and the official pronouncements of the IOC from the inception of the modern Games to the Moscow Olympics will confirm the persistence of such contradictions.

Although the IOC has asserted repeatedly over the last thirty years that the Olympic Games are "contests between individuals and not between nations," [27] they have never been conducted upon such a basis. At the founding Congress of Sorbonne in 1894, the selection of competitors was made the responsibility of member states and participants were declared to be national representatives. Prior to 1914, Olympic rules even permitted a ranking of nations based upon the number of medals won.[28] Beginning in 1955, the IOC attempted to create at least a rhetorical separation between national Olympic committees and their respective governments when it adopted a rule that required all national committees "be completely independent and autonomous and entirely removed from political, religious or commercial influence."[29] Several years later the IOC reiterated its insistence that any relationship between an Olympic committee and a given state was nonsubstantive when it declared that "Recognition of an Olympic Committee does not imply political recognition as this is outside the competence of the International Olympic Committee."[30] This is a rather curious statement considering that "the Olympic system almost exactly duplicates the names and territorial jurisdiction of states." In fact, "In order for a national Olympic committee to be recognized by the IOC it must represent a viable political unit with a stable government";[31] indeed, there are few substate units recognized by the IOC.[32] As one analyst noted, "In effect, the recognition of a national Olympic committee is tacit recognition of a government and existing boundaries."[33]

The steadfast refusal of the IOC to make the structural changes required to transform the Games in practice into "contests between individuals" was seen in its refusal to allow individual entries not approved by a potential participant's respective Olympic committee. Just as the IOC refused to revamp the organizational structure of the Olympic movement in 1976,[34]—in particular, failing to reduce drastically the power of national Olympic committees—it similarly rejected such a proposal in 1980.[35] Since adoption of a measure allowing individual entrants could have significantly curtailed the extent of the boycott, the IOC had every reason to act at that moment if it was in fact serious about promoting an individualistic orientation for the Games. That was not the case. Just as the "IOC insists that NOCs [national Olympic committees] be structurally separate from their governments, but makes no complaint if they are under the *de facto* control of political authorities,"[36] the leaders of the Olympic movement were willing to insist rhetorically that the Games were competitions among individual participants, while perpetuating an organizational structure intimately connected to the state system, and designed to insure that the Games were contests among national representatives.

Although the IOC and its leaders failed to display either a consistent philosophical perspective or a concerted policy position related to the issue of politics and nationalism in the Olympic Games, it is noteworthy that the framework in which these topics were considered varied over time as the Games evolved into an ever larger and more politically attractive event. In the early years of the movement, it was the *IOC* that was worried about intruding into the affairs of states; the question of states influencing the Olympics was not considered. Future IOC president Edstrøm of Sweden sought to curb potential political actions of the International Committee when he warned in 1923 that "the IOC must avoid all interference in the political sphere."[37]

However, in 1956, in response to the boycotts of the Melbourne Games, IOC officials began to lament the intrusion of national politics into international sport. Avery Brundage, in words that would echo yet again in 1968 and 1972, questioned, "In an imperfect world, if participation in sport is to be stopped every time the politicians violate the laws of humanity, there will never be any international contests. Is it not better to try to expand the sportsmanship of the athletic field into other areas?''[38]

As the Games became ever larger and more commercialized, its value as a political forum grew, thus forcing the IOC to abandon any remaining vestiges of concern about the possible political ramifications of its actions on national governments and to concentrate instead on the behavior of states with potentially injurious consequences to itself. Lord Killanin reflected the reorientation of IOC officials during the last eight years when he remarked, ''Clearly politics are 'in' sport and have always been. Everything in our lives is governed by political decisions. We have varying degrees of freedom, but that freedom is obtained by political decision. Yet what we in sport need is the interest and support of politicians, not their interference.''[39] Thus, the leaders of the Olympic movement came to exhibit a heightened degree of respect for the power and influence that could be exerted by members of the community of states upon their actions; correspondingly, concern over the IOC engaging in behavior detrimental to state interests evaporated.

Paradoxically, perhaps, it was the growth of the Olympics into a worldwide spectacle of unprecedented proportions that forced the IOC to recognize a vulnerability to external manipulation and interference that previously had not existed. After conducting the 1976 Games, the Montreal Olympic Organizing Committee accurately focused on the factors fueling the rapidly changing character of the Olympics when it declared, ''With the eyes of the entire world focused upon them, the Games become a readily available stage upon which to parade the tensions and frictions of a tormented society. Their very importance makes them a prime showcase for social injustice and discontent.''[40] In addition to its enormous popularity, the fact that the ''Olympic system is an expression of the political *status quo*'' has transformed the Games into a global phenomenon highly susceptible to political intrusions.[41] With the attention of the world media focused squarely upon it, the Olympics offers to virtually all levels and elements of the political process, including states, terrorists, and minority groups, the opportunity to redress grievances or pursue political objectives by nontraditional means. It was with this relatively new set of circumstances that the IOC tried to cope.

NATURE OF SPORT AS AN INTERNATIONAL POLITICAL TOOL

In order to realize precisely why sports is used for political ends, first we turn to the candid pronouncements of official Soviet literature. In an explicit enunciation of the interconnectedness of politics and sports, the 1980 handbook for Soviet Communist party activists pronounced: ''The decision to give the honor of holding the Olympic Games in the capital of the world's first Socialist state was convincing testimony to the general recognition of the historic importance and correctness of the foreign policy course of our country, of the enormous services of the Soviet Union in the struggle for peace."[42]

That Soviet leaders do not attach merely rhetorical significance to sports as a political tool is evidenced by their development of an elaborate sports structure, which lavishly rewards the best athletes with a very high standard of living and with guaranteed time to train. Article 41 of the Soviet Constitution states that the "mass scale [development] of sport" is a citizen's "right." The Committee for Physical Culture and Sport, a subunit of the Council of Ministers, is entrusted with ensuring this right. After grade school, nearly two million children are selected as promising candidates to attend over 5,000 special schools for a ten-year course aimed at athletic development.[43] When Soviet officials declared that "The view popular in the West that 'sport is outside politics' finds no support in the U.S.S.R.,"[44] it reflected long-standing governmental policy.

Although the Soviet Union has been the least reticent in officially linking politics and sports, it is cited here as exemplary proof of the norm, not as an exception. Despite U.S. protestations to the contrary, every state with appropriate resources attempts to manipulate international sport in a manner as advantageous as possible. Whether through governmental appropriations, such as the 1979–80 $16 million grant by the U.S. Congress to assist in the grassroots development of sport,[45] or through the offer of travel subsidies by host governments to teams unable to attend international meets because of financial constraints, as in the West German efforts to bolster the number of competitors at the 1972 Munich Olympics,[46] government leaders attempt to maximize the potential political returns associated with an identification with international sport. Thus, when Carter said, "In the Soviet Union international sports competition is itself an aspect of Soviet government policy, as is the decision to invade Afghanistan," or when Vice President Mondale asserted that it was the Soviet Union which was responsible for erasing the "line between sports and politics,"[47] one must question the objectivity and accuracy of such official comments. It should be kept in mind that the differences in the utilization of sport derive more from a variance in methods than from a divergence in objectives. The Soviet example, since it provides the foundation for analyzing the use of sport for state ends, is thus useful; however, it should be remembered that, while Soviet tactics may be somewhat unique, their strategic goals are much the same as other states.

If we are now prepared to acknowledge the near universality with which states use sports as a tool of national policy, we must then question why this is so. Is it because the essence of sport so closely parallels that of international politics? Or, rather, has the ideal of sport been impinged upon, and perverted, by wicked statesmen? Perhaps a combination of the two factors is most likely at work. Far from being an idle question, the reasons for the political manipulation of sport must be found if we are to have any hope of comprehending the events of 1980.

Without doubt, the nature of sport and that of international politics is strikingly similar. The fiercely competitive aspect of sport correlates closely with the environment in which world leaders must function. States locked in struggle bring to bear all available and appropriate resources to any given contest. However, one significant difference exists between the two types of competition: in sports, there is a clear dichotomy between winner and loser, as only one individual or team can be victorious; in international relations, there are seldom unambiguous results, and the best one can usually hope for is a marginal improvement of position.[48] While states may seek clear advantage, they seldom can expect such results. Also, when statesmen attempt to utilize sport to establish or to increase contacts with other states, they must accordingly tone down the "win-lose" competitiveness of sport or risk producing results contrary to their intentions. If, on the other hand, sport is to be used to punish or to establish superiority, then all that need be done is to avoid inhibiting the true expression of sports' competitive essence. As one astute observer noted, "When sport is used for the improvement of diplomatic relations, it is by design; when it is used purely for the demonstration of superiority, it is by its nature."[49]

In addition to certain intrinsic similarities between sport and international politics that tempt leaders to utilize sport politically, sport is also attractive as an instrument of diplomacy that can be wielded with significant effect at relatively low cost. Since sport is "peripheral to the international political system" in that its use seldom results in a heightening of the risk of war or in a break in diplomatic relations, it is a safe way for one nation to express its displeasure with another's policies. The curious fact that sport "has no intrinsic political value" allows it to be used for political purposes without the usual commensurate costs.[50] Thus, the Netherlands could boycott the 1956 Olympics to protest the Soviet invasion of Hungary without fearing a break in relations or a severe Soviet response. In a world order in which realist assumptions about the nature of the international system and about the utility of force as an instrument of power are under intense scrutiny,[51] the peripheral characteristics of sport offer statesmen an attractive alternative tool to address unacceptable behavior.

While certain aspects of sport naturally lend themselves to political use, statesmen have proven capable of exploiting sport to a far greater degree than one might expect possible. Not only has sport been utilized in specific international instances to reflect or to influence the tone of relations between countries, it has also been employed to effect two additional state aims: to bolster domestic support for, and identification with, a ruling government; and to enhance a country's prestige in the international arena.

The effort to employ international sport as an instrument to increase the domestic popularity of a government is intimately associated with exploiting its nationalistic components. The Olympic traditions emphasizing national flags, national anthems, and team sports provide for a ready identification of a country's nationals with their fellow countrymen who are actually competing. It takes little effort on the part of governmental leaders to associate themselves with those athletes representing their country, and thus to benefit from the athletes' success. Patriotic fervor tends to be a contagious phenomenon that is all-inclusive and nondiscriminatory in its scope and focus. Politicians, even the less astute among them, thus seek to exploit any national success to the greatest possible extent.

No more graphic example exists of political leaders' willingness to transform sporting success into increased popular support for themselves than that of the events following the triumph of the U.S. hockey team over the Soviets in the 1980 Winter Olympics. The euphoria that swept the entire country following the victory at Lake Placid far superseded any reaction based purely on sporting considerations. Persons who had never before watched a hockey game were enraptured by the never-ending highlights. Bantam Books produced its ''journalistic commemorative,'' *Miracle on Ice*, only forty-six hours after receipt of a manuscript, and the book was on sale by March 1.[52] The American Broadcasting Corporation revealed plans to make a movie about the victory, while Volkswagen immediately signed the team to an advertising contract.[53] The American Institute for Public Service gave the first group prize in its history to the entire team in honor of its achieving the ''impossible dream''; the official category under which the prize was given was that for the ''greatest public service performed by an individual 35 or under.'' *Sports Illustrated* likewise broke with precedent and named the team ''Sportsmen of the Year,'' an honor previously bestowed only upon individuals.[54]

President Carter lost no time in associating himself with what was to become the national mania. He immediately telephoned his congratulations to Herb Brooks, the coach of the team. Later, at a White House reception, Carter toasted not only the hockey players but all other medalists from the Winter Games as ''modern-day American heroes.''[55] Not to be outdone by the efforts of the chief executive were lesser political figures in a variety of positions. The mayor of New York City, Edward Koch, gave Brooks the key to the city.[56] Representative Frank Annunzio from Illinois was prepared to give both the hockey team and Eric Heiden, winner of five gold medals in speedskating, a symbolic key to the country. He also introduced legislation that would authorize congressional gold medals for these champions. Lest anyone be ignorant of the purpose of such medals, Annunzio announced that they ''will be coming from the *American people* as a sign of our appreciation and recognition for outstanding performances.''[57] That the various politicians were correct in assessing the magnitude of the impact of the victories at Lake Placid on the national psyche was most cogently attested to in a letter to the *New York Times* that concluded, ''The gold medal won by the American hockey team is probably doing more to bolster the morale of Americans vis-à-vis our international problems than any words or action of our President and other leaders.''[58]

Unable to resolve effectively pressing foreign policy issues, and perceived as incapable of assuaging a sense of national impotence and frustration,[59] Carter, as well as lower ranking politicians, were willing to permit sporting victories to reinvigorate their constituents' national pride and self-esteem. Hoping to derive personal benefits from an upbeat electorate, government leaders sought to identify themselves as closely as possible with Lake Placid. Although "riding the coattails" of the athletes may have indicated acceptance of a passive leadership role, elected officials nevertheless allowed public opinion to assume an unusually dominant role in directing their behavior; it was prudent political maneuvering. In this case, political wisdom dictated that if you were unable to lead, at least follow as closely as possible.

One problem with encouraging the identification of national pride with sporting achievement is that once such a policy is adopted, it is difficult to abandon. As Carter was to discover in the course of his boycott campaign, nationalist sentiment often resulted in a desire of individuals and nations to go to Moscow to prove themselves on the aggressor's soil. Such sentiment was expressed by two former U.S. Olympic champions, Al Oerter and Bob Mathias. Oerter, four-time gold medalist in the shot put, observed, "The only way to compete against Moscow is to stuff it down their throats in their own backyard."[60] Mathias, winner of the Olympic decathlon in 1948 and 1952, echoed Oerter's sentiment, "Our people want to go to Moscow to beat the hell out of those guys and tell them face to face what's wrong with them."[61]

Patriotic feeling is thus a double-edged sword. It can be harnessed by a government's leaders to enhance their own aura and position; however, it can also restrict the range of choice available to statesmen, or damage efforts, such as a boycott, perceived as thwarting the expression of national virtue.

In addition to the enhancement of domestic popularity,[62] sport can also be manipulated by state leaders to create a particular image of their nation within international circles. Thus, in 1952 when the Soviet Union first sent a squad to the Olympic Games, it insisted that two separate Olympic villages be available, one for the socialist countries, a second for the remaining participants. Yugoslavia, unwilling to retreat from its break with Moscow and submit to Soviet dictates, defiantly camped between the two hostile villages.[63] Far from being the petulant behavior of children, the Soviet and Yugoslav actions represented the pursuit of international recognition through the vehicle of Olympic sport. The Soviet Union was attempting to demonstrate its leadership position as the head of the anti-imperialist Cold War alliance, while the Yugoslavs sought to carve out a nonaligned niche in a rigidly bipolar international order.

Lest it be thought that only major actors in world politics seek to elevate their stature through international sports, one need only analyze the behavior of the smaller members of the Olympic movement to find evidence to the contrary. Lord Killanin accurately observed that "there are many NOCs that do not have athletes of Olympic standard but have created NOCs partly for prestige, and to assist in developing sport."[64] Another commentator noted, "Those few sub-state units in international sport cling to their separate Olympic status, making use of it in the search for domestic and international legitimacy."[65]

Perhaps the most obvious manifestation of the efforts exerted by government leaders to promote their country's international reputations through the vehicle of the Olympic Games is the attention focused by leading nations on the "medal count" of each Olympiad. As an expression of intense national rivalries, the tally of medals won is equated with a country's international prestige and standing. In 1952, the Soviet team posted a large scoreboard at the entrance to its village to display the daily medal standings. However, when the United States overtook the Soviet delegation with two days left in the competition, the scoreboard was taken down.[66] Reflecting a favorable turn of events over the ensuing twenty-five years, Moscow, prior to the 1980 Games, pointed to the fact that between its first Olympic competition in 1952 and the Montreal Games of 1976, it captured 683 medals to only 606 for the Unites States.[67] It was implied that such athletic prowess reflected directly upon the relative merits of the two states' economic, social, and political systems. Similarly, the rise of East Germany to second place in the medal standings was parlayed by government officials into an exaggerated impression of the GDR's political strength;[68] indeed, sporting achievements have been considered a major instrument of East German foreign policy.

While sport may well be a "form of competitive exchange between states interested in the expression of national pride and the accumulation of national prestige,"[69] it is not the opposing state's government which is of vital concern to political leaders, rather it is the opposing state's spectators. The easiest and most successful international relations campaign may well reside in a state's ability to target spectator interest in various countries where it would like to improve its public image.[70] In the international arena, sport may therefore be utilized more effectively on a popular level than on a strictly state-to-state basis because leaders tend to be more impressed with hard "reality" and "facts" than with athletic displays that are at best only vicarious expressions of national virtue.

That sport may be employed by states of whatever persuasion to establish the merit of their human resources and of their particular ideology and value structure means that absolutely no state is barred from implementing sport to garner international acclaim and recognition.[71] However, certain observers have emphasized that sport has been primarily a tool associated with the East-West struggle in general, and more notably with U.S.-Soviet relations. Lord Killanin, president of the IOC during both the African boycott of 1976 and the U.S. boycott of 1980, declared as early as the Munich Olympics of 1972, "At the moment we have the big shots, America and Russia, trying to prove their way of life is better because of the number of medals they win. It proves nothing of the sort."[72] While the significance of Olympic victories may have been lost upon Killanin, this hardly prevented statesmen from recognizing their political value and from attempting to maximize it.

Moscow's policy of using athletics to promote a certain image to the rest of the world, as well as to gain increased acceptance within the family of nations, was revealed most clearly in connection with the 1980 Olympic Games, the first Summer Games ever hosted by a communist state. In what many Western observers described as an effort by the Soviet government to allay its own sense of illegitimacy and insecurity relative to the Western democracies, Moscow put an enormous effort into securing the honor of hosting the Olympic Games.[73] Once that was achieved, the Soviets subsequently proclaimed the IOC choice to be "a convincing testimony to the general recognition of the historical significance and correctness of our country's foreign political course, the enormous services of the Soviet Union in the struggle for peace."[74] With expenditures on preparations for the Games estimated to range as high as $3 billion, the Kremlin was taking few chances that the world would have any cause to malign the accomplishments of the "peaceloving" Soviet nation.[75]

Declaring that "The Soviet people view sport as an instrument of peace,"[76] Soviet authorities went to great lengths to insure that foreign media covering the Moscow Games captured the proper spirit of the occasion. After all, if the media portrayed the militarization of Moscow, the forced exile of dissidents, and the generally "un-Olympic" spirit that existed during the Games, the Kremlin would hardly have succeeded in using this sporting extravaganza to help tilt the international political climate in its favor. Therefore, despite vehement protest, Soviet censors were directed to refuse to transmit a film about official Soviet views on the relationship between sports and politics produced by the West German television network, ARD. The Soviets declared that only material dealing exclusively with sport would be transmitted. This policy was also applied to all reports made by Eurovision, the European network pool; indignation and protest predictably resulted.[77]

American cognizance of the capacity of sport to be utilized to increase or to establish international prestige, or to prevent the erosion of world standing, was reflected in the tone of official remarks dealing with the prospect of holding the Olympics in Moscow subsequent to the invasion of Afghanistan. Secretary of State Cyrus Vance warned the IOC that "To hold the Olympics in any nation that is warring on another is to lend the Olympic mantle to that nation's actions." Czech dissidents echoed such views by declaring that "prompt moral sanctions," such as a boycott, "will prevent the aggressor from donning a halo of peace."[78] Any Soviet effort to legitimize their actions in Afghanistan through the vehicle of the Moscow Olympics, self-servingly dubbed "a major milestone in human history,"[79] would be countered vigorously.

We should not assume from this discussion that the United States acts only to insure that the Soviet Union does not reap the advantages offered by the political agency of sport. On the contrary, the United States likewise actively attempts to promote its own international image. U.S. athletic success is touted as an indication that its "free," "just," and democratic society is not only "right," but can also compete advantageously with the "evil" force of totalitarian, repressive communism. Vice President Hubert Humphrey, speaking in 1966, said that the United States had to prove that a "free society" could produce better athletes than a communist one.[80] President Carter, in referring to the Winter Olympians from Lake Placid, implied that the performance and behavior of U.S. athletes reflected positively on his nation's entire system when he stated, "here they are, and we're very proud of them. You have conducted yourselves in the finest traditions of our country and of the Olympic ideal."[81] That Carter was not overly sentimental about any "Olympic ideal," and indeed was more concerned with Olympic gold medals and the international benefits presumed to accrue from them, may be surmised by the fact that the ceremony at which he made his address was for medal winners only. Coubertin may have believed participation to be the highest achievement; Carter obviously thought otherwise.

One further demonstration of the significance of sports as a means of developing international respect, especially at the expense of an adversary, should convince even the most skeptical of its importance. Jimmy Carnes, the 1980 U.S. national track coach, was adamantly opposed to any boycott of the Games. His reasoning was not premised on a belief that the Games were above politics or that athletics should be left alone (comments frequently voiced by athletes and coaches), but rather on a desire to establish and promote the merits of the U.S. system. He observed, "I want to see the Olympics go on. I feel very strongly that the United States should develop its sports program and show the world that a free society has the best system."[82] Even those opposed to one political use of sport (a boycott), favored another (a demonstration of U.S. superiority).

CONCLUSION

It should now be apparent that sport has several areas of intrinsic congruence with the international political arena that commend it to statesmen seeking alternate means of pursuing national objectives. The competitive, "win-lose" nature of sport, while less appropriate in some political contexts than in others, is particularly valuable for punitive expressions of displeasure with another state. Also, the peripheral relationship of sport to international relations allows leaders to turn to it aware that its use will be relatively low risk, especially as evaluated against its potential benefits. Although the punitive political use of sport more closely resembles the athletic process itself, sport can also be employed in an effort to enhance a state's prestige and standing among other countries. Athletic success can often be transformed into increased respect for a country's foreign policy and diplomatic efforts. While such an effect of sporting prowess is essentially unquantifiable, one need only analyze the example of East Germany to establish a causal relationship. Finally, sport may be manipulated by political leaders to enhance their domestic popularity. This is most readily accomplished through an active identification between a government and the international sporting accomplishments of its citizens. Patriotic enthusiasm is sought to be redirected upon the government, which is self-portrayed as an ever-faithful supporter of athletics. Needless to say, increased popular support enables leaders to pursue more actively, and more successfully, international, as well as domestic, policy objectives.

2

The Boycott Decision

Jimmy Carter's decision to boycott the 1980 Summer Olympics was motivated by two main considerations. First, the Soviet Union was to be punished for its actions in Afghanistan. The White House sought to increase the political costs to be borne by Moscow, and determined that as Olympic host the Kremlin's investment in prestige, propaganda, and other resources was of such magnitude as to make a boycott especially effective. Second, Carter desired to show the rest of the world that the United States still had the will to resist Soviet aggression. In the post-Vietnam era, American determination to act forcefully to protect and/or promote its international interests had become increasingly suspect both at home and abroad. The helpless position in which the United States found itself as a consequence of the Iranian hostage crisis only reinforced such perceptions. It was in an effort to counter this negative assessment of U.S. foreign policy that Carter moved to support the idea of a boycott. A U.S.-led disruption of the Moscow Olympics would not only punish the Soviet Union, it would also help restore respect for U.S. leadership.

Of the options the White House had at its disposal to punish Moscow, it determined that a boycott of the Olympics would have the most far-reaching consequences. Lloyd Cutler, counsel to the president, stated the administration's belief that the Moscow Games "may be the most important single event in the Soviet Union since World War II." It was thus logical, he continued, that to disrupt the Games would "deny them what was going to be an enormous propaganda victory."[1] It was this belief that Moscow was going to achieve a propaganda coup of global proportions that would confer legitimacy not only upon the regime and its political system but also upon its actions in Afghanistan that made the boycott idea so alluring. Carter could thus declare, "We have no desire to use the Olympics to punish, except the Soviets attach a major degree of importance to the holding of the Olympics in the Soviet Union."[2] The Olympics was not to be used to "punish," unless Moscow was to be the target.

Carter reiterated his desire to punish the Soviets via boycott in a letter of January 20, 1980, to Robert Kane, president of the U.S. Olympic Committee. In the letter, made public at the time, Carter stressed, "We must make clear to the Soviet Union that it cannot trample upon an independent nation and at the same time do business as usual with the rest of the world. We must make clear that it will pay a heavy economic and political cost for such aggressions."[3] In the context of such sentiment, it becomes apparent that the White House never sought to use the threat of a boycott as a means of forcing the actual withdrawal of Soviet troops from Afghanistan. That the desire was to punish, rather than to coerce, was revealed by the timing and the nature of Carter's boycott deadline.

Secretary of State Vance, with the full support of Carter, set a mid-February (later to be clarified as February 20) deadline for the full withdrawal of the estimated 85 to 100 thousand Soviet ground troops in Afghanistan. This deadline was publicly promulgated January 15, although not formally conveyed to Moscow.[4] It appeared that Carter, as well as Vance and other administrative officials, had few illusions regarding either the ability or the will of the Soviet leaders to effect a complete and total withdrawal in such a brief period of time. Carter realized that even if the Soviets were inclined to retreat from Afghanistan, it was virtually impossible that they would be able to do so within the space of four weeks. Also, the decision to announce what amounted to a public ultimatum severely circumscribed the possible Soviet courses of action. With the U.S. position so well publicized, Moscow could change its policy only at an extreme political cost. The Soviet Union would be internationally humiliated through the exercise of U.S. pressure. No Soviet leader, especially since Khrushchev,[5] could ever accept such a scenario.

Warren Christopher, deputy secretary of state, argued that "This [threat of a boycott] is the strongest single step we could take to persuade them to withdraw their troops from Afghanistan,"[6] but, in fact, such a threat, especially made within the context of a U.S. ultimatum, insured Soviet intransigence. Carter betrayed his own awareness of the effect of the February 20 deadline when he told Gene Edwards, a member of the United States Olympic Committee Board, "I don't want to mislead you about our chances for competing in the Olympics this year."[7] Clearly, Carter intended from the outset to wield the boycott in a punitive fashion. Any talk regarding a "deadline" was, if anything, a rhetorical ploy to attempt to create the impression that the United States was willing to give the Soviets a chance to mend their ways before proceeding in a decisive fashion. However, as we have seen, any public ultimatum could never produce such results, and indeed was never so intended.

In addition to its punitive aspect, the boycott was meant to be a demonstrable show of U.S. will to the rest of the world. The United States would make a moral stand, suffer the associated costs, and thereby exhibit both its moral integrity and its capacity to endure sacrifice for a just cause. No longer would the United States be liable to accusations of being unwilling to shoulder its burden in the fight against Soviet transgressions of international civility. The Kremlin would be shown that America could no longer be discounted as a "paper tiger"; it was a force with which to be reckoned.[8] While, in fact, a boycott would cost the United States very little, and affect only a few hundred athletes and an insignificant number of businesses, it would create the perception that the United States was willing to sacrifice for its principles.

Carter felt that only through a firm and unyielding stance could U.S. world leadership be bolstered. Warren Christopher accordingly proclaimed the U.S. position in none-too-subtle terms:

We must convince the Soviets that we are willing and able to respond to their aggression, whether in Afghanistan or elsewhere. If we permit sports to go forward as usual, after we have said there will be no business as usual, we will be sending out a contradictory signal, and one which could call into question the firmness of our resolve.[9]

Vice President Mondale endorsed a boycott as a means of establishing U.S. credibility when he declared such a step to be "an unambiguous statement of our national resolve."[10]

One of the major obstacles that confronted the president in his effort to convince both U.S. citizens and foreign nations of the sincerity and depth of the U.S. commitment to a boycott was that the recent record of the government in general, and of the Carter administration in particular, was not one to inspire confidence in American willingness to fight for a policy to its bitter end. There was an attempt to overcome this credibility problem through pronouncements that stressed that the United States was prepared, if necessary, to "go it alone" in its boycott effort. Carter attempted to lend the weight of his office and personal integrity by declaring forthrightly his intentions to act unilaterally, if required, to counter Soviet behavior: "We make our position very clear, and it's predicated not on what other nations might do but on our own decision. If all of the nations go to the Moscow Olympics, we will still not go."[11] Such steadfast resolve may not, however, have existed except for public displays and speeches. Carter's statement of his willingness to act regardless of "what other nations might do" was made January 20. Yet, on January 2, Carter entered in his diary, "Only if many nations act in concert would I consider it [a boycott] to be a good idea."[12] Either Carter developed a much firmer opinion regarding the position the United States should, and could, assume during those three weeks, or else he was attempting to lure other nations toward the U.S. position by posturing an extreme stance that would not have been adhered to had significant support not emerged. Regardless of whether or not a ''fall-back'' position existed, Carter was determined to adopt publicly an intransigent position, and Lloyd Cutler transmitted to the media the unwavering nature of Carter's commitment.[13]

3

The Domestic Campaign

In order for a boycott to accomplish the dual, interrelated objectives of punishing the Soviet Union while demonstrating the ability and the will of the United States to utilize its full diplomatic resources to assume a leadership position on a pressing world issue, Carter was required to act on two broad fronts. First, the United States Olympic Committee (USOC) had to be "convinced" that its support of governmental policy was crucial, and accordingly agree to abide by White House decisions. Failure to gain solid domestic backing would cripple the strategy as a whole, and particularly efforts in the second arena in which the boycott scenario was to be played out. This second front was the international one. As we have seen, Carter was, with good reason, reluctant to undertake any action on a unilateral basis. Not only would such efforts likely be ineffectual, they would also leave the United States in an isolated, vulnerable position. Soviet propaganda would exploit any unsupported action, rendering U.S. policy counterproductive. It was essential to rally as much worldwide support as possible, presenting Moscow with a united front of Western, and hopefully Third World, nations.

Although the process by which the boycott was effected was marked by a complex interplay of domestic and international maneuverings, in the interest of analytic clarity these two processes will be treated independently. While such an analysis may distort reality, it will allow us to grasp more readily the divergent obstacles faced by Carter in the two distinct milieux in which he was forced to operate. Because the barriers to success were different in nature, tactics had to be formulated independently in order to influence domestic policy and to direct international sentiment toward a common position.

INFLUENCES UPON THE USOC

Subsequent to the Soviet invasion of Afghanistan, President Carter determined that a disruption of the Moscow Olympics was an appropriate response. Although initially conceived as an effort to move, postpone, or cancel the Games, a boycott was the policy eventually adopted.[1] The domestic component of the boycott movement consisted of three main elements: direct governmental pressure on the USOC and its athletes, coupled with a combination of more subtle means of coercion and certain "incentives" to act properly; mobilization of public opinion through White House statements and congressional resolutions; and specific, binding legislation affecting U.S. businesses supplying the Games and network television coverage available to the U.S. public.

Direct Government Pressure

Despite the fact that IOC rules prohibit national Olympic committees from succumbing to governmental dictates,[2] in the real political world a government willing to accept certain costs can, in the final analysis, implement its policy decisions. In a democratic society, however, it is preferable for a government to "persuade" its Olympic committee to follow its lead, rather than have to resort to forcible measures that could have severe political repercussions. Thus, the Carter administration pursued a relentless effort to direct USOC policy without employing mandatory measures.

Immediately after the president broached the idea of moving, postponing, or cancelling the Games, it was communicated by USOC leaders to the White House that such a policy had very little support within their organization. Robert Kane and Donald Miller, president and executive director, respectively, of the USOC, were quick to point out the sheer logistical impossibility of moving the Games on such short notice. Kane observed, "Anyone who knows anything about it . . . should realize there's no other city in the world that could take this year's Summer Games at this late date. The sports facilities might be usable, but no city except Moscow has an Olympic Village now that could house and feed 15,000 athletes, coaches and other personnel."[3] Miller added that, in his estimation, it would cost $250 to 350 million, and take two years, to change sites.[4]

Not only did the USOC believe that moving the Games was a physical impossibility, it also felt that the IOC would never adopt such a course of action. Kane stressed that "The IOC owns the games, . . . and they're not about to make a choice like that."[5] Kane and Miller likewise doubted that the IOC would ever postpone, or cancel the Games unless there was a severe deterioration in the political situation in the Persian Gulf; perhaps only war could cause the IOC to act in such a manner.[6]

In the face of such opposition, the White House felt it necessary to deal directly with Kane and Miller. The administration, whether wanting to proceed in a step-by-step fashion or actually believing that it could get the IOC to adopt its proposals to move, postpone, or cancel the Games, desperately sought to get the USOC to present its position at the executive meeting of the IOC in Lake Placid prior to the opening of the Winter Games in mid-February. Carter, who had ignored the USOC leaders' repeated requests to express their views, changed tactics and asked Kane and Miller to attend a meeting at the White House on January 18 with Secretary of State Cyrus Vance, deputy counsel to the president Joseph Onek, and counsel to the president, Lloyd N. Cutler. The two-and-a-half-hour meeting, characterized as "informative" by Kane, did not produce its desired effects.[7]

Whereas Kane and Miller had previously declared that they would not defy the White House if a boycott was called for, after the White House meeting their position seemingly became more uncertain.[8] No longer was the president's position acknowledged as decisive, but was rather only one factor to be considered. The USOC leaders stated:

If our Government advocates a boycott, our athletes, under Olympic rules, must decide whether or not they wish to comply. . . . If the President of the United States advocates a boycott, we will immediately poll prospective members of the U.S. team to ascertain their feelings about such an action. . . . Based on the collective view of the athletes, the USOC executive board will then make a decision on whether or not to enter athletes in the Games.[9]

Miller, however, was careful to stake out for the USOC only as much freedom of action as he felt it could protect. He thus conceded, "If the President called for a boycott, that would have a tremendous impact on any decision made by the USOC and the athletes."[10]

Realizing that he had lost momentum, Carter wrote a personal letter to Kane. Carter characterized the step of moving the Olympics as one whose impact "will reverberate around the globe."[11] He deemed a boycott necessary in order to "make clear to the Soviet Union that it cannot trample upon an independent nation and at the same time do business as usual with the rest of the world," and added that a failure to boycott would undermine "our other steps to deter aggression."[12] Carter's direct approach, coupled with certain indications he provided of a willingness to respect the decision-making procedures of the international sporting community, reaped dividends.

The USOC, desirous of maintaining its good standing and influence with the IOC, had repeatedly expressed concern for avoiding a "confrontation within the Olympic community" by working through channels.[13] In addition to acting within the accepted parameters of the IOC, the USOC also sought to avoid being pressured into an immediate decision about the most extreme potentiality, a boycott. Thus, when Kane and other USOC officials came to the conclusion, perhaps optimistically, that they would be given adequate time to pursue objectives within the organization "in a proper way" and as "part of the decision-making [process]," they agreed to try to rally support among other nations to move the Games.[14] Kane also agreed to bring Carter's proposals to the attention of the USOC executive board scheduled to meet later that week in Colorado Springs, Colorado.

At that meeting, the USOC executive board voted 68 to 0 to ask the IOC to move, postpone, or cancel the Games. The board failed to propose a boycott or to set any deadline for action. As Kane candidly acknowledged, they were "playing for time" and wished to avoid any irrevocable or injurious action.[15] One concern was that any boycott decision before the Lake Placid Games could precipitate a withdrawal of up to one-quarter of the thirty-seven teams entered in those Games.[16] The resolution adopted by the board further stated that the United States would continue to select a team, and also that no decision would be adopted at that time as to the actions that would be pursued should the IOC refuse to act. All that was agreed upon was that, in the case of such an eventuality, "appropriate action" would be considered. Despite the tentative nature of the USOC resolution, it was, as Joseph Onek observed, "precisely what the President requested."[17]

In the two-week interval between the USOC resolution and the meeting of the IOC, Lloyd Cutler worked to solidify support for the administration's position within the leadership ranks of the U.S. committee. He conveyed to Kane that the Olympic Committee would be given "reasonable" time to review the situation once the IOC decision was made. Miller came to believe that the government was as interested in taking its time regarding any final action as was his committee.[18] It was largely as a result of new-found respect for White House methods that Miller was prompted once again to revert to his previous position that the USOC would abide by whatever decision the president deemed appropriate and necessary. He privately concluded, "We would never defy an order by the President."[19]

Carter had succeeded in his first major battle of the domestic campaign; U.S. Olympic officials would present his proposals to the IOC. Kane, accompanied by four associates, appeared in Lake Placid before the meeting of the executive board of the IOC prior to the start of the Winter Games. The U.S. delegation castigated the Soviet invasion as an "act of war," and claimed that the aggression constituted a violation of the contract between the Moscow Olympic Organizing Committee and the IOC. Kane stated, "I request that the Games be postponed until such time as an alternate site can be found and prepared to host the next Olympic Games. If neither of these alternatives [transfer or postponement] are feasible, I suggest that the 1980 Olympic Games be canceled."[20] As expected, the IOC unanimously rejected the U.S. resolution; Moscow was to be the site, period.[21]

White House reaction to the February 12 decision by the IOC was one of "regret." In contradictory statements concerning its new expectations for the USOC, the government pressed the committee leaders to support promptly a boycott while at the same time reassured them that they would have a "reasonable time" to act after expiration of the February 20 troop withdrawal deadline.[22] In what had to be seen as a positive development for the Carter administration, Kane reaffirmed his recent support for government policy: "We must remain open to the President's views of what is best in the international interest and to the will of the American people. . . . Of course, the U.S.O.C. will accept any decision concerning our participation in the games the President makes in view of his analysis of what is best for the country."[23]

However, despite the ostensible solidarity of the Olympic Committee and the White House, certain fissures began to become noticeable. Miller announced that no decision would be made until the April 11-13 meeting of the committee. While he said he had not been told that this date was unsatisfactory, the White House could hardly have been pleased. Neither Carter's idea of "prompt action" nor of "reasonable time" corresponded to a seven or eight week delay; a final decision by the USOC was of critical importance in enlisting foreign support.[24] An additional note of discord was evidenced over Carter's February 20 proclamation that a boycott was now "irrevocable." Dissatisfied that his Olympic Committee was now relegated to a rubber stamp, Kane criticized such an intransigent position and said that a degree of flexibility should be maintained.[25] A Soviet source quoted him as saying, "Nothing is irrevocable but stupidity and death."[26] Carter may have forged a temporary alliance, but its durability and foundation were becoming increasingly suspect.

Regardless of the emergence of potentially divisive attitudes, Carter appeared confident that USOC compliance had been assured, and turned his full attention toward efforts to broaden the boycott internationally. This decision to take the USOC for granted proved to be a nearly fatal mistake, and one which would again require intensive, direct intervention by top government officials to rectify.

As the meeting of the USOC House of Delegates drew near, the administration correctly recognized that support within that body for a boycott was waning rapidly, and that some counter-offensive was called for. Miller indicated to the White House that many of the delegates were advocating an early rejection of the boycott proposal, and that the new strength of this sentiment made it impossible for him to predict the outcome of any vote. Miller himself, while never reneging on his personal pledge to support a boycott should Carter make such a request, nonetheless displeased the White House by taking the lead in advocating that any decision be deferred until May. After all, he reasoned, why should the USOC act at its meeting on April 12 when the IOC did not require a decision until May 24? Not only was "The international situation . . . fluid," but American popular opinion could also change in the six week period.[27]

Although remaining publicly confident that the Olympic delegates would not defy the president, the White House sensed that it was in trouble and had to act quickly and decisively. It was with this objective in mind that fifty members of the U.S. Olympic Committee were invited on April 3 to meet with top government officials, including Deputy Secretary of State Warren Christopher and Secretary of Defense Harold Brown. Adjudging it best to show the firmness of the government's resolve, the invited guests were told in no uncertain terms that a failure to boycott would "be damaging [to] our national security" and would not be tolerated. They were told Carter was determined, if necessary, to utilize whatever legal measures were required to prevent the athletes' participation.[28] While the government officials expressed satisfaction with the meeting, feeling they had succeeded in conveying the administration's resolve, it was far from certain that they had accomplished the ultimate objective of preempting a revolt by the U.S. committee.

Kane and Miller emerged from the White House session obviously resentful of the pressure for an early decision, and adhered to their position that no action need be taken before May. Not only were they opposed to immediate action, the two top USOC leaders no longer professed the ability, or necessarily the will, to act to avoid an outright rejection of a boycott at the April 12 meeting.[29] The success of the uncompromising, strong-arm tactics employed by the White House remained at best problematic, at worst counterproductive.

Carter determined to bolster his standing within Olympic circles through two additional, pre-USOC conference, efforts. First he arranged for thirty-six out of the eighty-two-member USOC executive board to attend yet another White House meeting, this time with Secretary Vance and General David C. Jones, chairman of the Joint Chiefs of Staff. These two men stressed the administration's belief that not only was a boycott the strongest peaceful measure available to respond to the Soviet aggression, it was also essential for national security.[30]

The second tactic pursued by Carter focused not on the leaders of the Olympic movement, but on the actual delegates to the April 12 meeting. Attempting to build grassroots support within the Olympic organization, Carter, along with Senate majority leader Robert C. Byrd and Speaker of the House Thomas P. O'Neill, Jr., sent all 300 delegates telegrams or letters urging their support for a boycott.[31]

The position of the USOC was still obscured amid internecine divisons, at least partially engendered by what many perceived as undue government pressure. Carter determined to mount a final, all-out campaign when the hope that Miller and Kane could obtain approval for the latest government-sponsored proposal—that would defer formal acceptance of a boycott until May—appeared doubtful. A contingent of White House and State Department officials, headed by Vice President Walter Mondale, and including White House counsel Lloyd Cutler, deputy White House counsels Joseph Onek and Dr. Robert Berenson, and State Department members Nelson Ledsky and Jane Wales, was sent to Colorado Springs, Colorado, to attend the USOC House of Delegates' meeting.[32] Carter realized that the outcome of the conference might well decide the fate of the entire boycott campaign; he was not about to spare any resources.

Before a closed session of nearly 300 athletes, sports officials, and businessmen composing the USOC House of Delegates, Mondale gave what may have been the decisive appeal for Carter's boycott. In an emotional, yet nonthreatening and mild-mannered speech, the vice president drew upon the 1936 Berlin Olympics as a guide for present policy. He posited the view that Hitler had used the Games as a means of globally ratifying his policies and of legitimizing his regime. The failure to boycott was implied to be one causative element in the events precipitating World War II; it was argued that today the United States must refrain from conferring similar benefits of legitimacy and acceptance upon a Soviet regime engaged in blatant aggression.[33] Mondale went to such lengths as to state, "History holds its breath; for what is at stake is no less than the future security of the civilized world."[34] The supposedly apolitical delegates were burdened with an enormous responsibility as the fate of Western society was placed squarely upon their shoulders. Careful to give the athletes a measure of dignity and respect, Mondale "recognize[d] the enormous price" they were being asked to pay and said their sacrifice would be appreciated by all.[35] Much to the administration's delight, the delegates voted, according to a complex, weighted system, 1,604 to 797, with 2 abstentions, not to send a team to Moscow.[36] Carter had scored a major victory.

One further step taken at the meeting, and in line with administration efforts to reduce U.S. visibility at the Games to an absolute minimum, was to provide no financial assistance to technical committees involved with the Moscow Games. U.S. officials would attend various international sporting congresses held in Moscow before, during, and after the Games, but in no way judge, or even spectate, at the Games themselves.[37] The White House approved of officials being sent to international conferences, despite their being held in Moscow, reasoning, "To not allow these people to go would cause them to lose positions on important committees to Cubans and Russians. . . . We'd be in even worse shape than we were before."[38]

Moral Responsibility

In addition to the use of high government officials, Carter's domestic boycott campaign sought to invoke the concept of "moral responsibility" in its efforts to "persuade" the USOC to accept its policy. The White House exhibited little reticence in presenting the boycott question in patriotic terms; a dissenting opinion became "un-American." Early in January, Secretary of State Vance used such a tactic when he equated the Berlin Olympics of 1936 with the Moscow Games of 1980. Categorizing the decision to attend the Berlin Games as one which flew in the face of American ideals, Vance thereby indicated his view of a similar action today.[39] President Carter, in acknowledging the efforts of the USOC to get the IOC to move, postpone, or cancel the Games, likewise described its attempt in such terms. He "thanked the committee for its earnest and patriotic efforts."[40] In a March 21 speech to representatives of U.S. teams gathered at the White House, Carter again returned to the theme of the "athlete

as patriot.'' While telling the athletes their decision on a boycott was ''a decision for [them] . . . to make,'' he thanked them for meeting with him on ''a
very serious matter as equals, as Americans who love our country, who recognize that sometimes we have to make sacrifices and that for the common
good, for peace and freedom, those sacrifices are warranted.''[41]

However, it remained for Vice President Mondale's address to the April 12
meeting of the USOC House of Delegates for this strategy to receive its fullest
expression. Setting the tone of his address by solemnly affirming, ''I know that
everyone in this room loves our country [and are] citizens dedicated to America's best interests,'' Mondale proceeded to state that going to Moscow was an
act of ''complicity'' to which the U.S. public was adamantly opposed. The
delegates were urged to unite behind the President and the American people as
their decision was, in addition to a test of American values, a ''referendum on
freedom'' in general. Although such a postulation hardly needed reinforcement,
Mondale concluded with one final effort to stir the conscience of the delegates
and to inspire guilt for a nonboycott decision they had yet to make. He declared, ''some goals surpass even personal achievement. To any young athletes
who feel singled out for suffering, I say, it is war above all that singles out our
young for suffering. And it is war that our peaceful resolve can prevent. Everyone across the board is being asked to sacrifice.''[42]

Nongovernmental sources reinforced the idea that the boycott issue had attained a symbolic significance grounded in its supposed moral and ideological
qualities. No longer could one take a position on the matter without his degree
of ''American-ness'' and patriotism being open to judgment. The two distinct
concerns of the Olympic boycott and of one's national loyalty merged into one,
the result being the imposition of extreme pressure on all to *prove* their patriotism by supporting nonparticipation in the Moscow Games. Newspaper editorials and letters admonished the athletes to stop being selfish and to accept
the fact that governments often, especially in times of war and international
crisis, demand more of some citizens than of others. Athletes should be happy
that they have not been asked to sacrifice their lives, as have many before
them. Once athletes transcend their egoistic self-pity, they will conclude that
their obligation to their country is really most important.[43] Finally, perhaps
Bernard Levin, although addressing British athletes, best captured the moral
and nationalistic flavor that the boycott assumed when he wrote: ''By going to
Moscow . . . they [the athletes] will be condoning tyranny, disgracing themselves and betraying the ideals of sport. They may . . . win medals of gold,
silver or bronze. But not all the skills of alchemy will ever transmute their
prizes into anything but tarnished badges of shame.''[44]

The impact of this none-too-subtle moral suasion was readily apparent. Athletes, who for years had trained on their own at great personal sacrifice and
with little financial support, were suddenly castigated as unpatriotic and selfish.
To make matters more difficult, these were the same individuals who had, prior
to Afghanistan, been idealized and praised without reserve. Most athletes were

dismayed at the criticism, and somewhat perplexed that apparently they had been singled out to bear the brunt of the sacrifice and were then told they were being unpatriotic by those with absolutely nothing to lose. Bruce Jenner, the 1976 U.S. Olympic decathlon champion, symptomatically lamented the athletes' plight when he noted the numerous "letters and flak" he had received from people telling him he was "un-American" for opposing the politicizing of the Olympics.[45]

That the "patriotization" of the boycott decision had an influence upon the USOC leadership was obvious if one examined the statements made by Robert Kane, president of the committee, both during and after the boycott campaign. In the initial phase of the Carter administration's efforts to develop a variegated response to the Afghanistan invasion that incorporated the Olympic weapon, Kane made no secret of his feelings regarding such maneuvers. He stated that he did "not favor the concept of an Olympic boycott" and "hate[d] to see the games used as a ploy." [46] Yet, only two weeks later, he was forced to defend his committee's actions not from a policy-oriented perspective, but rather with a rationale that would be accepted as "American" by the general public: "We are patriotic Americans trying to do the best we can for, not only our country, but also our athletes, who are potential Olympians." [47]

In the face of imminent congressional approval of a resolution advocating that the Olympics be moved, postponed, or canceled, Kane saw fit to eliminate any mention of looking out for athletes' interests in conjunction with larger national concerns, and instead stressed only the overriding significance that both he and the USOC attached to the entire country's objectives. Thus, only five days after his previous statement in which at least some balance was struck between the athletes and the country as a whole, Kane stated, "I can't imagine that, with the national interest involved, the United States Olympic Committee would ever be in a position other than in accord with the Congress of the United States." [48] Especially revealing of the pressures brought to bear upon Olympic leaders was the admission by Kane, after the April 12 USOC decision to boycott the Games, that "More than anything else, the preservation of our patriotism and support of the President of the United States had to be reaffirmed." [49]

Alternate Games

In an effort to make a boycott more palatable to potential Olympians and to members of the USOC, some congressmen, with the support of the president, proposed to have either a national sports festival or an alternate "Olympics" as a way of providing some high level competition that summer. The Olympic Committee had initially announced that, regardless of any boycott action, the selection of a team would still be made.[50] Nonetheless, it was felt that choosing a team that had no place to compete would not be sufficient to endear athletes to the president's position.

Prior to the IOC decision in early February to proceed with Moscow as the site of the 1980 Summer Games—despite U.S. arguments to the contrary—a House subcommittee had already begun hearings on a possible national sports festival should a boycott occur. Governor Brendan Byrne of New Jersey, in conjunction with New York City mayor Edward Koch, submitted a written statement to the subcommittee supporting alternate Games and offering the facilities of the New York City area for those competitions. Koch subsequently appealed directly to the White House to implement any "counter-Olympics" using the athletic facilities of the New York, New Jersey, Pennsylvania, and Connecticut regions.[51] Carter soon realized the value of some alternate competition as a means of attracting both domestic and foreign support for abandoning Moscow. He promised, soon after his February 20 troop withdrawal deadline had passed, to meet with "a representative group of our summer athletes . . . [in order to get] an alternative world-class competition for them this summer that does not harm Olympic principles and will not harm future Olympic Games."[52] Carter's felicity about maintaining the sanctity of the Olympics resulted from USOC concern that any "counter-Olympics" could irreparably damage the Olympic movement.

While the USOC initially supported exploring the possibility of staging a national sports festival as "a viable activity for our governing bodies and our athletes," a "counter-Olympics" never had any backing.[53] A sports festival may have been no substitute for the Olympics, but at least it was a forum in which competitions could be held without resulting in, as Donald Miller feared, a "schism . . . throughout the world [that] would be the demise of the modern Olympic movement."[54] USOC officials continued to endorse a national event, although somewhat tentatively, until mid-February when Robert Kane came out firmly against both a sports festival and an international competition. Categorizing both as "disloyal" to the Olympic movement, Kane stressed his personal conviction that either U.S. athletes would go to the Moscow Games or they would go to nothing at all. It was not, however, until early April that Kane's position was accepted by the USOC as an organization.[55] As Robert Helmick, president of the Amateur Athletic Union, correctly discerned, "For the athletes, there simply is no alternative to the Olympics."[56]

The fact that the idea of a national sports festival had little allure for either the athletes or the leadership of the Olympic Committee prompted the government to abandon its efforts in that direction. In July, Congress appropriated $10 million for summer competitions in a number of Olympic sports, but this was not meant to be comparable to the grandiose plans once envisioned.[57] The attempt to use the assumed attraction of an alternate sports competition to entice the athletic community to support a boycott was ill-conceived and of little effect.

Other "Reward" Incentives

Additional incentives, of both a financial and nonmonetary nature, were offered to the athletes and the USOC to woo them toward Carter's position. The White House, in announcing on February 20 its decision to boycott Moscow, also urged "all American citizens to continue their financial and moral support of the committee [the USOC]."[58] The president continued to make vague references to providing financial support to those sports likely to suffer economically in the wake of a boycott, but failed to make any concrete proposals until the decision was made to utilize all available means to insure USOC obedience. Mondale was then instructed to offer, in his speech to the USOC House of Delegates prior to their April 12 meeting, to provide both financial and symbolic compensation in return for a decision to boycott. Mondale promised to increase contributions to the USOC, whose donations had fallen precipitously subsequent to the initiation of the boycott campaign. Implicit in this offer was a pledge to disburse the $16 million already appropriated in principle by Congress for amateur sports development. This financial commitment was supplemented by a promise, perhaps felt by the athletes to be nearly as significant as the monetary one, to come up with a "suitable honor," possibly even a Congressional medal, for those athletes deprived of their Olympic dream.[59] It was guessed correctly by the president that the leadership of the USOC would be more willing to boycott if their organization was not forced to suffer economically, as well as athletically. Also, the USOC was given, through Mondale's offer of symbolic recognition, a means of allowing its athletes to salvage a degree of dignity and to earn some public respect and applause.

While the use of monetary and symbolic "rewards" was originally intended by the administration to be one means of assuring USOC compliance, after the boycott decision was ratified by the Olympic Committee both the government and the committee itself turned to those devices to reduce the costs they would be liable to bear for their actions. Carter made good on his promise to help ease the USOC's financial plight by obtaining $10 million for them, the first federal money the committee had ever received.[60] Additionally, Carter vowed to help raise another $20 million from the private sector.[61] At the administration's urging, Congress overwhelmingly approved a $50,000 expenditure to strike gold medals for the 650 athletes selected for the 1980 Summer Olympic team. Senator Gary Hart, who introduced the appropriations bill in the Senate, eulogized the athletes as "deserv[ing] recognition not only for their talent but for their great personal sacrifice and dedication to the spirit of the Olympic Games."[62] In a ceremony on the Capitol steps July 30, the president presented the "Olympians" with their medals; the athletes were then treated to a variety show in their honor at Kennedy Center.[63] Such governmental efforts, while appearing to many to be a manifestation of guilt and an attempt to salve troubled consciences, were intended to show the American people that the government truly cared about those it forced to suffer. As an exercise in public relations, such demonstrations of goodwill were generally received positively and were very cost effective (after all, the congressional money had already been appropriated and only $50,000 was spent for medals).

The USOC, quick to learn from the government's example, sought to mend its fences in similar ways. Inevitably, the committee had by its boycott decision alienated many, if not most, of the athletes it ostensibly represented and found itself badly in need of reestablishing intraorganizational rapport. Miller concurred that the awarding of congressional medals was appropriate, and went so far as to say that not only the athletes should receive such commendation, but that sports officials who supported the boycott should be honored as well through some type of ceremony. The USOC fully agreed with Miller's sentiments. It committed between $5 and $6 million to national governing bodies for both athletic and ceremonial functions. While most of the money funded various international competitions, an estimated $950,000 was destined for such non-sporting purposes as a "Recognition Day" in Washington, numerous parties, and gifts.[64] Although the sense of betrayal felt by so many athletes toward their Olympic Committee and its leaders could hardly be assuaged so easily, the post-boycott efforts of the USOC were at least a start in that direction.

Threats

Implementation of "persuasive" measures by the White House, including "advice" rendered by governmental officials, invocation of moral and nationalistic imperatives, and various athletic, monetary, and symbolic incentives, were used in conjunction with outright threats. Often in somewhat veiled form, those threats nonetheless were understood by those to whom they were directed, namely the USOC; they may well have been the decisive factor in the Olympic Committee's acceptance of Carter's boycott proposal.

To understand the effectiveness of the coercive tool relative to the USOC, it is crucial to be cognizant of the committee's particular vulnerabilities. Without question, the organization's financial condition offered the broadest target to those seeking to exert leverage. The committee was the principal fund-raiser to train, outfit, and transport Olympic athletes. Almost one-third of what it anticipated to be a $26 million budget for the 1980 Games was to be obtained through corporate contributions, given in return for the right of a business to use the Olympic symbol in its advertisements and on its products. The remainder of its funds were to be derived from private donations.[65] Heavy reliance upon individual contributions meant that public perception of the value of Olympic endeavors was crucial. Should any grave doubts be cast upon the Olympic movement, or on the 1980 Games in particular, there could be little doubt that contributions would be adversely affected. One additional monetary concern was that, with sufficient negative publicity about the Games, the one-time $16 million appropriation before Congress designed for grassroots athletic development would be defeated.[66] That the USOC's financial position was tenuous, and liable to serious deterioration under certain circumstances, was borne out by the course of events. Donald Miller lamented, several months after the Moscow Games had been contested, that "contributions almost stopped cold because of the boycott"; indeed, the USOC went $11 million into debt.[67]

Although most susceptible to economic coercion, the USOC was also vulnerable in areas dominated by presidential and congressional power. Specifically, while only the USOC had the constitutional authority to adopt a boycott, the president could order the revocation of passports, thereby effecting the same result. On a more basic level, the USOC, incorporated through an act of Congress, could conceivably have its charter threatened.[68] Likewise, Congress had the power to alter the committee's tax exempt status, a move that would strike a severe blow to its financial solvency.[69] Yet another ploy was possible should the government deem it necessary to circumvent USOC authority, and that pertained to the implementation of emergency powers delegated by Congress to the president.[70] While all these moves against the USOC and/or its policy decisions would be extreme, they were far from implausible.

We now turn to an examination of those threats that were actually directed against the USOC during the course of the domestic boycott campaign; it should then become possible to determine the relative significance that coercive pressure played in the committee's final decision. In the first weeks following [fjCarter's decision to utilize the Olympic Games politically, the White House circumspectly conveyed to the Olympic Committee, in a series of ever more direct threats, its inferiority and impotence in the face of government power. The committee was informed that any attempt to thwart the will of the president would be futile. Submission would be exacted; the USOC had only the choice of presenting the appearance of making the proper decision itself, or of having that decision made publicly for it and implemented against its wishes.

Secretary of State Vance initiated the campaign to undermine the self-confidence and will to resist of the Olympic leaders as early as January 15. Responding to a question regarding the ability of the government to compel a boycott, he hinted that such power was available in sufficient magnitude to make its actual use unnecessary: "If the Government expressed its views, I believe that our citizens would follow that view."[71] Shortly thereafter, but prior to the Olympic Committee's decision to present the IOC with the government resolution requesting that the Games be moved, postponed, or canceled, presidential counsel Lloyd Cutler intimated that passport restrictions could be used to enforce a boycott, but that he did not "think that contingency would arise."[72] Attorney General Benjamin R. Civiletti moved beyond acknowledging the mere existence of tactics alluded to by Vance and Cutler. He explicitly stated that, although the USOC was expected to comply voluntarily with White House policy, in the event that a problem arose the Justice Department was studying the legal means available to it to enforce a boycott.[73]

In further efforts to ensure that the USOC would agree to present the government's position to the IOC, as well as to acquiesce in all future administration decisions, threats became far less discreet. White House aides warned Olympic leaders that they would, if necessary, request Congress to amend the USOC charter and to withhold its pending $16 million appropriation.[74] Cutler reemphasized the administration's readiness to use coercion when he noted, in connection with Carter's desire for the USOC to act as his liaison with the International Committee:

The President has made a request, he's not given an order to the U.S.O.C., even though it is a committee that is incorporated by an Act of Congress. . . . We don't think the need is going to arise to consider further measures of a compulsive character, but you have only to look at that vote of 386-12 [on a House bill supporting Carter's position] to see what the Congress might wish to do should it become necessary.[75]

Carter attempted to tone down his subordinates' zealousness, but still made it clear that he contemplated the use of obligatory measures should they be required, when he stated, "I would prefer *at this time* not to exercise legislative authority over the U.S.O.C. or American athletes."[76]

Over the next six weeks, the administration became noticeably more tactful regarding the use of coercive measures. Civiletti no longer spoke of passport revocation, but instead emphasized "consensus and cooperation."[77] If at all possible, Carter wanted to win his fight on the home front without resorting to "force" and with as little blatant intimidation as necessary. Such a victory would be viewed with considerably more weight abroad, as demonstrable of true American opinion, and would entail less domestic political risk. A democratic leader, after all, must always resort to compulsion with the knowledge that electoral suicide may be the result.

As the USOC vote on participation loomed near, Carter abandoned caution and wielded threats with impunity. At a March 21 meeting at the White House, which over 150 athletes and coaches attended, Carter stated policy without attempting to persuade. His guests were told, "I cannot say what other nations will not go. Ours will not go."[78] He told them that he could, should the IOC authorize athletes to compete under the Olympic flag, stop all movements to the USSR by declaring a national emergency.[79] Although Carter assured that such an action "would be a drastic step I wouldn't want to face," he refused to forego such an option.[80] Willie Davenport, the 1968 Olympic hurdles champion in attendance at the meeting, communicated the effect of Carter's message with absolute clarity: "The President closed the door. . . . And not only did he close the door, but he locked it and threw the key away."[81]

Once again, USOC leaders were warned by government officials that Carter would use whatever means necessary to prevent teams from traveling to Moscow, including blocking currency transfers, proposing changes in the statute under which the USOC was organized, and implementing various import-export restrictions. Carter was reticent about barring individual athletes from competing, which would require the lifting of passports, but did not rule it out should the IOC change its guidelines to allow individuals to compete without national affiliation. Although Warren Christopher claimed that the USOC was not being "threaten[ed]," that organization's leaders clearly believed otherwise and expressed dismay at the intensity of White House pressure.[82]

Perhaps most distressing to USOC leaders was Carter's willingness to strike directly at the heart of the committee's financial stability. Ann Wexler, a White House official acting as assistant to the president for public liaison, began to exert direct pressure on corporate donations to the Olympic cause. She made a "request" to Edward R. Telling, chairman of Sears, Roebuck and Company, to withhold the final $25,000 of a three year, $75,000 contribution until the committee authorized a boycott. Sears agreed to the government request.[83] Donald Miller, who accused the White House of "sheer blackmail,"[84] indicated that sixteen corporations followed Sears's lead, resulting in a loss of more than $200,000 in pledges. In addition to that, five more firms with contracts with the USOC for endorsement privileges were delinquent in payment. The net result of the government's intimidation, according to Miller, was that the committee's fund-raising campaign was $1.2 million short of its projected quarterly intake of $4.2 million. Although most of the companies involved rejected any causal relationship between White House pressure and their failure to make good on agreements with the Olympic Committee, their denials were far from convincing.[85]

In the days preceding the April 12 USOC convention, Carter, rather than having second thoughts about the potential backlash his coercive policy might cause, redoubled his efforts. He met with congressional leaders Byrd and O'Neill to assess the feasibility of amending the 1978 Amateur Athletic Act as a means of preventing the athletes from circumventing government policy. The 1978 act was the statute that officially authorized the USOC to field teams for the Olympics. It also approved government subsidies for training facilities as well as providing other forms of support. Carter made it known that he contemplated taking the drastic step of certifying the existence of a national emergency to enable him to utilize the emergency economic powers authorized by the International Emergency Economic Powers Act of 1977 to forestall any and all U.S. participation at Moscow.[86]

In a final attempt to convince even the most die-hard opponents of a boycott that any USOC decision that countermanded the president's wishes would be unceremoniously overridden, Carter made a speech hours before the USOC meeting was to begin in Colorado Springs that clearly outlined his intentions. The simple declaration, "If legal actions are necessary, then I will take those actions," said it all.[87] Nothing more was required to demonstrate to the Olympic delegates the utter futility of opposition.

Summary

The decision by the House of Delegates not to send a team to Moscow was a complex one, predicated on a number of factors. The influence of prominent governmental authorities was utilized; such persuasive efforts carried considerable impact. The need to reaffirm a dedication to national honor and to a patriotism that transcended individual interest was another important ingredient. Likewise, monetary and symbolic incentives offered in return for supporting the president held a certain sway over the Olympic Committee.

Nonetheless, in the final analysis it was the ability of the White House to convince the athletes of its determination and capacity to exploit its sheer strength, as contrasted to the USOC's relative weakness, that was the decisive factor behind the decision of April 12. Carter's persistent repetition of both overt and thinly veiled threats, whether through his own statements or through those of his subordinates or key congressional sympathizers, served its purpose, despite leaving a legacy of bitterness. This sense of government power, and of the athletes' impotence, was captured by the president of the Amateur Athletic Union, Robert Helmick, when he bemoaned, "We cannot allow the government to set a precedent here, because the precedent is pure coercion. Should government influence corporations on how they donate to charities? Should we stand for selective tax-exempt status? Selective lifting of passports?"[88] The answer sought to these questions was obviously "no," but the dilemma of how to effect that reality was one the USOC was unable to solve.

PUBLIC OPINION

The domestic boycott campaign involved additional aspects beyond the government's attempts to secure the compliance of the USOC with its policies. The White House realized that it was important not only to get the support of the Olympic Committee, but also to obtain the consensus backing of the people of the United States. Only through such a combination could the administration most forcefully present its case to foreign nations. Carter's leadership qualities were somewhat suspect in the international arena, and other states sought as firm an assurance as possible that Carter's policies reflected U.S. public opinion, and could therefore be relied upon to be effectively pursued, prior to committing themselves to the U.S. position. It was with this in mind that Carter sought to harness and to develop further what soon emerged as the strong popular support for utilizing the Olympics as a political weapon.

Although initially uncertain of public reaction to intimations that the Olympics was under consideration as a possible retaliatory instrument against the Soviet aggression in Afghanistan, the White House was quickly overwhelmed by a flood of support. A *San Francisco Examiner* poll of January 11, based on a random sampling of 16,393 persons, found 75 percent in favor of a boycott.[89] Shortly thereafter, Gallup conducted a poll for *Newsweek* and found similar sentiment. With a margin of error of plus or minus 5 percent, the poll found that 75 percent of those surveyed favored a shift in sites, and, should that fail, 56 percent supported a boycott. Not only was a boycott endorsed, but it was also felt by 52 percent of the respondents that such an action would directly affect Soviet foreign policy.[90] The *Washington Star* conducted a survey that revealed even more partisan results; 86 percent of those responding endorsed a boycott, 80 percent favored relocation.[91] The Olympic House in Colorado received hundreds of telegrams, the vast majority of which called for a boycott.[92] That public opinion remained firm, even with a U.S. boycott looming ever more certain, was confirmed by a *New York Times/CBS News* poll conducted between February 13 and February 17. In a survey of 1,536 adults, the poll strongly reaffirmed public support of a boycott: 72 percent endorsed such a policy, only 21 percent were opposed.[93]

Offering a multifaceted array of arguments, the leaders of public opinion, at least in the arena of mass circulation newspapers and magazines,[94] reinforced public opinion as it had first been expressed. Red Smith, the influential *New York Times* sportswriter, immediately declared his support for utilizing the Olympics in a retaliatory fashion. He wrote a number of articles in which he proffered the view that the athletes must accept the fact that the Olympic Games was inherently political and as such was subject to external manipulation. Such a situation should not be resented, it was argued, since it allowed the United States to take meaningful measures without resorting to war.[95] Even were a boycott to have little actual effect, it was said to be an intrinsically just action. After all, Smith observed, "It is unthinkable that in existing circumstances we could go play games with Ivan in Ivan's yard and participate in a great lawn party showing off Russian splendors to the world."[96] *Sports Illustrated*, agreeing with Smith's basic premise, declared its support of the Carter position and admonished all Americans to rally to their President's side.[97] Pete Axthelm, a well-known commentator, implored athletes both to recognize that "their problems tend to pale next to those of people dying in various corners of Afghanistan" and to sacrifice for a cause greater than their own.[98]

That the written mass media was not the only influential source affecting the formation of a public opinion that was generally supportive of a boycott can be seen through two brief examples. First, the AFL-CIO reaffirmed what had been, long before events in Afghanistan, its opposition to Moscow as a site for the Olympic Games. Its leaders unanimously adopted a resolution going beyond calling for a boycott of Moscow to include advocating the contemplation of complete withdrawal from the IOC.[99] Second, and of potentially greater influence, were the pronouncements of Tatyana Yankelvich, the stepdaughter of Andrei Sakharov. Speaking in New York City, she related the efforts by Soviet authorities to rid Moscow of dissidents before the Games, and called upon the United States to keep its athletes home.[100] The effect of such words upon an American populace already keenly sensitized to Soviet transgressions of internationally acceptable behavior was significant.

One further manifestation of the state of U.S. public opinion could be gleaned from a cursory analysis of the editorials and letters printed by the *New York Times*. Even taking into account the arguably conservative orientation of the paper, the pro-boycott position affirmed in the majority of letters contributed by the public and chosen for publication lent credence to the observation that

Americans generally accepted Carter's proposals. Numerous arguments were cited in support of the editorials' views: the cost a boycott would inflict upon the Soviets; the idea that the sacrifices of past athletes in World War II, such as Ted Williams and Joe Louis, should be respected and followed by today's Olympians; the idea that the Olympics had become unredeemably corrupt and should be abolished altogether; the belief that participation would be a humiliation to the president, and the USOC therefore should submit to public dictates and desist from trying to conduct an independent foreign policy; and, simply, that sometimes "the show must *not* go on." [101]

Lest it be thought that Carter was content to ride passively this wave of public approbation for his boycott, we turn now to an examination of active measures pursued by the White House to solidify and expand popular support. The first avenue pursued was to capitalize on the apparent eagerness of Congress to become identified with the boycott. This interest was all the more important because it was bipartisan in nature.[102] Prominent Democrats, including New York Senator Daniel Patrick Moynihan and Senate majority leader Robert C. Byrd, were outspoken advocates of Carter's policy. Moynihan, appearing on NBC-TV's "Today Show," accused the Soviets of creating an "outrageous violation of the United Nations Charter of every principle of peaceful international relations" and concluded that it was inappropriate to go to their "festival." [103] Byrd concurred, and advocated that the Games either be moved, or, failing that, that the United States should abstain from participation and encourage other states to do the same. He argued that the Games "constitute a political windfall for the Soviets in the wake of their outrageous invasion of Afghanistan," and urged that the reality of the political interpenetration of sports be acknowledged.[104] The Republican National Committee adopted a similar stance, approving a resolution calling upon the USOC to move the Games from Moscow.[105] Even Bill Bradley, the Democratic senator from New Jersey who was the only member of the current Congress personally to have participated in the Olympics, announced that he "would probably support a [boycott] resolution." [106]

With the probability of getting a congressional stamp of approval for his policies virtually assured, Carter urged immediate legislative action on a resolution calling upon the USOC to ask the International Committee either to move, postpone, or cancel the Games. The Foreign Affairs Committee of the House rushed through a nonbinding resolution—with only one dissent—and the full House of Representatives immediately gave its approval by a resounding, and in recent years unheard of, vote of 386 to 12.[107] Although the Senate was somewhat slower to act, it went even further than did the House. The Senate Foreign Relations Committee unanimously approved a resolution calling for the postponement, relocation, or cancellation of the Games, and, failing IOC approval of such measures, endorsed a complete boycott by athletes and spectators. The Senate as a whole adopted the Foreign Relations Committee's proposal by an overwhelming margin, 88 to 4. It should be noted that the Senate made no mention of a possible Soviet withdrawal, unlike the House which had made U.S. action predicated on the Soviets' failure to remove their forces by February 20.[108] With little effort, Carter had secured an endorsement of his plan of action that was unequivocal, and that could be parlayed readily both into mobilizing the public and into pressuring the USOC.

In addition to utilizing Congress to bolster public enthusiasm for a boycott, Carter established special White House and State Department units which were charged with, among other boycott-related duties, presenting a positive image of Carter's policies to the people of the United States. Lloyd Cutler was to lead the ad hoc working group within the White House, while Nelson Ledsky chaired the State Department task force. While such groups were directly in charge of organizing and supervising the boycott campaign, Carter was not reluctant to call upon other government officials to promote his cause. The boycott was too important to exempt any person from its facilitation.

These prominent government figures were instructed not merely to identify themselves with the massive outpouring of support for the boycott, but to generate additional interest and to provide themes with which public sentiment could identify. They were to transform amorphous public sympathy for administration policy into solid backing premised on an association of the boycott with specific policy objectives. These objectives included providing symbolic sympathy for Afghanistan, mobilizing world outrage, checking future aggression, preventing the Soviets from achieving a propaganda victory, and inflicting immediate political costs upon the Kremlin.

Carter himself capped the administration's attempts to direct public opinion when he authorized the White House to issue a statement in late March that declared Soviet aggression to be "an unusual and extraordinary threat to the national security, foreign policy and economy of the United States." [109] Such a dire assessment was designed to reinforce natural predilections against Kremlin actions in Afghanistan, while also providing broad justifications for such reactions that could be assimilated into the public's understanding of the situation. The antecedents to this climactic phase of the public relations campaign could be found in early January, and provide important insights into the goals and strategies of the effort itself.

In the United States, the public was targeted by the White House to be prepared carefully over a period of time to accept the idea of a boycott and to share the government's rationale for such a policy. On January 11, Vice President Mondale and first lady Rosalyn Carter both declared, speaking to separate audiences, that, in their "personal" opinion, the Games should be moved.[110] This was the first, somewhat tentative, attempt to evoke public reaction to the idea of threatening the Moscow Games without, it should be stressed, committing the government in an official context to such a policy. During this early phase, the government maintained a restrained, moderate position. Carter said nothing publicly, while Vance stated that the United States still preferred to have the Games in Moscow, although the Afghan situation would have to be the determinant of U.S. policy. A State Department spokesman likewise claimed that "The President believes and views this as an open question," with the U.S. response still predicated upon the final policy decisions of the Kremlin.[111]

As an American consensus began to emerge that the Olympics was an appropriate weapon for retaliation against Moscow, the White House became less oblique in its pronouncements. A more strident tone was adopted that reflected Carter's belief that the American people were behind him on this issue, and that therefore he could "lead" with little risk. By the latter part of January, Carter personally identified himself with efforts to move, postpone, or cancel the Games. He appeared on NBC-TV's "Meet the Press" and declared, "Neither I nor the American people would support the sending of an American team to Moscow with Soviet invasion troops in Afghanistan."[112] This direct association of government policy with public opinion was also seen in statements by Deputy Secretary of State Warren Christopher. He observed "a growing feeling [in the United States] of the inappropriateness of holding the games in Moscow and [a] feeling that they should be held in some other place." He added, shortly thereafter, that, although the United States should be prepared to act alone if necessary, he felt that "a great many nations" would stand behind U. S. policy.[113] Carter and other government officials had waited for public sentiment to become manifest, and then had sought to line up behind it and, if possible, to encourage its development and focus.

In the course of what was a complicated interplay between government policy and public opinion, in which it was often far from clear as to who was leading whom, Carter finally emerged as a force to solidify and focus an already supportive popular sentiment. His success in this endeavor enabled a unified front, consisting of the president, Congress, and the American people, to be presented both to the USOC and to other nations.[114] The USOC was placed in a position whereby defiance of Carter would be equated with disdain for the wishes of the public in general. Meanwhile, such a solid domestic base would be an asset in efforts to sway foreign states toward accepting the U.S. boycott. After all, the president, in an election year, had committed himself to such a policy, and he had the firm support of the electorate. Under those circumstances, it was unlikely that Carter would waver from his stand and leave nations which had expressed solidarity with the United States to fend for themselves. As noted previously, the analytic distinction drawn in this study between the domestic and international components of the boycott campaign is not to be accepted as one reflective of events as they actually transpired; indeed, a very close interrelationship existed between the two milieux.

LEGISLATION

Apart from its direct efforts to influence the USOC and to channel public opinion, the government also wielded its power over commercial matters to affect the amount of U.S. business support provided to Moscow and the possibility and extent of television coverage made accessible to the American audience. This executive action, as distinct from the threats already enumerated, was relatively restricted in scope. It nonetheless had a significant impact.

Desiring to minimize any benefits Moscow might obtain through U.S. corporate support and expertise, Carter requested, via the Commerce Department, approximately thirty U.S. companies to withhold voluntarily $20-30 million in exports related to the Games. This request, made March 12, placed the companies involved in an awkward position, while hardly ensuring that Moscow would be seriously hurt. The businesses, because of the voluntary nature of the embargo, were confronted with the dilemma that adherence to Carter's "request" could result in legal action stemming from breach of contract, not to mention the fact that their reputations as reliable suppliers would be tarnished, while defiance of the embargo could be seized upon as unpatriotic and as catering to Soviet interests, with the attendant damage to their images. The Soviets, meanwhile, could turn to other states to supply most of the lost products, thereby rendering the U.S. action ineffective.[115]

It was with these potential problems in mind that Carter, on March 28, made the embargo on the export of Olympic-related products mandatory. In addition, the White House promised to try to coordinate its efforts with other countries that could act as alternate suppliers so as to avoid making the sacrifice by U.S. businesses a purely symbolic one. This ban, affecting such companies as Levi-Strauss and Pepsi-Cola which were to supply merchandise and products to the Games, also included payments to be tendered to the Soviets in return for television rights. NBC-TV, which had already forwarded $61 out of $87 million to the Soviets for that purpose, was prevented from sending the Soviets the remaining payments, as well as from shipping further equipment to Moscow to be utilized during the course of coverage.[116]

NBC-TV, realizing that the chance for U.S. participation was bleak and that the image of the Moscow Games had been irreparably damaged, readily agreed to comply with the embargo. The network had, from the beginning of the debate on the Games, chosen to remain in the background, repeatedly stating that its actions would be guided by government policy. Although the Games had been hoped to be a financial windfall, not to mention a major ratings boon, for the last place network, NBC realized that covering the Games in the absence of the United States not only would have minimum viewer appeal, it could also foster a negative image of the company. Thus, it sought to dissociate itself from the Games as soon as practicable, the only major obstacle being the terms of its insurance policy (which necessitated it waiting until government policy had been irrevocably decreed, and been accepted in principle by the USOC, before it could cancel its contract with Moscow and collect damages).

The White House had to deal with some complaints regarding the embargo, but on the whole it was accepted without much protest. In fact, probably the most vehement opposition came not from any of the companies actually affected, but rather from the American Society of Newspaper Editors, an organization concerned with the constitutional implications of the embargo. Specifically, it argued that such an action would result in the practical impossibility of NBC televising the Games had it so chosen; NBC denied the group's contention.[117] Thus, the White House was able to impose trade restrictions that, whatever their actual effectiveness, reinforced public perceptions that the administration was determined to do whatever necessary to reduce U.S. presence in Moscow to an absolute minimum, while simultaneously demonstrating to the USOC that acquiescence was the most prudent policy.

CONCLUSION

The varied approach adopted by Carter toward the domestic boycott campaign yielded its desired dividends. The combination of "persuasive" measures with threatening statements and actions forced a reluctant USOC leadership to accept the heretofore unthinkable. After all, the president and the executive director of that body had originally denounced any political manipulation of the Games. Kane, reacting to Carter's initial boycott warning, stated, "I'm a little bit shocked by his statements. I wonder if he understood all the implications." Miller, responding in kind, stressed, "if the Olympic Games are to survive, they must be apolitical and remain in the private sector."[118] Although USOC cooperation was the main objective, Carter's ability to capitalize on favorable public opinion was significant in that it softened the perceptions of what many saw as the strong-armed tactics utilized against the Olympic Committee. The government could hardly be accused of being overly coercive when it was just trying to ensure that the public will was being respected. Public sentiment was used to isolate the USOC, and would force it either into submission or into the position of being a recalcitrant who must be dealt with summarily. In addition, the consensus nature of American popular opinion was a positive factor in attempts to rally international support. Finally, direct executive action, primarily in the form of an embargo of goods and services destined for Moscow, completed the effective termination of any significant U.S. association with the 1980 Summer Olympics.

4

The International Campaign

We now turn to the international element of the boycott effort. Despite oft-repeated protestations to the contrary, the United States was vitally concerned that it act in concert with as many states as possible; it is only with a firm grasp of this fact that one can appreciate the importance placed by Carter upon international acceptance of the U.S. initiative. The White House possessed no illusions as to the futility of any unilateral action. Not only could such an endeavor produce no positive results, it would subject the nation and the government to worldwide ridicule and to accusations of "warmongering" by the Soviets. The Kremlin's skill and expertise at propaganda dissemination required that a diverse spectrum of states coalesce against the Moscow Games; only such a variegated array of nations could effectively rebut Soviet attempts to paint the boycott in terms of yet another ill-conceived Cold War plot instigated by the United States and designed to undermine the peace-loving efforts of the Soviet Union.

The White House was cognizant of the fact that, in order to inflict punishment on the Kremlin, a boycott had to be both quantitatively and qualitatively supported by foreign states. This required an all-inclusive campaign to bolster the number of states involved, while it also demanded an intensive effort directed at enlisting the cooperation of the preeminent sporting nations. Only such a dual-oriented approach could achieve both the semblance of a global condemnation of Soviet aggression and a significant reduction in the quality of the Games. It was with this strategy in mind that Carter requested over 100 foreign leaders to reject participation at Moscow;[1] this general communique was hoped to elicit support from all areas of the globe, and from as many countries as possible. At the same time, however, the limited amount of diplomatic resources that could be utilized for this matter required a prioritizing of government effort. Thus, the approximately twenty nations with the premier athletes, excluding, of course, the Eastern European states, were selected to receive the greatest attention.[2] It was felt that should a majority of those countries accept a boycott, the IOC could well reconsider its refusal to abandon Moscow as the site of the Games; failing that, at least the level of competition would be seriously affected. One thing was certain, however, and that was that the United States would never act unilaterally. As Lloyd Cutler revealed, "Do not infer from what you read that we'll be doing anything alone."[3]

MEANS UTILIZED

In order to effect a boycott on an international scale, the White House resorted to four separate techniques: "conventional" diplomacy; the use of private persons as unofficial ambassadors; the promise of support for an alternate sports competition; and direct pressure on the IOC. As discussed in the previous chapter, any success at securing foreign support was predicated largely on the U.S. domestic response to Carter's proposal. Therefore, it should be remembered that the various schemes to rally international enthusiasm for a boycott had a clearly American component that could not be discounted. The significance of this factor was a driving force behind the administration's efforts to get the USOC to make a quick decision. As Mondale stated to the American committee, "Athletes and sports organizations and national bodies around the world await your lead to mobilize their commitment."[4] Carter correctly believed that without a firm endorsement of a boycott by the USOC the Europeans would be reluctant to act, and, accordingly, the numerous states which looked toward Europe for guidance would be hesitant to declare their support.

"Conventional" Diplomacy

State-to-state contacts, or "conventional" diplomacy, was one instrument Carter employed in his efforts to gain international acceptance for his Olympic policy. While stressing different themes depending on the country he was addressing, Carter used this technique on a global scale. As noted above, Carter contacted over 100 heads of state; in addition, he sent 150 governments a copy of his letter to the USOC in which he urged the committee to attempt to move, postpone, or cancel the Games.[5] Various government officials, including Cyrus Vance and Warren Christopher, were dispatched in the course of the campaign to numerous states to solicit support. Since the United States sought the backing of both its allies and the nonaligned Third World, its approach had to be tailored to the specific country with which it dealt.

When conferring with its Western allies, including Japan and Canada, the White House emphasized the importance of presenting Moscow with a unified front. Mondale characterized the boycott as "a keystone in our call to our allies for solidarity."[6] Carter was prepared to make acceptance of his position a litmus test of allied relations, and made it obvious that he would exert whatever pressure he could muster to increase "cooperation."

Although Carter's position was clear, the allies' initial response was hardly overwhelming. The State Department pronounced reaction to be "most encouraging" and stated that "We have been promised support from our traditional allies," but the facts belied such optimistic assessments.[7] Great Britain exhibited the most enthusiasm for Carter's policies, but was not prepared to make a definite commitment. Margaret Thatcher, the British prime minister, gave Carter grounds for hope, but little more, when she stated, "No one can do anything alone. We shall try to do it by taking concerted action with our allies to make a concerted approach to the International Olympic Committee."[8] Canada was supportive, but noncommittal, while West German and Greek reaction was lukewarm at best. France was hostile to the U.S. initiative.

As events unfolded, Carter's efforts at swaying U.S. allies toward his boycott yielded a sparse return. The British government became a fervent supporter of Carter, at least rhetorically, yet was defied by the British Olympic Association. The French, for appearance's sake only, made some moves toward endorsing a boycott, but remained in opposition. West Germany, with extreme reluctance and amid great controversy, became the only major West European country to boycott the Moscow Games.[9] Japan and Canada likewise came to accept nonparticipation. Needless to say, this outcome hardly fulfilled Carter's desire for a show of allied solidarity.

Since the boycott was to be presented to the Soviets in terms of a global response, not in the context of an East-West confrontation, the White House had to appeal for Third World support. This was done by emphasizing that the events in Afghanistan were a threat to world peace and were a morally reprehensible action that could not be accepted by any nation. Carter pleaded, "This is a morally indecent act . . . , and I cannot imagine the democratic or freedom-loving nations adding an imprimatur of approval to the Soviets' invasion by sending teams to the Moscow Olympics."[10] Carter's appeal could be interpreted in the broadest possible way. The Third World was offered an opportunity to join in punishing aggression, and thereby to establish some measure of credibility for the "freedom-loving" label which many of them had adopted. However, as with U.S. efforts aimed at the Western allies, attempts to woo the Third World had only mixed results. The African, Asian, and Latin American reaction to Carter's proposal will be explored in considerable detail in a later section of this chapter.

With the exception of such an athletic power as Kenya, Carter's state-to-state diplomacy focused primarily upon Western allies and friends, particularly Britain, France, West Germany, Japan, and Canada. It was these nations that had achieved the most Olympic success, and that would have the greatest qualitative impact should they boycott. Western solidarity was the theme emphasized in dealings with these powers. In the more limited state-to-state contacts with Third World nations, a universal moral imperative was stressed that was designed to enable these countries to act without becoming liable to accusations of toadying to U.S. demands. For reasons to be discussed later, neither of these governmental approaches was overly effective; in fact, such efforts were rarely the determining factor in the decisions of foreign Olympic committees regarding the participation issue.

Private Persons

In the Third World context, specifically in Africa, Carter opted for a rather unconventional tactic to enlist support. He commissioned a private citizen, former world heavyweight boxing champion Muhammad Ali, to visit five African states. Selected because of his enormous worldwide popularity, coupled with the fact that he was a black Muslim, Ali was sent to Tanzania, Kenya, Nigeria, Liberia, and Senegal. Lloyd Cutler characterized Ali's mission as one in which Carter sought to employ "useful contacts, both public and private," to further the boycott. Ali himself described his task in the following words, "President Carter has asked me to visit some of the African countries as soon as possible. . . . I have to explain the U.S. stand on the subject of the Moscow Olympics." [11] That the decision to use Ali was made at the highest levels was confirmed by the fact that the U.S. embassy in New Delhi, where Ali was conducting a charity tour at the time he was solicited for participation in the boycott maneuvers, knew nothing of the arrangement. When apprised of the situation, it could only plead ignorance, saying that "Ali's people have been dealing with Washington directly." [12]

The controversy provoked by Ali's appointment, and that which surrounded his travels, highlighted the problematic nature of using a private citizen for a delicate diplomatic mission. Confronted by hostile reporters who questioned the audacity of the United States to request African support for its boycott when America had failed to back the 1976 black African boycott, Ali appeared unnerved. He obviously had not been briefed on the matter, and declared that if he had known the "whole history of America and South Africa" he would have rejected undertaking such a trip. [13]

In addition to the candidness Ali exhibited, which created embarrassment for the White House, Ali's journey was also plagued by African resentment over Carter's apparent expectation that state leaders would consent to meet with an ordinary citizen. [14] Nigeria's president, Alhaji Shehu Shagari, refused such a meeting; he also exerted pressure on Nigeria's Olympic Committee to abstain from any contacts with Ali. Julius Nyerere, the president of Tanzania, refused to confer with Ali for similar reasons. [15]

In the final analysis, Carter's decision to act somewhat creatively by circumventing normal diplomatic procedure must be judged a failure. Ali did not generate increased support, while he may have created a degree of hostility to the U.S. position that had not previously existed. Carter's action signified his willingness to employ all possible resources in his fight, but lack of political insight and judgment doomed this particular endeavor.

Support for Alternate Event

Just as an alternate sports competition was offered to U.S. athletes as an incentive to cooperate with the president, so it was also presented, in somewhat different form, to entice foreign Olympians. Whereas domestic plans focused on a national sports festival, international efforts were directed toward multi-national competition open to all states, to be held after the Moscow Games. Both efforts sought to reward support for a boycott with some type of alternate event.[16]

Carter committed himself to providing the sportsmen of the world with a competition worthy of their participation well before his February 20 deadline for Soviet withdrawal had become operative. He declared, "I want athletes from all around the world to know that I am determined personally that they will have an opportunity to participate this year in international games of the highest quality, but unless invading forces in Afghanistan are withdrawn, in a location other than the Soviet Union."[17] The White House, in an attempt to imbue such sentiment with substance, said it was willing to ask Congress for up to $500 million either to help relocate the Games, or, if the IOC refused such a move, to subsidize a counter-Olympics. Lloyd Cutler indicated there would be ample support for such a bill.[18]

The State Department wished to avoid any misunderstanding as to the willingness of the U.S. government to play such an active role in any alternate competitions. It stated, quite frankly, that an international event "as broad and large as possible" was sought as a way of rewarding countries which aligned themselves with the United States.[19] After all, no concern for the welfare of athletes, much less of those representing foreign countries, could be expected to prompt the United States to commit a half billion dollars of its resources to their aid. Without pretense, Carter offered a simple quid pro quo: alternate event for boycott support.

The precise nature of any "Free World Olympics" or alternate international competition remained, during the period in which it was seriously contemplated, highly ambiguous. The range of options included a national sports festival incorporating international competition, a "Free World Olympics" held at a single site (possibly Montreal or Melbourne), and a series of events located in several different countries. It was finally determined that any such event should be held in more than one location. This would help forestall a polarization of the Olympic movement into "East" and "West" blocs. In another step designed to prevent such an eventuality, all participants in the Moscow Games would be invited to these international competitions.[20] A multitude of locations was to be coupled with geographic diversity of participants to create a broadly based event not susceptible to castigation by the Soviets as an exacerbation of the "new" Cold War by the United States.

What turned out to be the high-water mark of U.S. attempts to organize an alternate international competition was a meeting held in Geneva, Switzerland, on March 18 between spokesmen for twelve different countries, including representatives from Africa,[21] Latin America, Europe, America, Canada, and Australia. The meeting, largely the result of efforts by the U.S. State Department's Olympic task force, was, however, convened jointly by the United States, Britain, and Australia. These three states, as well as Canada, had discussed possible options among themselves prior to the conference in the hope that they, being among the most influential of those expected to attend, could present a unified position to the others.[22] The product of the multinational meeting was a pronouncement promising an international sports festival of two to four weeks in length. It was to occur after the conclusion of the Olympics, sometime in August or September, and would be held at a number of as yet undetermined sites on several continents. The competition would be built upon some already scheduled events, and athletes from any nation would be allowed to participate. The revenue from the sale of television rights would finance the event.[23]

Despite the apparent promise of this meeting, it had a number of fatal flaws. First, of the twelve participating countries, only a fraction were actually involved in the decision-making process. The major powers dictated terms and expected them to be carried out. This was not conducive to consensual action. In addition, there were too few governments represented to get such an ambitious project off the ground. Finally, and perhaps most significantly, the failure of the meeting to specify details, whether regarding dates, sites, financing, or expected levels of participation, left too much to be done in a limited amount of time. Generalities would never result in action; perhaps that was the true intention of the participants. Whatever the real aims of those in Geneva, by the beginning of April the United States had abandoned all plans for either a domestic sports festival or an international competition.

The impact of a proposed international sporting event in luring foreign commitment to the U.S. position was limited for several reasons. First, it should be remembered that this incentive would hold sway primarily over athletes and those directly responsible to athletes. This meant that in those states where a de facto separation between the government and the national Olympic committee did not exist, the offer of an alternative games had little effect. Governmental leaders based their decisions upon foreign policy considerations and potential domestic political consequences, not out of regard for their athletes' welfare. Second, in countries where national Olympic committees did possess a degree of independence, the lure of an alternate competition simply had little effect. Athletes in general felt that nothing could compare to the "real thing," so if there was to be no Olympics, they cared little if something else was offered as a replacement. Finally, since all states would be permitted to compete in any alternate event, the prospect of such a competition could not be expected to influence either a government's or a national Olympic committee's decision regarding the Moscow Games.

Government Pressure on the IOC

One final tactic utilized by the White House in its attempt to punish the Soviet Union vis-à-vis the Summer Olympics was to endeavor to exert direct pressure on the IOC to alter its oft-repeated declarations that the Games would proceed in Moscow, as scheduled, regardless of the events in Afghanistan. Efforts in this direction were most intense prior to the February meeting of the International Committee in Lake Placid, but continued intermittently, and in a less direct manner, until mid-May.

Carter, as evidenced by the diplomatic personnel employed,[24] placed considerable hope in persuading the IOC either to move, postpone,[25] or cancel the Games when that body met prior to the opening of the Winter Olympics. The administration had previously enlisted the support of the USOC for such a proposition, and would use the U.S. committee as a vehicle to present its proposal formally. In addition, top U.S. government officials were sent to the meeting to lobby for support, the most noteworthy of those being Secretary Vance.

In an unprecedented move, Vance made a direct appeal for support to the eighty-nine executive board members of the IOC in what traditionally had been a nonpolitical opening address reserved for government leaders of those nations hosting the Olympics. Vance declared, "It would be a violation of the fundamental Olympic principle to conduct or attend an Olympic Games in a nation which is currently engaged in an aggressive way and has refused to comply with the world community's demand to halt its aggression and withdraw its forces."[26] Castigating the Soviets as an "invading nation,"[27] Vance urged the IOC to respect the United Nations General Asembly's condemnation of the U.S.S.R. and to act immediately to remove the Games from Moscow. Failure to take such action would jeopardize future Games, Vance reasoned, because the broad base of support enjoyed by the Olympics would be undermined if the will of the vast majority of nations was ignored.[28]

The political thrust of Vance's speech alienated what had already been an unreceptive audience; the IOC leaders were unaccustomed to being the target of such overt pressure. Lord Killanin observed that "Vance was virtually ordering the IOC to cancel or postpone the Moscow Games"; he characterized the speech as "inappropriate to say the least."[29] Monique Berlioux, executive director of the committee, and Julian Roosevelt, an IOC member from the United States, refused any acknowledgment of Vance's address.[30] Vance had been placed in an even more untenable position when Joseph Onek, a White House aide, had, several days prior to the IOC meeting, threatened the International Committee with the destruction of the Olympic movement should it refuse to support the U.S. position.[31] Although Onek later apologized, the damage had already been done. Vance merely exacerbated an already uneasy situation.

Vance and Lloyd Cutler, White House counsel, attempted to salvage the apparent debacle by meeting with Killanin the following day. The effort proved futile. Expressing its belief that current world conditions presented "the most serious challenge to confront the Olympic Games," and indeed jeopardized the very existence of the Olympic movement and international federated sport, the IOC nevertheless unanimously reaffirmed Moscow as the site of the 1980 Summer Games.[32] It reasoned that a contract had been signed on October 23, 1974, awarding the Games to Moscow, and "all preparations have been made in keeping with the terms of that agreement and consistently with the rules of the IOC."[33] Reiterating its position that "The prime responsibility of the I.O.C. is to the young athletes of the world," the International Committee vowed to do whatever possible to promote the "right atmosphere" for the Games.[34]

Attempting to avoid an immediate confrontation that could jeopardize the Lake Placid Games, the IOC sought to placate both the United States and the Soviet Union. A statement was issued, in conjunction with the decision upholding Moscow as the site for the Summer Games, that successfully preserved a fragile balance between the two principal adversaries. It declared:

The IOC recognizes particularly the difficulties with the United States Olympic Committee and encourages it to continue its effort to make possible the participation of its athletes in the Games. Also the IOC urges the Organising Committee in Moscow and the National Olympic Committees [*sic*] of the USSR to inform the highest authorities in the government of the circumstances which have created these difficulties for so many NOCs.[35]

Thus, although the Soviet Union retained the Games, the IOC implicitly condemned the Kremlin's decision to invade Afghanistan, while the U.S. government was not reprimanded for its anti-Moscow position. Furthermore, the USOC's leaders were praised by Lord Killanin for their efforts to preserve the committee's independence.[36] That the IOC was successful in its efforts to maintain a nonconfrontational approach to the potential crisis was evident in that even the U.S. government entertained a glimmer of hope that its endeavors would eventually produce success within official Olympic circles. The White House stated that the IOC decision "left a door open" to subsequent adoption of the USOC proposal; many senior government officials more realistically surmised that there was little, if any, basis for such a hope.[37]

In subsequent months, the administration only half-heartedly continued its efforts to influence the International Committee.[38] Attention was directed more toward preserving U.S. influence in the Olympic movement than toward actually altering the stance of the IOC. On April 21, Carter sent a message to Lord Killanin assuring him that the United States was acting only in response to the events in Afghanistan and not from any malice toward the Olympic movement. The president expressed his continued support for the 1984 Los Angeles Olympics, and pledged to welcome all eligible national Olympic committees to those Games. In a May 16 White House meeting between Carter and Killanin, Carter again emphasized that the long-term U.S. commitment to the Olympics remained undiminished, and that the boycott action was a unique occurrence in response to exceptional circumstances. He also told the IOC president that "the American international federation delegates and press would be permitted to go to Moscow," and that steps were being undertaken to remedy the financial difficulties the USOC faced as a consequence of the U.S. boycott.[39] Finally, Carter declared his opposition to any efforts to establish a rival UNESCO Games or otherwise to subvert the present movement.[40] However, in what had become an obligatory reaffirmation of contradictory positions,[41] Carter emerged from the meeting stressing his determination to boycott, while Killanin melodramatically declared, "Even if I'm there alone competing, the Games will go on."[42]

The attempt to influence the IOC must be judged a total failure. Were one to examine the history of the committee, this should hardly come as a surprise; renowned for its stubborn intransigence and determination to defend what it regarded as the sanctity of sport from political corruption, one should be surprised only that the White House bothered to exert such energy in this direction. If anything, the administration only alienated supporters of the Olympic movement by appearing to feel it could manhandle the IOC as it had the USOC. Such a perception hurt efforts to gain the support of national Olympic committees throughout the world, while accomplishing nothing in a positive vein.

AREA ANALYSIS

We now proceed to a more detailed analysis of the United States-sponsored boycott on an area-by-area, country-by-country, basis. Through such an examination we will be able to discern why particular countries acted as they did, what the relative impact of U.S. efforts was, and what accounted for the successes and the failures of the campaign. This will provide a foundation upon which to evaluate the U.S. initiative; accordingly, this should permit us to reach some tentative conclusions regarding the efficacy of any such efforts in the future.

Western Europe

The somewhat unique nature of Western Europe forces one to examine its reaction to the events in Afghanistan on two distinct levels: "Western Europe" as a cooperative, partially integrated entity; and "Western Europe" as individual states comprising a larger whole.[43] This distinction, similar to that already made between the domestic and international aspects of the boycott, is an artificial one, although useful as an analytic tool. All national responses were formulated with an eye toward simultaneously satisfying the needs both of the greater "community" and of the individual states. With this reminder, we first turn to "Western Europe" as a whole.

White House officials initially expressed optimism that "substantial support" would be forthcoming from the European allies, particularly from Great Britain and the Federal Republic.[44] As diplomatic proddings proceeded throughout January and February with no concrete results, administration spokesmen continued to express the conviction that the Europeans were just "hanging back" waiting for a diplomatic resolution to the entire affair, but that, when forced to take a stand, they would align themselves with the U.S. position. It was predicted that England, Italy, West Germany, Portugal, and even France would fall into line.[45] That this failed to occur was the result of a number of factors, one of which was the inability of the United States to appreciate the European perspective on events in Afghanistan and the Soviet Union, and thus to identify issues that would attract European support.

From the standpoint of Western Europe, the invasion of Afghanistan represented a predominantly East-South, as opposed to East-West, issue.[46] The Soviet Union had invaded a Third World state, and it was felt that a response to such aggression should come from the leaders of the South. The West could support any anti-Soviet action, but events did not warrant the assertion of non-Southern leadership. Only with the January 22 sentence of Andrei Sakharov to internal exile in Gorky was there an opportunity presented to the White House to enlist Western European support for a boycott on a grand scale. The Sakharov case, precisely because it stressed human rights as opposed to the events in Afghanistan, was an extremely sensitive issue in West European politics. Yet, despite the popular uproar and the governmental reaction to the Kremlin's verdict, the United States never accorded a priority status to Sakharov's exile,[47] and thereby forfeited an enormous opportunity to capitalize on anti-Soviet sentiment.

A second reason for the failure of Western Europe to support a boycott was intra-European efforts to create a position distinct from that of the United States which would show displeasure with the Afghanistan invasion, while not seriously jeopardizing relations with the Soviet Union. It was this necessity to formulate an independent position that caused Western Europe generally to prefer to act through the European Community rather than through NATO since the European Community was removed from direct U.S. influence.[48]

In an early attempt to reach a consensus position, the Common Market foreign ministers debated the boycott issue during the first week of February. On February 5, Attilio Ruffini, chairman of the meeting, reflected general agreement when he declared that the Soviets had "destroyed the conditions that ought to exist for holding such games."[49] The European Parliament, although only an advisory body and of limited significance,[50] followed the lead of the foreign ministers and likewise endorsed a boycott.[51] The U.S. initiative appeared to be gaining momentum. However, only two weeks after the ostensibly successful February 5 meeting, a subsequent meeting revealed the existence of divisive tendencies. Prompted by French objections to a boycott, the foreign ministers could produce no common position.[52] In response to the collapse of a unified West European stance, a meeting scheduled between U.S. Secretary of State Vance and the foreign ministers fell through and Vance was forced to conduct negotiations on an individual basis.[53]

Seeking to reestablish their earlier consensus, representatives from the United Kingdom, France, and West Germany met in Paris at the beginning of March. They failed to secure their objective. Great Britain was inclined to side unreservedly with the United States, while the other two refused to adopt such a course. Meanwhile, the Netherlands and Luxembourg had already intimated that they would support a boycott, and Italy indicated it would join any Common Market action. It was assumed that Belgium and Denmark would follow the general line.[54]

Despite the repeated failures of the Western European governments to forge a common position, the foreign ministers convened another meeting on the boycott in mid-March. Held only two weeks after the meeting between France, the Federal Republic, and Great Britain had broken down with no substantive progress, this effort likewise fell short of its objectives; the only clear result was the absence of a pro-boycott consensus. West Germany, Denmark, and Belgium were particularly reticent about accepting a boycott. They argued that Carter's policy would unnecessarily hurt their relations with the Soviet Union, and that they would be forced to bear the brunt of the sacrifice for the U.S. action. France reiterated its opposition to a general boycott and refused to allow the issue to be mentioned in the meeting's final communiqué.[55] What supposedly had been a meeting to clarify the issue served instead to further cloud the matter. Although the European governments could only give advice on Olympic questions since the final decision regarding participation was reserved for their national Olympic committees,[56] their failure to take a concerted stand helped to embolden the Olympic committees to act according to the dictates of their athletes. In the following months, no clear line emerged from the Common Market nations,[57] and the athletes indeed acted as they so desired.

Prior to the failed attempts to forge a united coalition of West European governments, the national Olympic committees representing individual European states attempted, unsuccessfully, to develop a common response to the boycott issue. On February 1, the heads of eleven national Olympic committees met in Frankfurt, West Germany, for precisely such a reason. Yet, after more than five hours of discussion, no decision was reached except to convene in Belgium once again the following month.[58] European sports officials appeared to be unwilling to make a firm decision in the hope that either the controversy would be resolved diplomatically or that some common response would be formulated by the governments of the European Community.

When neither of these eventualities appeared likely, the Olympic committees took decisive action on their own. At the March meeting of the committees' representatives, eight participants agreed to go to the Moscow Games regardless of the positions advocated by their respective governments. This coalition included France and Italy, as well as the United Kingdom.[59] Such a pronouncement was an extremely serious blow to the entire boycott effort. Great Britain, led by Prime Minister Margaret Thatcher, had been Carter's staunchest supporter, while France was viewed by many as a pivotal nation in determining the momentum of the international campaign.[60] Although the leaders of the Olympic committees could express only their personal sentiments, such a united declaration proved to have a decisive impact. Following adoption by the IOC of provisions to reduce the expression of nationalism in the ceremonial aspects of the Games,[61] national Olympic committees in thirteen West European states eventually voted to send their athletes;[62] West Germany was the sole major nonparticipant.[63]

Great Britain. Prompted by outspoken support within Parliament for a determined response to Soviet aggression, and one which included using the Olympic Games, Prime Minister Margaret Thatcher assumed a leadership role in supporting the Carter initiative among European and other world leaders. Within a week of the events in Afghanistan, members of Parliament [MPs] began to express their desire to wield the weapon of sport in a retaliatory manner. Conservative MP Neville Trotter condemned the Soviets and admonished Thatcher to attempt to move, postpone, or boycott the Games. He stressed the efficacy of a boycott in unambiguous terms: "This [a boycott] is the one lever we have to show our outrage at this naked aggression by Russia. We should do all we can to reduce the Moscow Olympics to a shambles."[64] Moderates of both the Conservative and the Labour parties endorsed Trotter's position, and the momentum behind the boycott position proceeded to grow rapidly. Former Labour Defense Minister James Wellbeloved led an all-party group in an effort to persuade Thatcher to put pressure on the British Olympic Association to abandon any plans for participation. Within two weeks, over 100 MPs had called for either a boycott or the transfer of the Moscow Olympics.[65]

Thatcher, hardly one to be characterized as overly indulgent toward the Kremlin, soon abandoned her previous reticence toward co-mingling politics and international sport. In an address before the House of Commons on January 17, she endorsed any attempt to move the Games "if it is possible to do so."[66] While avoiding mention of a boycott should the Games remain in Moscow, Thatcher nonetheless subsequently gave substance to her advocacy of moving the Olympics when she promised to write the British Olympic Association to urge it to press the government's position on the leaders of the IOC. She also offered Great Britain as a possible venue for some events should a series of alternate sites be adopted by the International Committee.[67]

In a characteristic manner, Thatcher, upon seizing the idea of using the Olympics to punish the Soviets, became ever more pronounced and intransigent in her advocacy. Whereas Lord Carrington, British foreign secretary, presumably had echoed Thatcher's position when he rejected, in a speech made on January 24, outright cancellation of the Games as "a bitter blow to the dedicated athletes, in Britain and elsewhere,''[68] Thatcher had far transcended this moderate stance within little more than a week. The prime minister, despite the protests of the aides who recognized the final authority of the British Olympic Association, declared that she would pull the British team out of the Games. Lord Carrington, now thrust into the role of trying to soften the impact of his leader's remarks, said that no decision would be finalized until after the meeting of the IOC in Lake Placid the following week. He further stressed that the United Kingdom would not act alone; ''a continuing discussion about Western reaction'' was required prior to any British action.[69] Refusing to give ground, Thatcher announced to the House of Commons on February 14 that ''we [the government] have decided to advise British athletes not to go to Moscow.'' Seeking to dispel any potential opposition, the prime minister injected a patriotic tinge to her address when she observed, ''Athletes are just like any other kind of citizen. They have the same rights and responsibilities toward freedom and its maintenance.''[70]

While Thatcher and the British government wasted little time in making their position known, this hardly insured that the British Olympic Association would adhere to a similar policy. Although avoiding a confrontational attitude in the initial discussion over possible nonparticipation, the Olympic Association never supported a boycott.[71] It indicated that it would listen to the government's perspective, and then, in all likelihood, vote to attend the Games.[72] Once Thatcher formally announced that the government would request the athletes to refrain from competing, the head of Great Britain's Amateur Athletic Board declared that all athletes who desired to compete would receive its support, while those who chose otherwise would not be pressured.[73] The International Athletes Club, representing track and field athletes, supported the Amateur Athletic Board and said it would raise $125,000 to field a fifty-member team should the Olympic Association back the government. Virtually the only concession that British athletes appeared willing to make was to agree to stage a limited political demonstration at the Games themselves; such an action presumably was to be focused upon the opening and closing ceremonies and on the use of the national anthem.[74]

The British government, realizing that sentiment within the Olympic Association was against a boycott, requested the Association defer any decision until an as then unspecified date. Scheduled to meet on March 5, the Association acceded to London's wishes. Thatcher immediately renewed her efforts to mobilize both the Parliament and public opinion, and thereby to influence the Olympic Association. In a highly controversial action, she decreed that members of the armed forces were prohibited from participating at Moscow and that no civil servants would be granted leaves to compete. Since most athletes had previously used their vacations in order to train, many Olympians would be forced to choose between participating and keeping their jobs. Thatcher also withdrew the services of Douglas Martin, a British diplomat, who was to have acted as an attaché to the athletes during the Games.[75] In a vote in which no party discipline was enforced, the House of Commons added its support for a boycott by more than a two to one margin.[76]

In the face of such pressure, the British Olympic Association only stiffened its resolve to attend the Games. Thatcher's coercive tactics polarized the situation and forced her to contemplate extreme measures, including revocation of passports, as the sole means of attaining her objectives. Any hope for persuasion had been lost. On March 25, the Olympic Association formally voted to send a team to Moscow. Denis Fellows, chairman of the association, said the invitation to compete would be "accept[ed] forthwith." [77] Fellows observed, correctly, that in Great Britain "This idea of a boycott was an absolute non-starter from the beginning." [78] British athletes, as well as the general public, had never supported the idea.

Thatcher accepted defeat, and refused to resort to preventing athletes from traveling to the Games. The government did halt its nominal contribution to the Olympic Association, but this was of minimal significance. Most medal hopefuls, including Steve Ovett and Sebastian Coe, eventually chose to compete; only the yachting, equestrian, field hockey, and fencing teams elected to boycott.[79] That Great Britain chose to participate was an extremely serious setback for Carter's boycott campaign. Thatcher's wholehearted support was something Carter had failed to elicit elsewhere; her inability to induce the Olympic Association to cooperate was thus of added significance.

In assessing the impact of U.S. pressure on the British government, one must conclude that, while far from negligible, it was not the decisive factor influencing policy. The British government, particularly the prime minister, sought to maintain allied solidarity, especially in opposition to the Soviet Union. However, it was domestic pressure that ultimately determined the government's position. Parliament's early, vocal support for using the Olympics in a punitive manner was crucial in prodding Thatcher toward her eventual stance. It appears that the British government would finally have adopted essentially the same position regardless of Carter's initiative. White House policy may have coincided with that of London's, but it was not determinative in its formation.

West Germany. Perhaps in no other country did the question of a boycott create such severe dilemmas for the ruling government as it did in West Germany. The decision regarding participation in the Moscow Games was one which had numerous international and domestic ramifications: the tenor of relations with the Soviet Union, an issue of great import, was directly affected; solidarity with the United States was at stake; and the issue soon became a dominant one affecting national elections slated for that year. The complex array of factors which had to be considered helps to explain why the Bonn government displayed a vacillating reluctance to commit itself in either direction.

Ironically, and much to the embarrassment of government leaders, it was the West German ambassador to an emergency NATO meeting, convened in order to formulate a response to the invasion of Afghanistan, who first broached the possibility of a retaliatory boycott.[80] Interior Minister Gerhart Baum quickly disavowed support for such an action, declaring, "In the opinion of the Government, sports cannot be used as a means for political ends. Sports cannot solve problems whose solution can only be achieved politically."[81] Shortly thereafter, lack of a clear government position again became manifest when top officials expressed "great understanding" for Carter's stance.[82] This noncommittal sympathy became increasingly substantive when Foreign Minister Hans-Dietrich Genscher told the Soviet ambassador to Bonn that the Federal Republic expected Moscow to "create preconditions for all states to take part in the Olympic Games."[83] Thus, by early February the West German government seemed to have come full circle and appeared to be willing to support a United States-led boycott.

The position of Chancellor Helmut Schmidt, however, remained unclear. On an issue that portended only negative consequences for the West German leader, Schmidt sought to keep a low profile and avoid political exposure. Election-year politics soon precluded such an option. Conservative opponents of Schmidt's Social Democratic party, led by Franz-Josef Strauss, expressed vocal support for a boycott, while the defenders of "Ostpolitik," the basis for the government's foreign policy, strongly criticized the U.S. initiative.[84] Schmidt was forced to act despite his awareness that support for a boycott would jeopardize "Ostpolitik," and thereby the highly valued economic and political benefits expected to result from such a policy,[85] whereas a pro-Moscow stance would strain relations with Washington at a time when Bonn valued solidarity with the United States.

In such a no-win situation, Schmidt attempted to avoid antagonizing either of the contending parties. In a meeting with the Soviet ambassador on February 15, the West German leader indicated that participation in the Games was in danger, but that no firm decision had been reached. Several weeks later, Schmidt went to the United States to discuss the boycott with Carter. U.S. officials claimed he told the president that West Germany would eventually boycott; however, Schmidt announced only that conditions permitting his country's participation at Moscow "do not now" exist. Such a tentative endorsement of a boycott was abandoned immediately upon Schmidt's return to Germany where he proceeded to stress the potential "adverse affect [*sic*]" on East-West security talks that a boycott could produce. Schmidt's indecision continued to manifest itself until he finally yielded in late April to pressures to recommend acceptance of a boycott to the Olympic Committee.[86] Forceful and determined leadership by the West German government was conspicuously absent throughout the crucial phases of the boycott debate.

Initially, the West German Olympic Committee did not exhibit this same degree of equivocation; led by President Willi Daume, it stridently opposed a boycott. Daume originally attempted to downplay the possibility that the Games would be tampered with by government officials, but, when this restrained approach became overwhelmed by the tide of events, he took the offensive.[87]

He vowed, along with fellow officials, to "do all in our power to save the 1980 Olympics this summer in Moscow," and defiantly stated, "We [the Olympic Committee] are in no way, either financial nor in any other way, dependent on the Government for permission to send athletes to Moscow."[88]

Such firm resolve was soon shaken, and ultimately dissolved, amidst increasingly intense pro-boycott pressure. Reflected in a vocal public opinion,[89] in the platforms of the major political parties, and, to a growing extent, in the pronouncements of government officials, an apparent national resolve to support the U.S. initiative became manifest. A weakening of the Olympic Committee's previous consensus could be discerned through the vacillation of President Willi Daume. While he ostensibly ruled out any chance of nonparticipation in one speech, in the next he just as readily opened the door. For instance, immediately following his statement asserting the Olympic Committee's independence from the government, he admitted that the government's position would "be given great weight" in any decision.[90] By the middle of March, Daume appeared to have abandoned totally his earlier position and now expressed his belief that the Olympic Committee " 'probably' would accept any government recommendation to boycott the Olympic Games."[91] Daume subsequently reversed himself yet again, but was unable to convince the national Olympic Committee of the merits of his position. The West German sporting establishment, while originally more forceful and decisive in its evaluation of a boycott than the Schmidt government, eventually lapsed into confusion and hesitancy.

When Helmut Schmidt finally announced to Parliament on April 23 that he would ask the Olympic Committee to boycott, he was relatively assured of the Olympians' acquiescence.[92] Requesting that the decision be made as late as possible, Schmidt continued to act in a less than decisive manner. He observed that the government in Bonn did "not regard as appropriate the participation by German athletes at the Olympic Games as long as the Soviet occupation of Afghanistan continues."[93] This was hardly similar to Carter's firm February 20 ultimatum, and reflected the continuing hope of Schmidt and other government officials that the situation would somehow be resolved short of a boycott.

The executive committee of the national Olympic Committee, despite the renewed opposition of Daume, accepted the recommendation by Schmidt and voted, by a 12 to 7 margin, to recommend a boycott of the Games.[94] The full committee, meeting in Dusseldorf on May 15, followed the recommendation of the executive group. After four hours of nationally televised debate, it was decided, 59 to 40, to abstain from participation.[95]

Although the United States had a significant stake in the outcome of the boycott struggle in West Germany, its role in influencing the course of events was not singularly decisive; the position of the United States was merely one of three determining factors. These factors, enumerated previously, may be listed in relative order of significance: domestic political considerations; concern for maintaining good relations with the United States; and a desire to retain the fruits of detente.

Foremost, Schmidt and his government considered the boycott issue in terms of election-year politics. The strong support given to the boycott by the opposition Christian Democratic party, and its determination to stress the issue in the campaign, restricted the range of maneuverability available to Schmidt.[96] Schmidt was also worried lest his failure to boycott lead to a rift with the United States. Once a governmental decision had been reached, Foreign Minister Genscher expressed this concern when he stated, "We expect solidarity from the United States in Berlin, and we will not deny it in the question of the Olympics."[97] Finally, Chancellor Schmidt was in a dilemma because any recommendation to the athletes to boycott would be a direct reprisal against the Soviet Union, something which heretofore had been avoided. Schmidt and the Social Democrats had made improved relations between Bonn and Moscow a basic premise of their policies; a boycott would jeopardize gains already achieved, as well as impede future progress.[98] In the final analysis, domestic political factors, coupled with a desire to solidify relations with the United States, determined government policy. In this case, as contrasted with that of Great Britain, the Olympic Committee followed the government's recommendation. That the committee opted to support Bonn may be attributed to a number of influences, including public pressure, sympathy for the exiled Sakharov,[99] and resentment at attempts by East German Olympic officials to affect its decision.[100]

Seen at the time as a key country because of its potential influence on other undecided states, as well as on those who had only tentatively expressed their positions,[101] the decision by West Germany to boycott Moscow did not in fact produce a snowball effect. France, Italy, and Great Britain, not to mention the rest of Western Europe, eventually decided to participate; indeed, West Germany was left as the sole supporter of the United States among principal noncommunist European nations. Nonetheless, the Federal Republic was a major sporting power and its absence had an undeniable effect.

France. The Carter boycott initiative received considerably less support from the French government than from either the British or West German. The initial reaction from Paris regarding any boycott action was a firm rejection. The French Minister for Youth, Sports and Leisure expressed what could be regarded as the official government position when he declared simply, "France will continue to participate" unless the Olympic Committee decided otherwise.[102] The French government, with only minor deviations,[103] remained firm in its opposition to a boycott until mid-March. During these early months, government officials stressed their belief that, although the situation in Afghanistan was patently unacceptable and must be resolved, the Olympics was not "the appropriate means for attaining that goal."[104] During a foreign ministers' meeting of the nine Common Market countries held in mid-February, France was reported to be the single voice raised in dissent on the boycott question.[105] Whether or not this was true, the French did prevent the issue from being mentioned in the meeting's final communiqué.[106]

Toward the end of March, the French government appeared to have reconsidered its position and opted to join the boycott movement. Officials, while declining to make an authoritative statement, implied that President Giscard d'Estaing's recent meeting with German Chancellor Schmidt had resulted in an agreement to act in concert. *Le Monde* said that a boycott would be announced, but that d'Estaing would do so in a manner that would attempt to preserve at least the appearance that France was acting independently of the United States.[107] In fact, the government may well have desired a boycott, but it wanted to achieve it with as little direct involvement as possible. It was with this objective in mind that Paris elected to leave the decision up to the Olympic Committee. It was felt that the committee could be steered in the appropriate direction, and accordingly would vote to boycott. These maneuverings would allow France to avoid any possibility of being the lone Western participant, while permitting the government to distance itself from the actual decision, and thus avoid antagonizing the Soviets. The flaw in this involved plan was that the Olympic Committee did not prove amenable to government wishes.

The French Olympic Committee had accepted the Soviet invitation to compete the day after it was received. Thus, unlike most other committees, it had to overturn a previous decision in order to prevent its athletes from competing.[108] French public opinion never endorsed a boycott,[109] and in fact became more opposed to such an action as time passed.[110] Since the committee was never subjected to the degree of governmental pressure faced by its British, American, and, to a lesser extent, West German, counterparts, and since the public firmly supported participation, it was free to act solely in defense of its athletes' interests. In a unanimous decision, announced May 13,[111] it did just that. The committee voted to attend the Games, characterizing its decision as one made "on sporting grounds alone."[112] Although prefacing its announcement with a warning to the Soviets that they would have to accept certain steps designed to de-nationalize the Games,[113] it was understood that a firm decision had been made.[114]

While the French government attempted to chart a delicate course in the hope of minimizing any detrimental effects that it might incur as a result of a boycott, the Olympic Committee acted contrary to government expectations. The decision to attend the Games was not one desired by French leaders, and indeed created a rather embarrassing situation. President d'Estaing had assured Schmidt that the French would support the West German position, but that they would do so in a discreet fashion.[115] However, when the government's indecision and vacillation was interpreted by Olympic officials as an indication that they could act as they wished, the government inadvertently helped to shape a decision it had not desired.

The impact of U.S. pressure on the French decision was paradoxical. Carter viewed French support as crucial. He felt that should the French endorse a boycott, it would have a significant effect on other European countries, and in turn on nonaligned countries throughout the Third World. However, the strident tone assumed by the White House in its advocacy of a boycott did not solicit French cooperation. The French government, particularly since De Gaulle, had made it standard policy either to act independently of Washington or at least to present such an appearance. Thus, for French officials to endorse a boycott amid Carter's posturings would seem to indicate that Washington had the power to dictate policy to Paris. That was unacceptable, and forced d'Estaing to act in such a circuitous fashion that the whole scenario fell apart. U.S. policy had a decisive impact, but one contradictory to its intent.

Other Western European States. The remainder of noncommunist Europe, with insignificant exceptions,[116] refused to join the boycott. Despite strong pressure exerted both by government officials and by the Dutch Parliament,[117] the Netherlands Olympic Committee refused to abandon the Summer Games. As early as January 11, the government had terminated all direct financial assistance to athletes preparing for Moscow and repeatedly emphasized its desire that the Olympic Committee decide against participation. The committee, however, was reluctant to boycott, and indicated that it would be guided by the March 22 meeting in Brussels of the European national Olympic committees. Although it postponed a final decision until mid-May, the committee eventually adhered to the consensus of the European Olympic groups and voted decisively to attend the Games.[118]

Belgium's national Olympic Committee similarly rejected the boycott,[119] reasoning that such an action was "contrary to the Olympic charter."[120] Declaring that "Any attempt to use the Games for political purposes is regrettable," the president of the Olympic Committee surmised, "Someone always has a reason for boycotting an event in which those who do not share his ideas are participating."[121]

Italy's Olympic Association likewise elected to attend the Games. The Italian government, although nominally supportive of a boycott, refused to dictate policy to Olympic officials;[122] the final decision was reserved for the Olympic Committee. The government did effectively cut the Olympic team in half by banning members of the police force and the military from competing, and by refusing to alter exam schedules to permit scholar-athletes to attend,[123] but the final Olympic Committee vote of 29 to 3 in favor of participation was not circumvented by government action.[124]

With the Spanish government paying only lipservice to Carter's boycott request,[125] the Spanish Olympic Committee was free to act as it deemed appropriate; it accordingly voted to participate.[126] Sweden's Olympic Committee rejected any notion of politicizing the Games and renounced a boycott in a decisive fashion, "Sports should not take it upon itself to pass judgment on a country's political system or international behavior."[127] Both the Portuguese and the Irish Olympic committees reasoned in a similar fashion, and, despite having to defy their governments' position, opted to compete.[128] In an extremely close vote, the Swiss national Olympic Committee decided in favor of participating; the Swiss government had made no attempt to influence the outcome of the debate.[129] Denmark and Finland, for differing reasons, voted against a boycott.[130]

Greece, Luxembourg, and Austria completed the list of countries whose Olympic committees refused to accept the U.S.-sponsored Olympic initiative.[131]

Summary. The dismal fate of the boycott in Western Europe was profound; only West Germany, Liechtenstein, Norway, and Monoco finally sided with the United States. The reasons for this were twofold. First, the White House neglected to conduct substantive consultations with its European allies *prior* to announcing its intention to abstain from participation.[132] Carter chose to state U.S. policy first and then sought to enlist allied support, perhaps in order to establish a degree of international respect through an authoritative stand or because of the pressure exerted upon him by an increasingly vocal American public. This discouraged bilateral cooperation and created an atmosphere of resentment in which few governments, with the exception of Great Britain's, were willing to put significant resources behind securing the support of their respective Olympic committees for any boycott action.

The second factor which contributed to the failure of the boycott in Western Europe was the attitude of Europeans, as contrasted with that of Americans, toward amateur sports in general, and toward the Olympics in particular.[133] Europeans tended to identify more closely with the Olympics than did Americans, and thus were more reluctant to abstain from competing. The lack of public support for a boycott evidenced throughout Europe contrasted sharply with the overwhelming enthusiasm for such an action exhibited by American public opinion.[134] This lack of grassroots support circumscribed the scope of action available to government leaders sympathetic to the U.S. policy. Since Olympic committees retained at least the formal right to make any decision regarding participation, governmental pressure had to be exerted upon these bodies in order to affect the outcome of events. However, such pressure, because of public sympathy for the athletes and the restraining influence of democratic tradition, could be of only limited intensity, and thus of little utility.

Canada

The Canadian response to U.S. overtures regarding a boycott of the Moscow Games must be analyzed primarily in terms of the domestic political situation. Prime Minister Joe Clark's defeat by Pierre Trudeau during the crucial mid-February period complicated what had been a hitherto resolved issue. We therefore must examine Canadian policy in two distinct phases in order to comprehend fully the reasons behind that country's eventual course of action.

One of the early proponents of using the Olympics in a punitive manner was Canadian Prime Minister Joe Clark. Clark expressed concern in the wake of Afghanistan over the "appropriateness" of Moscow as a host for the Games. He indicated that Canada was prepared to join the U.S. effort to move the Games, and offered the facilities of the Montreal area for a part of the relocated events. By the end of January, Clark's position had progressed to the point where he was in full agreement with U.S. policy. A deadline of February 20 was set for the withdrawal of Soviet troops; should this fail to occur, Canadian athletes would boycott the Games.[135]

Governmental policy was thrown into disarray when Trudeau triumphed over Clark in the February national elections. Trudeau had campaigned on a platform stressing independence from Washington and emphasizing Canada's role in preserving peace between the United States and Moscow. Prior to the election, he had cast doubt on his potential support of a boycott when he stated, "I think this kind of symbolic gesture of boycotting the Olympics is only effective if it shows that there is a massive participation by not only the Western nations but by a lot of the third world nations. Otherwise Moscow scores a propaganda victory."[136]

Once in power, the new prime minister refused to take a stand on the issue. He reiterated his belief that the effectiveness of any boycott rested on the extent of Third World involvement; however, he avoided any decisive commitment. It was not until April 22 that Trudeau finally announced, through an address delivered by the external affairs minister to the House of Commons, his decision to advocate a boycott. Trudeau emphasized that no coercive measures, such as revocation of passports, would be employed to prevent the athletes from participating; the government was prepared only to withdraw financial and moral support.[137]

Canada's Olympic Association was never an enthusiastic advocate of a boycott. Its initial policy statement was indicative of the prevailing sentiment within the group for the duration of the debate: "The Canadian Olympic Association does not agree that participation in [the] Olympic Games in Moscow represents an endorsement of the government of the Soviet Union or any of its activities."[138] In other words, the Soviets may have acted atrociously, but there was no link between the invasion of Afghanistan and the Olympics in Moscow. The Olympic Association seized upon the refusal of Trudeau to act decisively and voted to send a team to the Games. This decision was reached in early April.[139]

Once the Association's position had become known, it was subjected to intense pressure. The Olympic Trust of Canada, the Association's main fundraiser, admonished it to reconsider its decision.[140] Private groups, in particular the National Citizens Coalition, pursued a nationwide campaign to rally support for the boycott. Public opinion had already been disposed to accept a boycott; these efforts merely reinforced its predilection.[141] Dick Pound, the Association's president, promptly retreated and shifted the burden of responsibility squarely upon Trudeau's shoulders. He stated that the Association had decided in favor of participation, but would act according to any decision ultimately reached by the prime minister.[142] It was therefore no surprise when the Association reversed itself—by the lopsided vote of 137 to 35—following the government's eventual recommendation to abstain from competing.[143]

Although the Canadian Olympic Association finally supported a boycott, it did so in an equivocal fashion. It would still select a team, not, as in the United States, so as to allow the athletes an opportunity for recognition, but so as to

be ready to field a squad if "the international situation improves." This reluctance to make an irrevocable commitment reflected a similar reticence on the
part of the government. Trudeau had implied that should Moscow create "conditions in which the Olympics can take place," which meant a substantial withdrawal of troops by May 24, he would be willing to change his position.[144]
This was not a resounding endorsement of U.S. policy, but it was infinitely
more desirable, from the standpoint of Washington, than a decision to the contrary.

The extent of U.S. influence on the Canadian decision was significant. The
White House placed a high priority upon securing Canadian support, and was
willing to exert considerable pressure to attain that objective. While Trudeau
had sought to forge a degree of independence from Washington, in the final
analysis he elected to adopt Carter's policy.

Although the impact of the United States was considerable, it should not
overshadow the domestic aspects of the decision. The boycott became a significant question at the height of the election campaign, and as such was imbued
with additional interest and attention. Vocal citizens' groups coalesced in favor
of a boycott and focused a public opinion already inclined toward supporting
such a policy. The final decision to refrain from competing was a derivative of
both international and domestic influences; these factors were of comparable
significance.

Asia

The response by Asian states to the United States-sponsored boycott initiative was generally quite supportive. Not only did a significant number of countries decide against participation, but those states with the strongest athletic
traditions opted to remain at home.[145] Although the idea of a boycott was well
received, the United States had little influence over the question. Most Asian
nations acted as a result of varied considerations which included Islamic solidarity, opposition to Soviet aggression, and a desire to act in accord with the
consensus of world opinion. However, with the possible exception of Japan,
concern with backing the United States per se was not a factor which impacted
heavily upon states' decisions.

Japan. From the U.S. perspective, Japan was critical in determining the
success of the Asian component of the boycott. Not only was it a populous
country with enormous economic strength, Japan also was renowned for its
excellent gymnasts and long-distance runners. In the 1976 Montreal Olympics,
the Japanese had won twenty-five medals. In addition, Japan was the most
Western-oriented of the Asian states; should it fail to follow the U.S. lead, the
U.S. initiative could well be stillborn throughout the rest of Asia. Prime Minister Masayoshi Ohira, in a stance that was to become characteristic of that
assumed by most Asian states, refused to make a definite commitment on the
question of participating at the Moscow Games. In early January he stated that

he "would have to wait and see what other countries do" before he could make a decision.[146] Ohira wanted to gauge the world response in general, but most critically the position of the oil-exporting states upon which Japan was so dependent, before making any final determination.

Despite reiterating that they must pay "serious concern to world opinion," by the beginning of February Japanese leaders appeared to have reached a tentative decision to support U.S. policy.[147] Government officials implied that at an appropriate time, Japan would elect to boycott. By the end of March, any remnants of uncertainty were removed when Ohira's chief cabinet secretary announced that the government had firmly decided against participation.[148] Soon after, Saburo Okita, the Japanese foreign minister, told the Diet that it was "undesirable" to attend the Games, and intimated that the government would consider such coercive measures as revoking athletes' passports in order to enforce its policy.[149]

The Japanese Olympic Committee, while initially expressing reservations about a boycott,[150] refused to take any action until the end of May. The committee, cognizant of the fact that the announced position of various governments throughout the world was not a reliable indicator as to the eventual outcome of debate within national Olympic committees, sought to delay a commitment for as long as possible; despite governmental pressure, the committee refused to act prematurely. Katsuiji Shibata, the chairman of the Olympic group, expressed their understanding when he stated, "The Government position cannot be ignored although a decision on whether to take part in the Moscow games will [be] made independently" by the committee.[151] The Olympic representatives did not allow themselves to be forced to act before it was absolutely necessary. When such a time arrived, however, the Olympic Committee respected the dictates of the government and voted to boycott the Games.[152]

China. The readmission of mainland China to the Olympic movement in December 1979, ended its more than two decade exile from competition. The battle for the right to represent China that had been waged between Communist China and Taiwan had been intense and of great symbolic importance. Thus, when Beijing finally triumphed and was allowed by the IOC to send athletes to the 1980 Games, it was viewed as a great victory and as an opportunity to vindicate its supporters; one can imagine the torment that the idea of a boycott was bound to inspire. Nonetheless, when this possibility arose, it was not rejected outright, but rather received close scrutiny. A spokesman for the Olympic Committee announced that "China will take the same attitude as the majority of the national Olympic committees of all countries."[153] The deputy chairman of the Olympic Committee, Li Menghua, reaffirmed this position in an interview given to the New China News Agency in late January. He declared:

The proposal to boycott the Summer Olympic Games in Moscow or change the venue is reasonable. The Chinese Olympic Committee is watching the developments and will take the stand of the majority of the Olympic committees of other countries . . . We will make our own decision in accordance with the principled stand to safeguard world peace and in the Olympic spirit.[154]

Since there was no meaningful distinction between the government and the Olympic Committee in China, as there was in the West, we need not approach the two as separate entities capable of acting in a countervailing manner. Government thinking may be assumed to be reflected in the statements of Olympic officials; correspondingly, members of the Olympic Committee must be expected to act in observance of government policy. It therefore was significant when Li Menghua, upon arriving in Lake Placid prior to the beginning of the Winter Games, said he personally believed it to be "inappropriate to have the Summer Games held in Moscow under the present conditions." [155] Such prominent officials were not at liberty, especially when addressing a worldwide audience, to expound upon their own analysis of an issue of international consequence.

It therefore was no surprise when a few days later the Chinese government announced that it not only supported a boycott, but would also "work to promote such a decision." [156] The Chinese Olympic Committee subsequently reaffirmed the state's commitment to boycott the Moscow Games, reasoning that "so long as the Soviet authorities refuse to respect the noble ideals of the Olympic movement and to withdraw all of their troops from Afghanistan by May 24," the deadline for acceptance of Olympic invitations, it would not compete.[157] Much to the relief of the White House—and, it should be noted, without concern for U.S. policy preferences—China added its weight to the boycott movement.

Other Asian States. Pakistan, one of those states most directly affected in a geopolitical sense by the Soviet invasion of Afghanistan, was quick to respond to the boycott initiative. In private conversations the week following the attack, government officials indicated their willingness to use the Olympics as a means to punish the Soviets; however, this tentative decision was premised on the boycott achieving a wide acceptance among the nations of the Third World.[158] When an emergency meeting of the Islamic Conference, held in Islamabad at the end of January, issued a call to all members of the Islamic world to boycott, Pakistan's chief adviser on foreign affairs indicated that his government would respect the plea.[159] Pakistan's Olympic Committee accepted its government's position and voted unanimously to boycott the Games.[160]

The Olympic Committee of Turkey likewise voted to abstain from participation. It refrained from making a decision until the May 24 deadline, when it then announced its acceptance of the government's recommendation to boycott.[161] Saudi Arabia, in an attempt to assume a leadership position among Moslem nations, declared on January 6 its intention to boycott. Prince Faisal bin Fahd, the head of the Olympic Committee, said such an action was "in protest over the Soviet aggression against the friendly and brotherly Moslem nation of Afghanistan.''[162] The absurdity of such an assertion notwithstanding (Saudi Arabia had indicated it would not participate in Moscow several months prior to the events in Afghanistan), the Saudis were able to derive considerable political capital from appearing to be the first country to boycott as a punitive measure against Moscow.

Summary. Although the populous, politically significant state of India refused to act against the Soviets,[163] the boycott attracted a diverse Asian following which was both quantitatively and qualitatively impressive; nearly twenty nations, including Japan and China, supported using the Olympics in a punitive fashion.[164] One would be remiss, however, to assume that these states acted as a result of U.S. persuasion or intimidation. While Japan certainly was concerned with its American image, it was also careful to act only in concert with a significant number of Third World nations. Chinese policy emerged as a result of several factors. The Chinese were never hesitant to act against the Soviet Union. Sino-Soviet tensions were high, and any vehicle which provided a means to discredit and embarrass the Soviets would be looked upon favorably in Beijing. Also, Beijing's leaders desired to regain a measure of leadership in the Third World that had been forfeited both as a result of the chaos of the Cultural Revolution and as a consequence of Khrushchev's Third World initiative. It was felt that a strong response to the Afghanistan invasion, of which an Olympic boycott was one element, would indicate Chinese readiness to defend the interests of the developing nations against Soviet encroachment; hopefully, respect for Beijing's leadership would thus increase.

The Pakistani and Saudi actions, as well as those of other Muslim states, were predicated primarily on a desire to act in unison with their co-religionists.[165] It was the decision of the Conference of Foreign Ministers, at which thirty-six Muslim countries and five Islamic groups were represented,[166] that was the decisive factor regarding the boycott question. For Muslims to act against the conference's call to boycott would be to ignore the plight of those Muslims killed in Afghanistan, while also undermining Islamic solidarity. Iranian Finance Minister Abolhassan Bani-Sadr captured the importance of religious identity when he questioned, "How can we go to Moscow when we know Soviet troops are killing our *Moslem brothers* in Afghanistan?''[167] One must conclude that while the boycott attained a high level of popularity and backing among the Asian states, the United States had at best a peripheral role in decisions which were premised primarily on domestic, regional, and religious factors.

Africa

Despite the fact that the superpowers devoted more attention to Africa than to any other area of the Third World—in large part because of past African willingness to boycott the Olympics, as well as because of the athletic prowess of several states[168]—neither the United States nor the Soviet Union achieved clear supremacy in efforts to win support for their respective positions among African countries. Washington's reliance upon Muhammad Ali's five nation tour of Kenya, Senegal, Tanzania, Liberia, and Nigeria, both to influence these nations and to sway the rest of black Africa, produced no net results.[169] Moscow succeeded in enticing some states to participate, primarily through monetary incentives,[170] but this was of limited attraction. No unified position was ever adopted throughout the continent; the final tally indicated that slightly less than half of black Africa decided in favor of a boycott, the rest elected to participate.[171]

Kenya. By virtue of its past athletic prowess, particularly in the area of long-distance running, Kenya's stance on the boycott was viewed by the United States as vitally important to the success of the overall campaign. After an initial period in which the concept of a boycott was critically evaluated and options reviewed, Kenyan President Daniel Arap Moi announced that his country would once again boycott the Games.[172] Moi, concerned about Soviet actions in the Horn of Africa and in South Asia,[173] reasoned, "it would be most inappropriate for any nonaligned nation to attend the Moscow Olympics while Soviet troops are in Afghanistan."[174] The Kenyan president, in an attempt to strengthen ties with Washington, then assumed the leadership role among African statesmen in supporting the U.S. initiative. Appreciative of Moi's influence, the White House accorded the Kenyan leader the greatest courtesy during his February visit to Washington.[175] It should be noted that the Kenyan decision to boycott was announced nearly a week before Ali's "unofficial" visit.

Nigeria. Nigerian cooperation was also considered crucial by U.S. diplomats. Aside from being the most populous country in Africa, and one of the most influential in intra-African policy formulation, a Nigerian was the president of the Supreme Council for Sport in Africa.[176] Although only an advisory body, the council's backing had the potential to be the decisive factor in countries vacillating on the boycott question. It therefore was a significant setback for Washington when Nigeria's president, in opposition to his counterpart in Kenya, declared that Nigeria would attend the Moscow Games.[177] A government newspaper, *New Nigeria*, provided a clue as to why such a decision was reached in an article that stated, "there is a distinction between our genuine sympathy for the Afghans and the pious rantings of Western leaders."[178] It was obvious that the Nigerian government sought to maintain its reputation for acting in a nonaligned fashion, and resented any pressure exerted by Washington. It should not have come as a surprise to informed U.S. leaders that Ali's mission would be viewed not only as an insult, since Ali was merely a former athlete, but also as a coercive act. Needless to say, Ali did not succeed in altering Nigeria's position.[179]

Other African States. Disparate responses to the boycott proposal were not restricted to the major African states. For example, while the prime minister of Morocco declared his complete "agreement with a boycott of the Olympic Games," Upper Volta reacted oppositely.[180] Similarly, Gambia's Olympic

Committee saw fit to denounce Moscow's invasion as a violation of human rights that required a firm, complex response, while Sierra Leone refused to use the Olympics in a politically punitive manner.[181] Not only was there a lack of consensus among different countries, there was, as usual, no unanimity within individual states. For instance, when Ugandan President Godfrey L. Benaisa was ousted by a military coup, his decision to boycott the Games was discarded as well.[182]

Not even the strident proclamations of the forty-nine-member Supreme Council for Sport in Africa led to the development of a concerted African response. The Council's president, Abraham Ordia, had stated unequivocally, as early as January 25, that "Africa will be there [at Moscow] in full force. We will not boycott the Games."[183] Even subsequent to the Kenyan decision to boycott, the council refused to endorse such an action. Rather, Ordia reiterated the importance of attending the Games, and attempted to portray the issue in terms of an East-West confrontation that had no relevance for nonaligned Africa.[184] He argued, "Africa cannot refuse to go to Moscow just because the United States and Britain are annoyed with the Soviet Union."[185] Despite such attempts at leadership, no consensus was ever forged.

Summary. Africa's response to the boycott initiative was predicated on a variety of considerations. A number of states were concerned with respecting the Islamic Conference's call for a boycott. Others sought to avoid becoming involved in yet another superpower tug-of-war in which their interests would be readily sacrificed without compensatory benefits. For some, "nonalignment" was a facade behind which they could hide while promoting their anti-Western feelings; these states were willing to participate in the Olympics if it would in some way thwart the objectives of the West. Those concerned with the prospects for African sport in the years ahead opposed a boycott on the grounds that a twelve-year hiatus from Olympic competition could irrevocably damage athletic programs and the morale of potential Olympians. In many states, the view that black Africa had no reason to support a Western-sponsored boycott when the West had exhibited little sympathy for the 1976 boycott achieved a great deal of currency. Internal upheavals and changes in leadership, as in Uganda, also affected the fate of the boycott.[186] Finally, for those states such as Kenya with a number of superior athletes, decisions regarding a boycott would substantively affect the quality of competitions in Moscow; this conferred a degree of regional leadership on these states, and caused them to act so as to maximize this influence.

Except in a negative sense, concern for the United States was a negligible factor behind African decisions regarding Olympic participation. Washington was able to exert little discernible influence over African policy; decisions were reached in the context of local, regional, domestic, religious, and sporting considerations. Carter could take no credit, nor need he accept significant blame, for the successes and failures of the boycott initiative among African states.

Latin America

Much like Africa, no concerted response to Carter's boycott proposal was ever formulated by Latin American states. The United States expended minimal resources in efforts to influence this area of the world; Washington hoped that Latin America would follow what it assumed would be the West European lead in the boycott campaign. When the Europeans deserted the White House position, Carter was forced to resort to last-minute appeals for cooperation. The Soviets, meanwhile, promised to help a number of states with the expenses of attending the Games; Moscow, like Washington, merely sought to add to its respective "body count" in the diplomatic war being waged over participation in the Olympics. Some states were influenced by the Kremlin's efforts; most, however, chose either to boycott or to compete not because of Soviet incentives, but rather because of regional and domestic considerations.

The final tally revealed about an even split between those states which chose to participate and those electing to remain at home. Argentina and Brazil, regional rivals, adopted contrary policies; Argentina joined the boycott, Brazil did not.[187] The military governments of Chile and Peru likewise chose different paths; Peru sent its squad, composed of a female volleyball team, male and female swimmers, and a few track and field athletes, while prospective Chilean Olympians were told that they could not participate.[188] Both the Mexican government and its national Olympic Committee were enthusiastic supporters of participating at Moscow. Mexico hosted the meeting of the Association of National Olympic Committees that rejected the U.S. boycott.[189]

The absence of a unified response from the region precluded either the United States or the Soviet Union from claiming a decisive victory. Washington, probably more through lack of effort than any other factor, was outmaneuvered somewhat by the Soviets' use of monetary inducements. Nonetheless, it would be an error to see the decisions of the majority of Latin American states as being based mainly upon East-West considerations;[190] domestic and regional concerns were of paramount importance.

Other Areas

Australia. Perhaps nowhere did the boycott issue generate such heated public debate and produce a comparable degree of enmity between government leaders and their national Olympic committees as it did in Australia. Prime Minister Malcolm Fraser was one of the first statesmen to declare his support for a boycott,[191] and his position remained unchanged throughout the boycott campaign. The Australian Olympic Federation, in contrast, was unwavering in denouncing the politicizing of the Games. The general manager of the Olympic team, reacting against the perceived use of "blatant political pressure" by the Fraser government, lamented that he and his fellow colleagues "are not only [being] asked to boycott the Moscow Olympics, we are [being] asked to contribute to the ultimate destruction of the Olympic movement." [192] Public opinion was also polarized on the issue; the intensity of feelings produced a series of violent demonstrations by both sides in major cities throughout the country. [193]

In a narrow six-to-five vote, the executive members of the Olympic Federation decided to reject Fraser's plea, thus allowing its athletes to compete. The president of the federation indicated that lack of worldwide support for the U.S. initiative rendered a boycott futile, and his committee therefore saw no reason to sacrifice its athletes. Fraser immediately condemned the decision as contrary to national security and to the country's vital interests. He further castigated the decision by comparing it to the failure of the world community to boycott the 1936 Berlin Olympics. He stated, "I pray that the Soviet Union will not interpret this and other decisions of Olympic federations around the world as a weakening of Western will as Nazi Germany did in 1936." [194] Fraser reinforced his verbal attacks by failing to provide any financial assistance to the Olympic effort. [195]

Refusing to accept the Olympic Federation's decision, Fraser appealed to individual athletes and to representative bodies within specific sports to boycott regardless of the decision of the Olympic leaders. Ruling bodies representing field hockey, yachting, and equestrian events responded affirmatively to the government's request; the women's volleyball team also opted to respect Fraser's policy. [196] Although reports varied regarding the precise numbers, a significant proportion of Olympians independently chose to boycott. [197] Thus, although the prime minister did not prevent his country from boycotting, he succeeded in convincing many of Australia's finest athletes to refrain from competing.

The influence of the United States upon the attitude adopted by the government of Malcolm Fraser was considerable. Fraser predicated his response largely upon his desire to maintain solidarity with Washington in what was perceived as a significant East-West confrontation. However, Fraser's inability to dictate policy to the Olympic Federation rendered his support of little utility to the United States. The White House exerted influence over government decision making within Australia, but such power was meaningless in the context of the boycott; failure to influence the actual arbiter of the issue, in this case the Olympic Federation, translated into a serious diplomatic setback.

Puerto Rico. Puerto Rico's decision to oppose U.S. policy and send at least one "symbolic" athlete to Moscow revealed the inability of Washington to achieve its objectives even where it exercised considerable influence. Carter exerted intense pressure on Puerto Rico's governor, Carlos Romero Barcelo, to act in accordance with U.S. desires. Barcelo proved amenable, although he was unable to secure the cooperation of the Olympic Committee. On two separate occasions it refused to endorse a boycott and decided instead to allow the twenty-four federations governing individual sports to act as they deemed appropriate. Despite Governor Romero withdrawing the government's $500,000 stipend and refusing to finance any travel associated with the Games, the Olympic Committee remained firm in its stance.[198]

Since Puerto Rico's Olympic Committee had no ties to the USOC, Carter was forced either to accept the committee's noncompliance or to resort to extreme measures. Such steps presumably would have involved the invocation of emergency economic measures, including controlling the transfer of currency, to prevent athletes from traveling to Moscow. Carter opted against such coercive tactics partly out of concern lest it create additional resentment against the United States among those advocating Puerto Rican independence.[199] Once again, as in the case of Australia, the United States succeeded in effectively influencing another government's attitude toward the boycott, but failed to convince the respective Olympic committee; the impact of Washington upon policy formulation was thus nonexistent.

CONCLUSION

Before we attempt to determine the significance accorded to the U.S. position in the decisions of those countries which chose to boycott, we should first detail the comprehensive results of the campaign. Of the more than 140 national Olympic committees fully accredited by the IOC, 118 were not members of the Communist "bloc."[200] Sixty-two states elected not to send teams to Moscow;[201] eighty-one countries participated in the Games, although sixteen of those staged some type of symbolic protest.[202] The boycott was most successful in the Far East and in many Islamic nations. Both Africa and Latin America split evenly on the issue. Western Europe rejected a boycott in nearly universal fashion.[203] Assessed in quantitative terms, national teams and sports federations not competing at Moscow accounted for about one-half of the non-Communist athletes who competed at the 1976 Montreal Olympics. A qualitative evaluation revealed that those teams and sports federations that chose not to participate captured 73 percent of gold medals, and a similar percentage of total medals, won at Montreal by athletes from nations outside of the Eastern bloc.[204]

Both the United States and the Soviet Union tried to manipulate statistics to their advantage. Washington expressed optimism that Taiwan and Iran would join the boycott, overlooking the fact that neither country had satisfied all of the IOC requirements and had not been invited to compete.[205] Similarly, the State Department issued a statement which would create the impression that the United States had achieved a resounding victory, if one were not familiar with the structure of the international Olympic movement. The release, issued on May 24, declared:

Some 58 Olympic committees have already reached this decision [to boycott]. They are joined by the governments of 15 countries, who lack formal Olympic committees but which indicated they support the boycott. There are 11 other governments, which publicly support the boycott even though their national Olympic committees have chosen to send teams to Moscow. This makes a total, so far, of 84 governments around the world that support a boycott.[206]

Since only Olympic committees possessed the authority to make decisions affecting Olympic competition, it was irrelevant how many governments expressed empathy for the U.S. cause. Moscow, for its part, consistently inflated the number of states indicating they would compete. For instance, as late as May 24, the Kremlin, although informed otherwise, still maintained that over 100 teams would attend the Games.[207]

If one transcends rhetoric and examines the facts, a clearer picture emerges. First, a number of smaller countries did not go to Moscow, but neither did they ''boycott''; financial constraints and lack of competitive athletes were the primary determinants of their actions.[208] Second, neither U.S. nor Soviet pressure succeeded in decisively influencing the decisions of many Olympic committees. When given relative freedom by their governments, committees tended to act to further the best interests of their athletes. In those circumstances where government leaders dictated policy, they behaved more out of regard for domestic, regional, local, or religious considerations than out of concern for either Washington or Moscow.[209]

In the final analysis, Carter's large expenditure of time, energy, and manpower had relatively little impact. Most of those states which opted against participation probably would have done so regardless of White House efforts; in some instances, administration tactics drove potential allies into accepting a pro-Soviet position.[210] It is a matter of debate to what extent Washington enhanced the probability of a general boycott becoming a reality by its decision to take such a strong leadership position. If Carter had indicated U.S. support for nonparticipation in a world forum such as the United Nations General Assembly, in all likelihood the idea would have been embraced with a similar degree of enthusiasm as it was after the long, drawn-out, tortuous process of the boycott campaign.[211]

5

Consequences of the Boycott

The political allure of hosting the Olympic Games began to fascinate Soviet leaders some ten years before the Moscow Games actually took place.[1] Intense lobbying for the right to host the Games was engaged in by state officials prior to the awarding of the 1976 Olympics to Montreal; subsequent to that IOC decision, the Kremlin redoubled its efforts and was rewarded in 1974 with the honor it so coveted. In the following six years, the feverish intensity of activity and the enormous sums of money devoted to preparing physically for the Games was exceeded only by the extent of the propaganda effort associated with Moscow's endeavors.[2] The Kremlin realized its opportunity to impress both its own citizens and those billions of viewers who for several weeks would focus their attention upon the Soviet capital; it was determined to exploit events to the fullest.[3]

One can only imagine the shock and horror with which Soviet leaders must have responded to Western intimations regarding the possibility of an Olympic boycott.[4] All of their elaborate efforts were suddenly jeopardized in the most extreme sense; the Games were threatened with becoming a farcical, intra-communist scrimmage which would receive no significant coverage, much less acclaim, by the world's media. Soviet leaders responded accordingly by waging an all-out counter-propaganda campaign against U.S. "politicization" of the Games, while also offering financial inducements to nonaligned states in order to bolster attendance.[5]

In actuality, neither the worst Soviet fears nor the most optimistic of U.S. hopes were realized. The Games did take place, and were of a consistently high athletic quality. Over eighty states participated, and in the course of events thirty-six world records and numerous Olympic marks were established.[6] The United States was, in the process, revealed to be incapable of forging a united Western response despite the grave importance accorded to the matter in Washington. On the other hand, sixty-two countries abstained from participation and precipitated a drastic reduction in the television exposure given the Games. Britain's two networks eliminated over 130 hours of coverage, while Japan elected to televise only 20 percent of the time it had originally allotted; West Germany and the United States restricted themselves to virtually no coverage.[7] Moscow would not be the focus of world attention; neither would the Soviet Union's appeal as a rival state and social system receive the corollary boost expected as a result of the Games. The Kremlin did not succeed in overcoming its inferiority complex relative to the West—through a hoped-for increase in international acceptance as a world leader on a par with Washington—after its anticipated successful hosting of the Olympic festival. Both Washington and Moscow had to be content with partial victory; at least neither suffered resounding defeat.

POLITICAL EFFECTS OF THE BOYCOTT ON THE SOVIET UNION

International Effects

In order to understand fully the international political ramifications of a boycott for the Soviet Union, one must first realize the significance attached by Moscow to hosting the Games. Briefly alluded to above, it should be stressed that the Kremlin viewed the Moscow Games as an opportunity to achieve a degree of legitimacy among the family of nations which heretofore had been lacking. Moscow would no longer have to feel itself an outcast. Also, the Olympics was a means of achieving at least symbolic parity with the West, and was therefore a vehicle through which other states would be forced to recognize Moscow as "co-dominant" with the United States. In the never-ending struggle to shift the correlation of forces in their favor, the Soviets imbued the Olympics with the profundity of a great mission, that of significantly enhancing Moscow's image and reputation both among Third World states and in the West. The 1980 edition of the *Book of the Party Activist* reflected such beliefs. It stated the theoretical position of Soviet officials when it declared, "the acute ideological struggle between [East and West] directly affects the choice of cities for the Olympic Games, the program of the competitions, the reporting of the preparations and the conduct of the Games."[8]

That the Soviets took such beliefs very seriously was reflected both in their preparations for, and in their conduct of, the Games.[9] According to Western estimates, the Kremlin spent approximately $3 billion on Olympic facilities, renovations of Moscow, and various other related projects.[10] Never before had such enormous sums been spent by a host country, not even for the extravagantly produced Montreal Games.[11]

Lest it be thought that the Kremlin would permit such lavish efforts to yield no results, one need only examine its initial response to the U.S. campaign. Once a boycott became a probability, the decision was made by Soviet leaders to secure the participation of as many countries as possible, regardless of the cost. Latin American and African states were told that they need only ask to receive free room, board, and travel for the Games. Costa Rica promptly reversed its previous decision to boycott. Jordan, in return for participating, was promised a visit by the Bolshoi ballet. Soviet efforts, although unsuccessful, also included offering travel incentives to Thailand and the Philippines.[12]

During the Games itself, Moscow sought to present as positive an image of events as possible. Cameramen were instructed to avoid showing all gestures of protest; this directive was carried out most effectively during the opening ceremonies when those state representatives who carried the Olympic flag or the flag of their national Olympic committee, rather than their national flag, were excluded from coverage.[13] Similarly, Soviet censors refused to allow their facilities to transmit any material deemed "unacceptable." In practice, this meant that any discussion about the boycott, whether focused upon its causes, its impact on competition, or its political ramifications, was considered grounds for refusing the use of Soviet transmission facilities.[14] If the Olympics could not be as the Soviets desired, they did their best to make them appear to the rest of the world as originally envisioned.

The boycott's most significant international political effect from Moscow's perspective was its crippling blow to Soviet efforts to enhance its prestige, influence, and sense of standing among other states. Not only was worldwide media coverage drastically reduced, the exposure that was given to the Games stressed its negative aspects, ranging from the effects of the boycott to the militarization of Moscow to the lack of spontaneity and warmth as contrasted with previous Olympiads.[15] Unable to obtain the benefits expected from the mass media, the Kremlin at least hoped to achieve some recognition and sanction through the attendance of various international diplomatic figures. Such was not to be the case. Kurt Waldheim, secretary general of the United Nations, declined an invitation to attend,[16] while the ambassadors to the Soviet Union from a number of states, including the United States, left Moscow before the Games began in order to avoid any association with the events.[17] The boycott effectively denied Moscow an international forum of the scope desired, and thus prevented it from realizing its primary political objectives.

Domestic Effects

Assessing the domestic political consequences of the boycott for the Soviet Union presents a somewhat greater challenge than similar efforts focusing upon the international arena. Nonetheless, it is apparent that the Kremlin's ability to manipulate the media and to control access to information allowed it to mitigate potentially severe internal repercussions. It appears that the boycott had little effect on the impression of ordinary Soviet citizens regarding their government in general, and their government's foreign policy in particular.

The Russian penchant for sport, and the intense interest of the majority of the populace in all sporting endeavors, led a number of observers to conclude that a Soviet failure to prevent a boycott could result in serious domestic unrest and instability. Within the Soviet Union, each major city had a task force specifically assigned to entice premier athletes to compete for it. Automobiles, money, and luxury apartments were offered in return for a particular star's services; when persuasive tactics failed, such extreme measures as kidnapping were occasionally employed.[18] It was hardly surprising that Soviet citizens awaited "their" Games with great eagerness; the Kremlin correspondingly anticipated a patriotic upsurge that would help to forge greater ties between the party and the people.

Carter placed considerable credence in the belief that the failure of U.S. athletes, among others, to participate in Moscow would become known to the Soviet people, and would result in intense feelings of betrayal being directed toward the Kremlin. The people would demand an explanation for events, and would eventually conclude that their government's policies were to blame. Soviet propaganda could not succeed in perverting the truth to such an extent that the government would be absolved from responsibility. Carter's evaluation reflected a certain naiveté: "if the Olympics are not held in Moscow because of Soviet military aggression in Afghanistan, this powerful signal of world outrage cannot be hidden from the Soviet people, and will reverberate around the globe."[19] He subsequently added, "I know that it will be a very difficult problem for the Soviet Union to explain to the rest of the world and to explain to its own citizens why 20 or 30 or 40 or 50 or maybe 70 other nations refuse to participate."[20] Events would reveal Carter's lack of insight.

Once a boycott became more than mere conjecture, the Soviet propaganda apparatus began to promote the idea that the U.S. initiative was premised on a hostility toward the ideals of brotherhood and humanity embodied in the Olympic Games. The boycott was said to be imposed by a U.S. president desperately searching for a means to forestall his eroding popularity in what was a presidential election year. No connection was ever posited, except toward the culmination of the anti-boycott campaign, between events in Afghanistan and the U.S. Olympic action.[21] The intensive propaganda effort produced its desired results.

As certain officials had predicted,[22] Soviet citizens professed to see little relationship between Afghanistan and the boycott. Carter was accused of "warmongering" at the expense of the Olympic movement and against the wishes of the American people.[23] Ordinary Soviets, while expressing some disappointment that a boycott had occurred, nonetheless were thrilled and proud once the Games were underway. The lavish preparations and the efficient organization of the myriad events and activities associated with the competitions were something which commanded respect from foreigners, but which elicited affectionate appreciation from the Soviet people.[24] The boycott did not cause the legitimacy of the state to be eroded in the eyes of the people, nor did its message succeed in circumventing the Kremlin and transmitting a non-Soviet version of events directly to the Soviet citizenry. Carter's belief that the average person would become cognizant of world reaction to Soviet behavior was mistaken; as a result, despite the Russian preoccupation with sport, the populace did not blame its leaders for the boycott and therefore could hardly feel "humiliated" or "betrayed."

While the boycott failed to produce an antigovernmental reaction among the population, it also precluded what many viewed as an opportunity to penetrate the Soviet Union's tightly controlled borders. An estimated 8,000 journalists, not to mention several hundred thousand spectators, would have "invaded" Soviet territory had there been no boycott.[25] Some observers posited a resultant collapse of the entire Soviet economic system and/or political apparatus;[26] others believed that, if nothing else, the West could more closely inspect Soviet society and detail its various shortcomings.[27]

Regardless of what might have occurred, it was evident that Soviet leaders were deeply concerned about the matter. The head of the KGB, Yuri Andropov, had taken over three years to develop procedures by which visitors would be separated from Soviet citizens;[28] the Kremlin clearly perceived a serious threat. The advent of the boycott relegated the effects of any "peaceful invasion" to the realm of the hypothetical. It also relieved the KGB of a huge responsibility, thereby allowing it to pursue with added vigor various "purification" measures designed to cleanse Moscow of all dissidents, derelicts, and potential troublemakers prior to the Games.

POLITICAL EFFECTS OF THE BOYCOTT ON THE UNITED STATES

International Effects

Although the United States did not succeed, as some government officials claimed, in reducing the Moscow Olympics to a mere "athletic event," the boycott was supported by a significant number of countries on every continent.[29] These states included ten that had won medals in the 1976 Games. Carter's initiative inflicted a significant, unexpected cost upon the Soviet Union for its invasion. Indeed, the boycott, for all its shortcomings, may well have "succeeded beyond any previous effort of this kind."[30] Despite the fact that many nations acted for reasons very different from those of the United States, sixty-two of them did indeed act. "The boycott" at times achieved a visibility of sufficient magnitude to overshadow the Games themselves. While exhibiting an inability in many instances to effectuate its policy, the United States nonetheless demonstrated a will to lead and persevere that many had thought no longer existed.

Such positive accomplishments were not achieved without significant costs. Administration officials could rationalize in whatever manner they desired the embarrassing failure of Western Europe to implement U.S. policy, but the reality was that the Common Market nations acted with near unanimity in a manner diametrically opposed to Washington's wishes. Lloyd Cutler attempted to foist the blame upon the various national Olympic committees, and thus away from government leaders, when he reasoned, "We [the U.S. government] are disappointed with the European teams who went against their governments, but this shouldn't be portrayed as our allies' [*sic*] deserting us because we did get support from the governments."[31] In fact, the boycott exacerbated strains in the Western alliance system and revealed a degree of disunity that could only be greeted with satisfaction by those in the Kremlin. The United States *may* have succeeded in reasserting a degree of dominance over leadership questions within the Western alliance, but it did so in spite of its fellow members, rather than with their cooperation.

Domestic Effects

Domestically, the boycott campaign had positive political consequences for the Carter administration. The widespread feeling that had existed among the U.S. public that the Soviets had taken advantage of detente and were exploiting the United States became intensified, and focused upon a concrete cause, subsequent to the invasion of Afghanistan. Punitive measures, especially those which affected only a few hundred athletes,[32] were embraced with great enthusiasm. Americans adjusted quickly to the idea that there would be, at least for the United States, no Olympics for another four years. The almost total lack of television coverage from Moscow reinforced the apathy of the U.S. public to the Games itself; after all, how could the average American be expected to take an interest in an event in which no Americans were involved, and about which little information was available?

The receptivity of Americans to Carter's boycott proposal presented the politically vulnerable president with a ready palliative. He could "get tough" with the Soviets, and thereby demonstrate both his resolve and his leadership qualities, while in the process incurring few political liabilities. While it would be wrong to imply that the boycott was seized upon primarily with an eye toward the fall election, it could not be denied that such a measure was likely to yield political dividends. The groundswell of support for the boycott also relieved Carter of many inhibitions regarding the use of coercive measures against the USOC to which he otherwise would have been subject. It is difficult not to conclude that the boycott effort was a clear success from a domestic political perspective.

ECONOMIC EFFECTS OF THE BOYCOTT ON THE SOVIET UNION

The economic ramifications of the Olympic boycott for the Soviets were far from negligible. Although figures released by the Kremlin claimed that only $375 million was spent on preparing Moscow for the Games, Western estimates were about eight times that amount.[33] According to those projections, Moscow spent the astronomical sum of $3 billion for projects expressly related to the Olympics; more importantly, approximately $500 million of that was in hard currency.[34] The Soviets thus had an enormous investment, much of which they had hoped to recoup through the large influx of Western tourists expected for the Games.

When a boycott was first suggested, tourists planning to visit the Games became hesitant about their plans. As the probability of such an action increased, initial skepticism and concern were replaced by wholesale cancellations of Olympic reservations. For many the Games had lost its original luster and was no longer considered to be the tourist attraction it once had been. The mayor of Moscow acknowledged that the number of foreign tourists expected for the Games had been downgraded from 300,000 to 70,000. Scarcely 1,000 out of an estimated 30,000 Americans originally planning to attend the Games actually went; figures for other boycotting nations, as well as for those states sending teams, were similar.[35] The fact that the loss of tourists was from those countries with hard currencies made the economic impact considerable. The Soviets had anticipated earning $150 million in such currencies; this income was relied upon to finance imports from the West, particularly technology and grain.[36] With the loss of this source of revenue, the already troubled Soviet economy was forced to absorb yet another setback. The punitive impact of the boycott extended to the economic, as well as to the political, realm.

ECONOMIC EFFECTS OF THE BOYCOTT ON THE UNITED STATES

Financial losses and economic dislocations were not borne by the U.S. government, but rather by selected corporations and private individuals. Washington refused to absorb the adverse monetary repercussions of its boycott policy, preferring instead to remind business that the government was not an agency responsible for insuring their profits, and that risk was an integral part of conducting profit-oriented enterprises. As for those unlucky enough to have made plans to travel to the Games and who now sought to change their minds, it was an unfortunate situation in which they too would be required to bear certain expenses.

Without question, NBC television was most adversely affected by the boycott decision. NBC, after a fierce battle with the other two networks, was awarded the television rights to the Games. Its contract with Moscow called for payment of over $87 million, $61 million of which had already been delivered prior to the events in Afghanistan.[37] The network also incurred expenses of $36 million for training, promotion, and the purchase of special equipment,[38] $4 million for insurance, and $7 million for negotiating the contract.[39] Additional costs included the loss of significant advertising revenue. NBC had sold 98 percent of the commercial minutes available during its coverage for an estimated $170 million;[40] despite a tight advertising market, it had to reduce substantially its fees in order to resell commercial time for non-Olympic programming.[41] Perhaps the most significant, although unquantifiable, loss was in the expected ratings boost the Olympics would have provided for the network's fall programming. NBC executives had planned to use the Moscow coverage to help propel the last place network into serious contention for the rating's leadership. The boycott precluded any such possibility.[42]

Although insurance policies with Lloyds of London and other underwriters allowed NBC to recover 90 percent of the $61 million it had previously paid to the Soviets, its losses were still estimated between $25 and $70 million.[43] In addition to the costs detailed above, NBC had spent a great deal of money to produce movies, as well as athletic features, to promote Olympic themes. Much of this effort was scrapped. Finally, NBC's affiliates were deprived of valuable local advertising time, and thus of an incentive to remain with the network. In a period in which the parent corporation was experiencing significant defections by its affiliates, this blow was particularly difficult to endure.[44]

Faced with few options, NBC executives had to accept the situation as gracefully as possible, and thereby salvage at least a measure of public goodwill. Thus, despite the magnitude of its potential losses, NBC maintained throughout the boycott campaign that it would "be guided . . . by government policy" and would not attempt to influence the course of events. One senior executive discounted the significance of NBC's difficulties when compared to the Afghanistan crisis, reasoning, "There is a higher calling here, obviously, than the interests of NBC."[45]

Another company which suffered significant losses as a result of the boycott was RTB Olympic Travel, a subsidiary of the American-owned Russian Travel Bureau. Designated by the USOC in 1979 to handle all arrangements for Americans traveling to the Games, the boycott nearly resulted in the company's bankruptcy. Prior to the events in Afghanistan, RTB had forwarded to the Moscow Olympic Organizing Committee nearly half of the $15 million already collected from the 10,700 Americans making travel arrangements through its agency.[46] In response to the deluge of requests for refunds that RTB received in the wake of Carter's intimations about the possibility of a boycott, RTB elected to put the $9 million still in its possession under the control of the Federal District Court in Manhattan.

When the Soviets steadfastly refused to refund the $7 million in down payments they had received from RTB,[47] two class action suits were filed in New York on behalf of all those who had made prepayments to Moscow through the representative U.S. travel agency.[48] In a decision rendered June 13, Federal District Court Judge Lawrence W. Pierce approved a tentative settlement that provided for an 86 percent refund to those 6,700 persons who had canceled their reservations prior to March 1, and a 63 percent refund to the remaining 4,019 people who had either canceled at a later date or who had never canceled at all. The decision required the 965 Americans who elected to go to pay an additional $250 apiece, $58 for the administrative expenses of the lawsuit and $192 for supplemental airfare.[49] More importantly for RTB's future was the judge's ruling that permitted the company to use the interest from the heretofore frozen funds to help cover operating expenses; this, coupled with an additional decision that allowed RTB to keep any profits earned from the sale of unused tickets to foreign tourists in Moscow, allowed the company to avert bankruptcy and continue operations. Although tourism to the Soviet Union remained nearly 80 percent below normal for a number of months, primarily because many Americans thought travel to the USSR was not permitted, RTB remained solvent.[50] Nonetheless, the boycott resulted in serious difficulties for RTB, not to mention considerable financial loss to most Americans who had planned to attend the Games.[51]

Among other companies affected by the boycott were Coca-Cola and Levi-Strauss. The former, seeking a toehold in a market dominated by Pepsi, had paid the Moscow Olympic Organizing Committee between $1.3 and $1.6 million for the right to sell its products during the Games. It was expected that 19 million drinks would be sold, worth an estimated $20 million.[52] The latter, meanwhile, in addition to being the official outfitters of the U.S. team,[53] had agreed to supply Soviet athletes and Olympic staff with some 23,000 pants, shirts, and denim jackets.[54] Both companies canceled their contracts subsequent to the U.S. boycott. Although neither was overly concerned about immediate financial loss, both suffered promotional setbacks and the loss of promising opportunities to penetrate the large Soviet market.

Small businesses, particularly those dealing exclusively with Olympic novelty items, were among the hardest hit by the boycott. Image Factory Sports, Inc., owners of the Western hemisphere merchandising rights for the Moscow Olympics, sold licenses to fifty-eight companies seeking to market Olympic-related products. Estimates of losses for these businesses subsequent to the U.S. withdrawal ranged between $50 and $100 million.[55] A number of these companies attempted to recoup a portion of their losses directly from Washington by establishing a group called Olympic Boycott Recovery to lobby on their behalf; after brief deliberation, the government flatly refused any compensation. At least two of these small firms were forced to declare bankruptcy when other efforts to salvage some of their investments proved unsuccessful.[56]

The economic impact of the boycott upon the United States was restricted to a relatively small number of private businesses and to individual tourists. The government forced those companies which had sought to profit from the Games to accept the risks associated with conducting international business. For larger firms, such as NBC-TV and Coca-Cola, this meant lost promotional opportunities and temporary obstacles to expansion; for smaller companies, their very existence was placed in jeopardy. Those who had planned to attend the Games as tourists suffered minor financial losses since the majority of their down payments were refunded. Washington thus succeeded in shifting the economic burden of the boycott to private sector businesses which were generally forced to accept their losses without protest in order to avoid appearing unpatriotic and thereby damaging their reputations, and to a politically insignificant number of citizens who had originally intended to travel to the Games; financial losses associated with the boycott were distributed so as to reduce political costs to a negligible level.

EFFECTS ON 1980 GAMES AS SPORTS COMPETITIONS

While the sixty-nation boycott of the Olympics unquestionably had an impact on the quality of competition at the Moscow Games,[57] its effect varied widely depending upon the particular sport in question. The glamour events of track and field, boxing, gymnastics, and swimming suffered a significant loss of top athletes, while noticeable absences were also apparent in men's and women's field hockey, water polo, women's volleyball, soccer, and men's basketball.[58] In the remaining events, the strong Soviet and East European teams were traditionally dominant, causing the boycott to have a minimal effect.

The 5,928 athletes from 81 nations who participated at Moscow represented teams that accounted for 70 percent of the medals won at the 1976 Montreal Games.[59] Although problematic and of a highly conjectural nature, informed estimates speculated that the boycott caused a shift of approximately 140 medals to the Soviet bloc.[60] Regardless of the precise numbers involved, it is obvious that the level of competition was seriously affected in those sports in which the boycotting nations excelled. Nonetheless, numerous world and Olympic records were established, and the Olympics as a whole was highly competitive. Neither the Soviet assertion that "their [the West German, American, and Canadian] absence will in no way diminish the sporting significance of the Games . . . [because] the Americans had already lost their leadership in world sports a long time ago,"[61] nor U.S. sentiment that the medals won at Moscow would necessarily be tarnished by the U.S. absence, accurately assessed the results of the boycott.[62] An objective evaluation indicates that both the Soviet and the U.S. contentions had a degree of validity, but neither was accurate for the entire scope of the competitions. The boycott had a differentiated impact that can not be generalized beyond an individual sport with any degree of confidence.

EFFECT ON OLYMPIC MOVEMENT

Despite U.S. assertions to the contrary, the boycott seriously damaged the Olympic movement.[63] Vice President Mondale could claim that "the Olympic movement will be forever strengthened'' by the U.S. action,[64] but such a statement was belied by the facts. As Robert Kane accurately predicted, the likely result of the boycott would be the ''retaliation by the Soviet bloc nations, who would boycott the 1984 Summer Olympics in Los Angeles.''[65] That this was probable was apparent from various Soviet statements at the time. *Sovetsky Sport* implied that Moscow would push for sanctions against U.S. participation in 1984 should a boycott occur, while the Moscow Olympic Organizing Committee Chairman, Ignati T. Novikov, hinted that, should Los Angeles retain the 1984 Games in the wake of a boycott, there could well be problems associated with Soviet participation.[66]

Kane was also correct in warning that the United States, unlike the Africans in 1976, had the ultimate power to destroy the Games.[67] This capacity resulted both from the sporting prowess of the United States and from its global political position. As one of the top three athletic powers in the world,[68] U.S. withdrawal from the Games would have a serious impact on competition. However, from a long-term perspective, the insertion of the Olympic Games into the East-West struggle in a direct, confrontational manner hitherto avoided set an extremely dangerous precedent. Whereas the Olympics had always served as an arena for superpower competition, political battles had been waged within the context of the Games itself. The boycott, in stark contrast, elevated the struggle to a plane in which mere participation became a political statement in the ongoing Cold War. No longer were political victories won on the playing field; rather, they were achieved before any medals were ever awarded.

The elevation of the East-West political struggle to qualitatively higher levels vis-à-vis the Olympics had effects which were being felt years later. The fragmenting of the Olympic movement begun by the 1980 boycott continued in 1984.[69] No longer was the Olympics a place where athletes representing the most divergent political persuasions competed simultaneously. In addition, the U.S. boycott significantly lowered the threshold at which either superpower might in the future resort to political manipulation of the Games, while also altering the rules according to which that struggle might be waged. The stakes have been raised so that participation in the Games, rather than simply the results of competition, are judged in political terms. Such a development does not bode well for an Olympic movement already unable to cope with its inherently political significance.

Not only did the U.S. action place the future of the Olympics in jeopardy, it failed to help rectify the numerous problems plaguing the Games before the Afghanistan crisis. Many statesmen, Olympic officials, and athletes urged the United States to make participation contingent on the enactment of fundamental reform measures for future Games. Such a policy would offer the opportunity for positive development; the inherently negative nature of a boycott would be transcended.

Proposals for improving the Games included their decommercialization and return to a simpler format, the elimination of team sports, thereby reducing the nationalistic fervor associated with the Olympics, and an end to the IOC's enforcing the artificial distinction between "amateur" and "professional" athletes that served in practice to bar only noncommunist competitors.[70] While these suggestions were the focus of significant attention, the major topic for reform was the establishment of a permanent site for the Games. An international movement to establish such a site had existed for a number of years, and many influential people sought to persuade the United States to utilize its boycott threat to force the IOC to alter its policy. It was suggested that the United States offer to forego hosting the 1984 Olympics in return for a commitment to make Greece, or another appropriate site, the permanent home of the Games. It was felt that should the United States condition its participation at Moscow upon such an agreement, a major flaw of the Olympics would be rectified and future crises avoided.[71]

Although both Carter and Secretary of State Vance publicly called for the establishment of permanent sites for both the Summer and the Winter Games,[72] the White House commitment to a boycott overshadowed any such concern. Carter did not seriously pursue a policy of linking U.S. participation to a Soviet commitment to work in the direction of establishing a permanent site; the boycott consumed all of the administration's time and effort.

One additional facet of the boycott that reinforced its perceived counterproductive character was the fact that it was the Soviet Union which was accused of aggression in violation of international law, yet it was the boycotting nations which were forced into a posture of self-denial. Some urged that the Soviets be barred from the Lake Placid Games and/or that the Moscow Games be canceled. This would, it was argued, rightfully deny Soviet athletes the opportunity to compete, while also demonstrating the U.S. will to resist aggression.[73] The boycott would no longer be perceived as such a self-defeating measure.

The effect of the boycott on the Olympic movement was a wholly negative one, the ramifications of which are yet to be fully realized. The boycott increased the likelihood of potentially disastrous East-West political intrusions into the Games, while at least temporarily splitting the Communist "bloc" from the United States within the context of the movement. The loss of a near universal Olympic Games was not accompanied by substantive improvements in problem areas.[74] No permanent site was established, efforts to curb nationalism were ineffectively pursued, and the extravagance of the Olympic spectacle was left untouched, a situation that precluded the possibility of hosting the Games for the vast majority of the world's states. The boycott exacted a heavy toll on the Olympic movement without offering commensurate dividends.

CONCLUSION

In assessing the varied impact of the boycott upon the numerous actors involved, one must realize that, aside from economic losses, it is difficult to delineate the effects of the boycott with any degree of precision; it is impossible to quantify losses of domestic confidence or international goodwill. At best, we can posit some tentative conclusions.

Domestically, neither the Soviets nor the Americans were forced to pay a heavy political price. Moscow succeeded in countering the boycott's anticipated effects on its population through a combination of intense propaganda and rigid security. The Soviet populace was undoubtedly dismayed that the United States did not participate, but this was soon forgotten amidst the pomp and pageantry of the Games; the Olympics was seen as a national accomplishment and elicited a significant degree of patriotic pride. In the United States, Carter restricted the harsh impact of his policy to a select segment of the population, thereby insuring that the administration's political costs would be minimal. The president was aided in this regard by the fact that an overwhelming majority of the American people supported his actions. Such a situation provided the White House with a wide degree of latitude in the tactics utilized to secure support, and meant that the use of coercive pressures would not precipitate a political uproar.

In economic terms, both countries suffered significantly. Soviet losses resulted primarily from the huge drop in the number of tourists who came for the Games, and in the corresponding reduction in the influx of hard currency. The enormous construction costs associated with the preparations for the Games had resulted in large foreign debts; thus, the unexpected loss of revenue was particularly distressing. Washington, in contrast to Moscow, foisted the costs of the boycott onto private sector businesses and prospective tourists who had already made down payments for Olympic trips. Depending on the size of the company, the extent of the losses incurred ranged from missed promotional opportunities to outright bankruptcy. Tourists were forced to absorb losses of several hundred dollars.

The most difficult area in which to evaluate the effects of the boycott was that of the international political standing of the two superpowers. Clearly, Moscow was denied an enormous opportunity to gain the degree of international acceptance and acclaim it had always sought. On the other hand, the Kremlin secured the participation of a majority of the Olympic community and foiled U.S. efforts to reduce the Games to an intra-communist fiasco. From the U.S. perspective, Washington succeeded in significantly diminishing the propaganda value of the Games, but failed to obtain the support of most of its West European allies. It thus increased the perception abroad that it could act with determination, while simultaneously exhibiting the lack of political skill and ability required to forge an effective alliance. The results in the international political arena were far from decisive.

The Moscow Games itself suffered from the boycott in a selective fashion. Sports in which the boycotting states were strong were no longer competitive; the remaining events were contested at extremely high levels. While the number of contestants and of participating states was the lowest in many Olympiads, the presence of the Soviet "bloc," Great Britain, and France meant that a quality Games could occur. The Kremlin did not succeed in hosting the greatest Olympics ever; neither did the United States create a "non-Olympic" Olympics.

Finally, the boycott must be adjudged to have had a deleterious effect on the Olympic movement in toto. The fractionation of the Games on "East-West" terms begun by the 1980 boycott continued in 1984, yet showed signs of improvement in 1988 under the influence of the image-conscious Gorbachev regime. The results of such political machinations on the future of the Olympics remain uncertain, but it is clear that any previous inhibitions which may have existed pertaining to political manipulation of the Games were destroyed by the boycott.

In order for the Olympics to entertain any hope of survival, it must respond to such coercive political pressures and attempt to forge an existence in which the political component of international sport will be kept within manageable control. The IOC must recognize that it oversees a highly political event, and that it must, at the very least, restrict the quest for national advantage through the Olympic Games to within reasonable parameters.

6

Endemic Obstacles
to the Boycott

The United States-sponsored boycott encountered numerous obstacles in the course of its implementation. Foremost among these barriers were difficulties endemic to *any* attempt to effect a boycott of the Olympic Games. These problems would have existed for any administration, and were not the result of incompetence or miscalculation. A second category of difficulties, however, stemmed directly from shortcomings associated with the White House. Errors were made, for a variety of reasons, which heightened the problem of developing a broadly based international response to the Afghanistan invasion focusing upon the Olympic Games. Once we identify the two distinct causes for the boycott's difficulties, we will be able to determine how the failure to implement the boycott appropriately compounded the problems inherent in this particular endeavor.

CONSTRAINTS IMPOSED BY THE STRUCTURE OF THE INTERNATIONAL POLITICAL SYSTEM

Lacking a centralized decision-making and enforcement body, the horizontally structured international system presents significant obstacles to those states seeking to act in collective fashion.[1] While powerful states can, if willing to expend the necessary resources, use force or the threat of force to gain the support of lesser states, such efforts are costly and create resentment. However, absent such tactics, collective action remains elusive; states tend to pursue what they perceive as their own short-term self-interest since each state is forced to perceive all other states as actual or potential threats.[2]

If such constraints to collective action have marked the state system since its inception, they have been exacerbated by the rapid transformation of the international arena since World War II. The dramatic increase in the number and diversity of the principal actors and the evolution of the nature of relations among those actors have been of particular import. With the end of World War II and the ensuing rise of nationalist movements throughout the colonial world, pressure was applied to European governments that forced their eventual retreat from overseas empire. The result was an enormous expansion in the number of sovereign states comprising the world community. In addition, transnational actors, particularly multinational corporations, grew at a spectacular rate. The consequence of these developments was twofold: first, an erosion of the capacity of the most dominant states to enforce the compliance of the weaker with their policies; and second, a more general diminution of the ability of states to dictate the course of international events.

While the quantity of states, coupled with the increasing significance of nonstate actors, has posed further obstacles to collective state action, an additional impediment must be mentioned. Curiously, this obstacle results from a rise in the phenomenon of complex interdependence. While interdependence signifies only the existence of mutual dependence (i.e., where one party's actions can impose costs upon another), complex interdependence is more multidimensional; three characteristics prevail. First, multiple channels, including transgovernmental, transnational, and interstate organs, connect distinct societies. Second, the agenda of interstate relations includes a multitude of issues not structured in any rigid hierarchy of significance. Finally, military force, while still a component of national power, is never threatened between complexly interdependent countries nor on inappropriate issues.[3]

Thus, while complex interdependence signifies a generally increased level of interaction and cooperation between certain states, it is the implicit restraint involving the use of force between those states that eliminates any certainty regarding "cooperation" on a given issue. Since force may no longer dictate acquiescence, cooperation must be achieved through negotiation; failing that, no further measures are available. Also, since the usability of force varies depending on the issue area involved, no assumption may be made that the militarily strongest state will automatically prevail on a specific question.[4] Therefore, the United States, in a complexly interdependent relationship with Western Europe, could seek to use such a connection to gain adherence to the boycott, but could not, once this failed, resort to force to gain its objective. The United States, although not complexly interdependent with the Third World, could not credibly threaten forceful action because of the nature of the issue and the general inability of militarily dominant states to link successfully nonmilitary matters to their military prowess.

Forced to implement policy within such a milieu, it is hardly surprising that the United States encountered such a degree of resistance. Third World states, aware of the limitations constraining Washington, could act as they deemed most advantageous without fear of extreme reprisal.[5] Similarly, Western Europe, secure in its particular association with the United States, recognized the tools available to the White House to exert pressure; beyond these, no viable means existed for the Carter administration to secure cooperation.

POLITICAL DIFFERENCES OF COUNTRIES TARGETED FOR BOYCOTT

Any international political action of such scope confronted the fact that regimes of vastly differing orientations, with objectives often diametrically opposed to one another, had to be forged into a unified entity. Not only were these targeted states often unsupportive of U.S. policy in general, they also had few common interests among themselves.[6] In order to overcome antipathies among these states, the United States had to identify individual sensibilities and policy goals. Without such a strategy, the sole thread of commonality among prospective boycotting nations was an opposition to "aggression"; yet, such sentiment rarely provokes states to act in a decisive manner.[7] Other ends besides the expression of moral outrage must be served to evoke a significant response. Thus, while the White House could stress in domestic speeches "the Soviet lunge toward the most strategic oil-rich spot on Earth,"[8] and its corresponding threat to national security,[9] it had to adopt a multifaceted approach when dealing with other countries with greatly differing concerns.

Western Europe was placed under pressure from Moscow to refrain from supporting the boycott in return for a continuation of detente. Soviet officials warned the Europeans:

One cannot, as some politicians in the NATO countries do, declare for continuing détente in Europe and simultaneously express solidarity with the U.S. policy directed at frustrating it, boycotting the Olympics and curtailing contacts with the Soviet Union. . . . Events in Afghanistan cannot and must not to any degree jeopardize the destinies of détente in Europe.[10]

Perhaps no European state was so caught between the superpowers as was West Germany. Chancellor Helmut Schmidt and his Social Democratic party had stressed the need for closer relations with Moscow, while refusing to act so as to create a rift with the United States. This dichotomous policy was possible because, prior to Carter's call for a boycott, the Federal Republic was able to support the United States without engaging in direct acts of reprisal against the Soviet Union. The boycott rendered such a delicate policy untenable. Schmidt was forced to accept a boycott, but for reasons far removed from those that had prompted Washington's actions.

Not only did the West Europeans have different political goals from the United States, they were also concerned lest they appear to be pawns at Washington's disposal. There were efforts in the initial phases of the campaign among

Great Britain, France, and West Germany to develop a common position apart from the United States.[11] France was most adamant that it act independently of the United States, and mistakenly carried this to the point of creating the false impression that the government had no preference as to how its Olympic Committee acted. This ultimately resulted in the committee proceeding contrary to the government's actual desires.

The Canadian government of Pierre Trudeau likewise sought to forge a more independent and balanced position between Moscow and Washington, and was forced to act in a hesitant fashion regarding the boycott. Trudeau's political mission was not one predicated upon Carter's goals, but rather was formulated so as to establish a distance between Canada and the United States. Lest it be thought that only the Western states were desirous of acting in an independent manner, one need only look toward Africa to see a wealth of such feeling. Countries including Nigeria, Tanzania, and Liberia explicitly expressed their refusal to be influenced by outside pressure. Regardless of their actual decision-making processes, these states sought to establish at least the appearance of independence.

When analyzed from the perspective of the boycott's relationship to substantive issues, it becomes clear that states predicated their responses to the boycott upon the most wide-ranging of concerns. The Islamic states sought to act on a common basis in response to the plight of a co-religionist. Japan was preoccupied with how its decision would affect access to natural resource suppliers.[12] Certain African states based their decision largely upon the international response to their boycott of 1976. If one can make any generalizations about the factors that weighed most heavily upon decisions concerning the boycott, it is that there was no consensus among states which ultimately acted in a similar fashion.

The difficulty presented by the fact that the boycott was global in scope was immense. No common political values existed upon which to base a working alliance. National objectives were unique, and often contradictory. Finally, even when some degree of commonality existed, states resisted conforming to what was perceived as outside pressure and attempted to create an independent position. Carter was confronted with a task of Herculean proportions for he not only had to weld the most disparate of states into a nominally cohesive unit, but this had to be accomplished in a brief period of time.

NATURE OF THE INTERNATIONAL SPORTS ESTABLISHMENT

One of the most difficult obstacles that the boycott campaign was forced to overcome was the complex, highly idealistic international sports establishment.[13] The component organizations of the Olympic movement included the IOC, the organizing committee of the host city, national Olympic committees in each member country,[14] twenty-six Olympic sports federations, and regional games federations.[15] The interactions among these organs were governed by explicit rules, such as those set forth in the Olympic Charter, and by custom and tradition. Decisions were not made with undue haste, and the sanctity of precedent weighed heavily on all matters. Not only was it difficult to discern the exact distribution of power among the distinct structures within the system, but it was problematic to assess the relative power possessed by individual members of each separate organization.[16] Thus, should a majority of the 137 states with accredited national Olympic committees have voted to relocate, postpone, or cancel the Games, this need not have occurred because of IOC statutes that gave special weight to those countries with more powerful teams.[17]

The problem of dealing with this labyrinthine establishment was compounded for the Carter administration by the fact that, according to Olympic rules, national Olympic committees must act independently of government influence. While it is unrealistic to expect any true differentiation between governments and Olympic committees in many, if not most, states,[18] Western committees in particular have succeeded in maintaining their independence to a surprising extent. This made it imperative for Carter to establish a constructive rapport with nongovernmental actors predisposed to resist political pressure. Carter was confronted with an unenviable task.

That at least some members of the administration were cognizant of the unique problems faced by Washington in any attempt to affect the sacrosanct symbol of the international sports establishment was reflected by one official's evaluation of the government's proposed effort: "The Olympics are only in a tangential way under the control of the Government. . . . We can't just go in and announce an embargo on the Olympics. This is largely a matter of leadership and persuasion that involves a lot of private people."[19] The White House may have been able to coerce the acquiescence of the USOC—despite the fact that that group had been a private corporation since its inception and was not dependent on governmental financial support[20]—but it did not possess such power relative to other states' Olympic committees. Perhaps the president of Israel's Olympic Committee most accurately assessed the feeling of many of the committees when he declared, "While we obviously sympathize with President Carter's position, we stand by the principle that any decision about a country's participation should be made only by that state's Olympic committee without any government interference whatsoever."[21]

While it was initially assumed that most Olympic committees would be opposed to any political action that would impact negatively upon the Games, the first concrete indication that such was the case was the action of the nineteen-member council of the Association of National Olympic Committees. Meeting in early February, the council unanimously urged the IOC to continue its support for the Moscow Games, while also calling upon the International Committee to resist all outside "political, religious or economic" pressures.[22] Such firm opposition to political manipulation of the Games was subsequently exhibited by a group of eighteen committees, including those representing all nine

Common Market states. On May 3, the group stated, "We appeal to the Olympic committees of all the countries in the world to take part" at Moscow because the boycott will not solve any problems and "would have disastrous consequences on international sport."[23]

That the committees indeed could act independently was evidenced by their defiance of government policy in a number of instances. The Olympic committees of Ireland, the Netherlands, Australia, Belgium, France, and Great Britain refused to succumb to varying degrees of governmental pressure to boycott and elected to send teams to Moscow. While eventually reversing its position, the Canadian Committee likewise initially voted, contrary to its government's wishes, to attend the Games.[24]

A further obstacle to the success of any action aimed at disrupting the Olympic Games was the power of both national and international sports federations.[25] These organizations' dedication to preserving the Olympics insured their steadfast opposition to any alternative event.[26] This predilection was reinforced by Article 24C of the Olympic Charter which called for sanctions to be applied against any nation not competing in the Olympic Games for political or racial reasons.[27] This created difficulties for Olympic committees otherwise inclined toward some type of action, whether it be the establishment of an alternate event or a boycott of the Moscow Games. Should a "counter-Olympics" be supported, a committee's athletes would be liable to future sanctions by international governing associations, while a boycott would place the committee itself in violation of the Olympic Charter.[28]

The question of the future position and degree of influence within the international Olympic structure of recalcitrant committees loomed as a crucial issue, and one which affected the willingness of committees to follow the U.S. initiative. Olympic groups correctly perceived the likelihood that any "anti-Olympic" action on their part would impact negatively upon their relative power within Olympic circles. Should a committee damage its relations with the IOC, it could impair the hopes of its officials to advance within international ranks, as well as reducing the prestige of that committee.[29]

The international sports structure further frustrated boycott efforts because members of the IOC are not considered as national representatives to that organization, but rather serve in the capacity of spokesmen for the IOC to their home country.[30] The constituency of IOC members is restricted to those associated with the Olympic movement, and does not include the populace or the government of their home state. Once it is realized that IOC members are only representatives to a given country, and not vice versa, it is possible to understand why the IOC remains such a difficult body for governments to influence. The IOC is fully aware of the unique, transnational,[31] independent character of its organization, and jealously seeks to guard this position against governmental encroachment.

The boycott campaign was confronted by a litany of obstacles: the complexity and variegated structure of the international sporting establishment; the refusal of national Olympic committees to submit readily to government coercion; the power of national and international sports federations and their firm commitment to the Olympic Games; the concern of national Olympic committees not to jeopardize their relations with the IOC, and thereby sacrifice their influence and power; and the particular organizational characteristic of the IOC whereby its members were considered transnational ambassadors above the interests of any one state. These features of international sport could not be dismissed by government officials seeking to act against the Moscow Games. Only through an understanding of such realities could one have any hope of reaching a modicum of accommodation with the world's sports establishment; without such mutual cooperation, any attempt to establish alternate Games and/or boycott Moscow was faced with prospects of at best limited success.

TIMING OF EVENTS

The sincerity of *any* U.S. response to the Soviet aggression was certain to be called into question because of the fact that it was a presidential election year and all prospective candidates, not the least of whom was Carter himself, had to be concerned with how their position would be perceived by the American public. The incumbent president was especially vulnerable to accusations that his boycott initiative was predicated not upon effectively rebutting the Soviet Union, but rather upon winning the upcoming election. The president's popularity rating had, except for brief interludes, followed a steady downward trend, while the Iranian hostage crisis was widely perceived as yet another manifestation of Carter's ineffectiveness and lack of resolve. Thus, a strong response to events in Afghanistan could indeed be interpreted as a show of force, aimed not at the Kremlin, but rather at the U.S. electorate.

Although Carter vowed to avoid "yielding to political pressures here at home,"[32] the boycott issue nonetheless became embroiled in the domestic political arena. The Republican National Committee voted in January to support a boycott.[33] This action served to delimit the parameters within which Republican candidates could address the issue, while it also acted as an impetus for Carter to adopt a firm, hard-line position at the earliest possible date in order to usurp any advantage his opponents might achieve.

That the individual candidates within each party were cognizant of the significance of the issue was evident in the tentativeness of their positions. Senator Edward Kennedy, Carter's most serious potential Democratic challenger, abstained from voting in January on the near-unanimous resolution of the Senate that called for all athletes and spectators to boycott Moscow. Kennedy sought to keep his options open by appearing loyal to his president in time of crisis, while at the same time expressing his belief that the boycott was only a symbolic gesture of little utility.[34] The Republicans likewise vacillated on the issue according to what was deemed politically expedient. Ronald Reagan, who initially supported the boycott unreservedly, later began to express doubt about the efficacy of such an action; finally, and only after Republican rival George Bush accused him of being "wishy-washy" on the issue, did he declare to be in favor of Carter's policy.[35] While Reagan was forced to adopt the party position, which paralleled that of the president's, he distanced himself from the Democrats by attacking the implementation of the boycott as likely to turn "the whole exercise into yet another failure in U.S. foreign policy."[36]

The international response to the boycott initiative reflected a keen awareness of the importance attached to the Olympic issue within U.S. political circles. The Soviet Union and its East European allies repeatedly asserted that the boycott was merely the action of a president in desperate electoral difficulty seeking to "manufacture" support by creating a foreign enemy around which to rally the nation.[37] A Budapest newspaper typically observed, "The Moscow Olympics cannot be thrown into the American election as some sort of miracle weapon."[38] Lest it be thought that the Soviets and their allies were creating propaganda which had no audience in the West, one need only examine statements by West European leaders, as well as Olympic officials, to prove the contrary. West Germany, Denmark, and Belgium were among those states whose representatives hinted that Carter's tough stance was at least partly a result of his reelection campaign.[39] Richard Palmer, general secretary of the British Olympic Association, perhaps expressed the thoughts of many when he attributed the boycott to "Carter's election bandwagon."[40]

Reflecting the belief that the U.S. boycott stemmed primarily from domestic political concerns was the posture adopted by Lord Killanin. The president of the IOC indicted Carter's integrity and motivation when he replied, in response to a question about a possible meeting between Carter and himself, "He has not requested to see me, and I have not requested to see him, and I don't have a vote in the United States."[41] Julian Roosevelt, an American member of the IOC, likewise accused Carter of acting on the basis of election-year politics, rather than on what was best for the country.[42]

Although the primary impetus behind Carter's action almost certainly rested on a sense of moral outrage and despair at Moscow's invasion, the president could not escape the fact that the unfolding events fell in the shadow of his reelection campaign. Carter could attempt to reduce the political nature of his policies, but he could never divorce himself from their context nor eradicate completely his less than noble political considerations. Such a situation inevitably produced both domestic and foreign accusations of political manipulation; doubt was cast on the sincerity of the entire effort. Carter was forced to confront such apprehension, and attempted to minimize it as much as possible. Thus, the confluence of events within a presidential election year presented yet another endemic obstacle to the success of the boycott campaign.

PAST U.S. FAILURES TO BOYCOTT

The White House faced a further difficulty in its quest to effect a boycott of the Moscow Games that could not be attributed to ineptness or miscalculation on its part. This problem centered upon the U.S. legacy of uninterrupted participation in the Olympic Games from the initiation of the modern Olympic movement in 1896 through the Montreal Olympics of 1976. U.S. teams had been fielded at every Olympiad regardless of the global political situation. U.S. competitors were present at the 1936 Berlin Games despite the declaration by Hitler that those Games were to showcase the supremacy of the German people, and the obvious implication that by attending the Games the United States would bestow a degree of legitimacy upon the Nazi regime. Likewise, the Soviet invasion of Hungary in 1956 precipitated no U.S. countermeasure involving the Olympics, despite the fact that Spain, Switzerland,[43] and the Netherlands withdrew their squads in protest.

Of most import to the 1980 campaign, however, was the failure of the United States to follow the lead of black Africa and boycott the 1976 Montreal Games in protest against New Zealand's participation. The African states had argued that New Zealand should be banned from competition because its rugby team had toured South Africa. They felt that any sporting contact with the apartheid regime, despite the fact that rugby was a non-Olympic sport, should be punished by the IOC. When the International Committee failed to act, the majority of African states boycotted; the United States expressed only verbal sympathy.

When the United States sought African support for its Moscow boycott, many African leaders recalled the American nonaction of 1976 and questioned the right of the United States to ask for solidarity on a moral issue it deemed significant when it had ignored similar African pleas four years earlier. Indignation by the United States appeared selective to many, hypocritical to most.

While it can be argued that there has always been some upheaval, threat to the peace, or actual war in every Olympic year, and that, in order to preserve the movement, the boycott weapon must be applied in a highly restrictive fashion, such reasoning held little sway over those who had sacrificed without support in previous years. Those countries had perceived an issue of vital importance to themselves, had acted accordingly, and had not been supported by the United States. An understandable reticence toward future cooperation was instilled. This was not to be overcome easily.

Carter's boycott campaign thus had to surmount the resentment engendered by previous administrations, particularly that of President Ford's. Carter had the unenviable task of persuading the world, but most particularly the Africans, that the United States had mended its ways and would now act to uphold moral principles in a more consistent fashion; mutual cooperation would begin presently, and would continue in the future. Promises of such an alteration of U.S. behavior were not considered reliable by foreign leaders; only through significant effort by Washington could American credibility be established.

HISTORY OF U.S. AGGRESSIVE ACTIONS

Another historical impediment to achieving wide-ranging international acceptance of a boycott concerned what many viewed as the U.S. propensity to engage in aggressive foreign actions. U.S. intervention in Cuba, Chile, and, most recently, Vietnam was hardly perceived as benevolent in the eyes of many world leaders, and called into question Carter's right to moral indignation.[44] The United States certainly would have opposed any Olympic boycott in protest against its extraterritorial endeavors; why, it was argued, should it expect such action against the Soviet Union for the same type of activity?

Carter was once again forced to convince foreign statesmen that the United States had adopted a new course of action. Should Carter's persuasive efforts fail, the United States would appear to be cynically manipulating world opinion in an effort to gain advantage in its struggle for supremacy with the Soviet Union; in that case, most countries would seek only to avoid involvement. Once again, the legacy of the past had bestowed upon the White House a problematic situation which served as an additional obstacle to the implementation of the Olympic boycott.

SACROSANCT VIEW OF THE GAMES

The final endemic obstacle faced by Carter, and in many ways the most difficult to overcome, was the cherished attitude held by many that the Olympic Games, if somewhat tarnished, represented the noblest of man's ideals and aspirations and as such should be above political manipulation. This highly idealistic perspective was displayed by the most disparate of people: international Olympic officials, athletes, and, perhaps most importantly, ordinary citizens. Endorsed by persons of virtually every nationality, the "Olympics above politics" belief was deeply held and presented government leaders and national Olympic committees otherwise inclined toward following Carter's initiative with great difficulties. Western statesmen, in particular, could afford to ignore public sentiment only at their own electoral peril.

The observation, "Throughout the history of the Olympics . . . politics and sports have always been intertwined, and anyone who denies that is simply molding history for their own convenience,"[45] dismisses as objectively false the widespread belief that in ancient times the Olympic Games was an apolitical affair. However, since man tends to act not upon the basis of objective reality, but rather upon subjective perception, the fact that the Greek Games were highly significant political contests is not of all-encompassing importance. Rather, one must deal with popular opinion, regardless of its erroneous nature, if it exerts effective pressure on governmental and/or Olympic decision makers. Once the pervasiveness of this idealism and its various manifestations in the boycott campaign is understood, one can grasp the magnitude of the difficulty that confronted Washington.

That the White House was cognizant of the potential of Olympic idealists to thwart the boycott was evident early in the campaign. Administration officials attempted to preempt the possibility that such sentiment would coalesce into concerted opposition, at least within this country, by portraying the boycott as the only available means by which to preserve the future of the "true" Olympic Games. Secretary of State Cyrus Vance described the history of the Olympics so as to portray the U.S. action as one of salvation:

From their beginnings in ancient Greece, the Olympics have symbolized some of humanity's noblest principles. Foremost among these is peace. . . . The United States deeply values the Olympic Games and the principles on which they rest. . . . But if the basic principles of the Olympics are ignored, the future of the games themselves will be placed in jeopardy.[46]

Deputy Secretary of State Warren Christopher similarly beckoned to Olympic idealists to embrace the boycott as a necessary step to preserve their institution when he chastised the Kremlin for its act of aggression and questioned, "Who . . . can believe the Soviets intend to host the Olympics as a celebration of the human spirit?"[47] By appealing to the lofty ideals supposedly represented by, and embodied within, the Olympic Games, the White House sought not only to defuse adverse reaction among Olympic "purists," but also to enlist these potential opponents as allies in the president's fight. That Washington chose to emphasize the ideals of the Games rather than its flaws attested to the strength of "idealist" sentiment and to the perceived need to coopt it in order to achieve success.

What exactly did the idealists espouse? While it is problematic to generalize when dealing with such an amorphous array of people, one may discern some general areas of agreement after examining a sampling of editorials that appeared over a period of time in the *New York Times*.[48] These editorials emphasized several themes. First, the Olympics was said to be one of the last available forums in which the peoples of the world could gather peacefully. This temporary assemblage of athletes was viewed as a conduit through which nations, regardless of past or present enmities, could begin to communicate with one another. Although only a tentative first step, such a dialogue was to provide a point of departure for substantive progress in the resolution of differences. Man was assumed to have had a natural regard for his fellow beings which had been suppressed and corrupted by the institution of the state.[49] If the people of the world could only rediscover their basic oneness, world harmony would be a viable possibility. The Olympic Games was the foundation upon which this edifice of hope was constructed.[50]

A second idea with widespread currency was that the Olympics transcended politics and, as the embodiment of an ideal, should continue despite the "petty grievances among nations of the world."[51] There was a pervasive sense of disgust and impatience with the endless conflicts between various countries and their respective leaders; the Olympics was an escape mechanism that allowed one to rise above petty differences and aspire to a loftier vision. The Greeks, it was argued, suspended wars and political battles during the Olympics in order to create a proper atmosphere for the Games. So, then, why couldn't we do the same?[52] The chairman of the U.S. Olympic Council on Sports Medicine went to such lengths as to submit a proposal to the USOC to develop a mechanism, using the influence of the IOC and the United Nations, to implement a global truce during the entire Olympic year. This period of peace would enable the Olympic Games to "be held in a spirit of peace while affirming the aspirations of individual man toward excellence."[53] Although an extreme expression of this position, the idea of an international truce was revealing. It showed the depth of conviction that, as one journalist observed, "political issues are . . . transient, . . . the Olympic spirit is transcendent."[54]

A final concern of Olympic "purists" was for the integrity of international sport itself. They placed great credence in the idea that international sport was an intrinsically worthwhile activity, one appreciated by true fans unconcerned with the nationalities of participants. Since the Olympics was not "owned" by the Soviet Union any more than the headquarters of the United Nations was "owned" by New York City or the United States, and since the Kremlin's actions were unrelated to the actual Games, a boycott was considered an inappropriate response with potentially disastrous consequences. Only if the Soviets attempted directly to politicize the Games should a boycott be considered, and even then the decision should rest with the athletes; as many argued, "Aren't the Olympics for athletes?"[55] If the Games was to succumb to the pressures of the outside world, should not those directly involved make that decision? As one former Olympian wistfully lamented, "Why not get the athletes together . . . and put on a great athlete-run Olympics? Boy, we'd do it right. . . . We could really run an Olympics like it should be run, where people represent themselves with no flag waving; sport for the sake of sport."[56] A naive and childish wish? Perhaps. But nonetheless it was one which represented the yearnings of many, and which came to impact heavily on the boycott campaign.

The most outspoken, and also the most influential, of those who stressed the sacrosanct nature of the Games were the representatives of the international sporting establishment; prominent among those was Lord Killanin, president of the IOC. Noted for his steadfast opposition to the "reality" of the progressive politicizing of the Olympics, Killanin fought fiercely to minimize what he regarded as the intrusion of politics into the hallmark of international sport. Killanin's predecessor, the much maligned Avery Brundage, likewise refused to permit the political disruption of the Olympics when he declared, subsequent to the killing of Israeli athletes by Palestinian terrorists at the 1972 Munich Games:

Every civilized person recoils in horror at the barbarous criminal intrusion of terrorists into peaceful Olympic precincts. . . . The Games of the XX Olympiad have been subject to 2 savage attacks. We lost the Rhodesian battle against naked political blackmail. We have only the strength of a great ideal. I am sure that the public will agree that we cannot allow a handful of terrorists to destroy this nucleus of international cooperation and good will we have in the Olympic Movement. The Games must go on.[57]

Killanin echoed the past president when he implored "the sportsmen of the world to unite in peace before a holocaust descends. . . . Sport and the Olympic Games must not be used for political purposes, especially when other political, diplomatic and economic means have not been tried."[58] He also warned that the very future of the Olympic movement would be jeopardized should "politicians continue to make use of sport for their own ends." Declaring the Olympics to be a "competition between individuals and not between countries"—conveniently ignoring the fact that the IOC permits only those politically affiliated to compete in the Games—Killanin then denied that attendance at Moscow would signal approval of the Soviet regime.[59] The Olympics was said to be a transnational event that was forced to find a temporary home every four years amid the jungle of nation-states. This did not indicate, however, that it had any inherent connection with the international political order.

Throughout the international Olympic establishment, national officials adhered to a similar line of reasoning. The president of the British Olympic Association stressed that the Games was "a competition between athletes and not between nations," while the French Minister of Youth and Sports declared the Olympics to be "a sporting event, not a political affair."[60] The president of the French Olympic Committee justified his country's refusal to boycott by arguing that the decision rested solely on "sporting grounds" and from a desire to prevent athletes from being "used in politics." Willi Daume, president of the West German Olympic organization, raised his voice with that of his international colleagues when he urged other national Olympic committees to resist "political pressure on international sports and the Olympics" since they were not the appropriate forums for the resolution of "political disputes."[61] Italy, Puerto Rico, Sweden, Switzerland, the Netherlands, and Finland were among the other states whose Olympic officials drew explicit distinctions between sports and politics, as well as between individual and national competition, in protesting against the United States-sponsored boycott.[62] The intensity with which these convictions were held was perhaps most clearly captured by the president of the Irish Amateur Athletic Federation, William Coghlan, when he defended his country's decision to attend the Moscow Games through a historical analogy: "It must be remembered that Great Britain, now supporting the boycott, herself invaded Afghanistan over the Khyber Pass something like 25 times. She's *still* in Ireland. Yet civilized people set that aside when we compete."[63]

The Carter administration could not hope to achieve any semblance of success in the promotion of a boycott without attempting first to neutralize and then, if at all possible, to coopt those clinging to an idealized Olympic conception. That the boycott did not become more universally accepted was due in large part to the inability of Washington to alter radically the views deeply cherished by many people throughout the world. Whether a misconception or not, the belief that the Olympic Games should be politically inviolable, since it symbolized the loftiest and noblest of man's aspirations, was one that had important bearing on the fate of the 1980 Moscow Olympics.

CONCLUSION

Assuming the absence of any miscalculation or error in the orchestration of the Olympic boycott, the White House nonetheless faced extremely difficult and wide-ranging obstacles. The decentralized nature of the international political arena, coupled with the enormous post-World War II increase in the number of both state and nonstate actors, precluded the easy realization of large-scale collective action. In addition, the increasing disutility of force, particularly on nonmilitary issues and between complexly interdependent states, prevented Washington from enforcing its will upon reluctant governments. Structural realities restricted both the effectiveness and the nature of the policy tools available to the White House, and thus mitigated against the achievement of an all-inclusive boycott.

The ambitious scope of the boycott presented another impediment to the realization of White House policy. It forced Carter's aides to deal with regimes of widely differing orientations and political cultures. A complex array of approaches was required in order to present each potential supporter with the most persuasive possible argument; disingenuous reasoning was necessary to avoid the appearance of outright deception and manipulation. After all, Washington sought the backing of regimes that were often in an antagonistic relationship with one another. Only through a careful process in which all nations' interests and concerns were identified could the White House hope to woo previously hostile states into some semblance of agreement by emphasizing areas of commonality, while ignoring, as much as circumstances permitted, issues of contention. The need to integrate appeals tailored to individual countries into a comprehensive schema was problematic, yet crucial for large-scale success.

A third barrier to White House efforts was that posed by the complex structure of the international sports establishment. Nearly impenetrable to the unfamiliar observer, the Olympic "organization," with its overlapping layers of administrative apparatus, in conjunction with its array of obscure rules, made an accurate assessment of how best to deal with the Olympic issue extremely difficult for administration officials. Yet without such knowledge, they were doomed to commit serious errors that could impact negatively on the entire effort.

The coincidental occurrence of the Afghan crisis in a presidential election year created further difficulties in effecting a viable boycott. Aspersions were cast upon Carter's motives and personal integrity, especially in the wake of the Iranian hostage crisis and his plummeting presidential ratings. Carter had become easy prey for skeptics who believed that those in power seek only to retain that power, whatever the cost. This created a situation in which foreign nations' distrust of the United States was heightened, and their receptivity to any concerted action sponsored by Washington diminished.

Two historical impediments existed to Carter's Olympic boycott initiative. The first was the failure of the United States to join other boycott efforts, either directed against such regimes as Nazi Germany and apartheid South Africa, or in protest of previous acts of aggression, including that of the Soviet Union against Hungary in 1956. Those who had taken part in these previous actions were especially reticent to join a boycott sponsored by a country that had never before lent its weight to Olympic protests. Many African states in particular emphasized the need for reciprocal support; they accordingly dismissed the U.S. appeal.

The second obstacle of a historical nature was associated with the United States' long history of intervening in the internal affairs of foreign countries. Many nations perceived as hypocritical the extreme reaction of the Carter administration to the Afghan invasion when the United States had fought in Vietnam for nearly fifteen years. These states refused to accept what they believed to be a U.S. double standard. The entire affair was seen only as the latest skirmish in the East-West rivalry, and as such of little relevance except to the closely aligned nations. Carter faced great difficulties in attempting to dispel this view of the United States, one that handicapped efforts to garner foreign support.

Finally, the White House was forced to overcome a global idealism reserved for the Olympic Games. The Olympics was considered to be qualitatively different in nature from ordinary political contests. It was imbued with the hopes and dreams of mankind, and symbolically represented the potential for cooperation and fraternity so desperately sought by the peoples of the world. Although somewhat corrupted, the Olympic ideal remained strong for many; they sought to preserve its existence and to shield it from the threatened encroachments of the "real" world. In order to transform his boycott into a truly global action, Carter had to neutralize the impact of such sentiment. This proved to be a task beyond the capabilities of any single person.

7

U.S. Shortcomings

LACK OF UNDERSTANDING OF THE INTERNATIONAL SPORTS STRUCTURE

> I personally think it's unfortunate that the President of the United States, on sporting matters, was not fully informed on the facts. . . . This led to the trouble. . . . They did not understand how sport is organized in the world. They did not understand how national Olympic committees work. They did not understand the workings of the International Olympic Committee. They did not understand the workings of the international federations and national federations. . . . To my mind they had virtually no knowledge other than about American football and baseball, which if they had been in the Olympic Games, perhaps we wouldn't have had the boycott.[1]
>
> Lord Killanin at final news conference
> as president of the IOC,
> July 28, 1980

With this scathing indictment of Carter and his White House aides, Lord Killanin identified the first of three major shortcomings of the boycott campaign directly attributable to the miscalculations and ignorance of those concerned with the policy's implementation—that of being fundamentally unaware of the structure of the international sports establishment and unversed in its methods of operation. Killanin accurately recognized the extent to which the Carter administration operated in a void of informed opinion about the Olympic Games and its numerous supporting administrative organs. It was far from simple vindictiveness that caused him to lament, "If they [the White House] understand other matters as well as they understand sport, God help us all."[2]

Carter appeared to become aware of the sparse and often inaccurate nature of the advice he received, and eventually sought to remedy the situation. Nonetheless, the severe time constraints confronting the boycott effort made any substantial rectification of the information shortage a low priority concern. It was far better to proceed with some plan of action, however misguided, than to sit idly by and be accused once again of indecisiveness and ineffectuality. It was to be a "learn as you go" operation, and thus one bedeviled by needless difficulties and unnecessary mistakes.

Before enumerating the particular failings of the White House that resulted from a lack of knowledgeable advice, we should first take a cursory look at the unique organizational arrangement of international sport;[3] this should allow us to realize better that which administration officials failed to understand. There are three primary institutional components of the international Olympic movement: the International Olympic Committee, national Olympic committees, and international federations associated with individual sports. Theoretically, the three organs have jurisdiction over all international sporting activities that fall within the scope of the Olympic Games, regional contests, and world, regional, and national championships in each particular sport. In fact, the international federations have usurped primary control over the organization and functioning of sporting contests. The IOC has been relegated to defending the "ideals" of amateur sport, as well as to selecting Olympic sites and choosing new members for its ranks, while national Olympic committees are chiefly concerned with the selection and preparation of national teams. Finally, any discussion of the structure of international sport would be incomplete in failing to note that the IOC is organized not as a collective body representing the world's states, but rather as a transnational organization functioning across national boundaries.[4] Members of the IOC only represent that group in their homelands; they do not act as agents of their state's interests to the IOC.[5] The IOC may be described most accurately as a fiercely independent, nongovernmental, transnational actor that utilizes the state unit not because it is subservient to it, but rather because such a structure provides an expedient means of organizing and conducting the Olympic Games.[6]

One manifestation of Washington's uninformed position on Olympic matters was the steadfast refusal of administration officials to concede that the IOC, barring a major war, would *never* consent to having the Games moved, postponed, or canceled. Killanin emphasized repeatedly that the International Committee had signed a binding contract with the Moscow Olympic Organizing Committee; only if that contract should be broken—which it had not been— would a change of venue be considered. Other IOC leaders also refused to admit to any possibility of alternative Games. Monique Berlioux, director of the IOC, declared, "Any 'alternative games' are completely excluded," while observing that the commitment of the international sports federations to the Olympics meant that there would be no experienced, sanctioned body to organize any such event even were some nations considering defying the IOC's position.[7]

Despite the unambiguous opposition of the IOC either to moving the Games or to establishing alternative competitions, members of the State Department and the White House staff most intimately involved with the boycott continued to express hope for cooperation until the end of March. In the early stages of the effort, prior to the Lake Placid Winter Olympics, Deputy Secretary of State Warren Christopher said the Games could be moved "if the will were there." Nelson Ledsky, director of the State Department's Olympic Task Force, likewise pronounced, "We have a very good chance of getting the international community to move the Games from Moscow."[8]

Nearly two months later, after it was apparent to all that no matter what the success of the boycott the Games would go on as scheduled, key administration officials refused to admit to the futility of their efforts to erode the IOC's commitment to Moscow. In a pathetic statement issued hours before the Olympic committees of eight European states, including Great Britain, France, and Italy, declared their intentions to attend the Moscow Games regardless of their governments' position, Joseph Onek, deputy counsel to the president, clung to groundless illusions. He implored, "I think there is a good chance that none of the major Western European countries will go and that their nonparticipation, especially that of the French, . . . might convince the IOC to cancel or postpone the Games."[9]

Despite the vehement opposition of the IOC to any "counter-Olympics," as well as the fact that such an event would probably not be sanctioned by the international federations—consequently nullifying all performances and exposing participants to the possibility of future suspensions and loss of eligibility[10]—Carter's aides remained insistent that alternative competitions could be established.[11] Dismissed as "no threat to the future" of the Olympic movement,[12] a "counter-Olympics" was embraced for its potential allure to those countries contemplating a boycott, but also concerned for the welfare of their athletes. The possibility for effecting such games was evaluated by men with no comprehension of the enormity of the logistical obstacles endemic to such a massive undertaking.[13] The arrogance of those responsible for adjudging the feasibility of non-Olympic competitions was evident from Nelson Ledsky's appraisal of the situation, "It seems almost beyond belief that, given the entrepreneurship of the Western world, a major sports event cannot be organized in six months."[14] The blissful certainty with which Ledsky spoke was symptomatic of the degree of ignorance with which he and his colleagues functioned.

A further indication that the Carter administration possessed inadequate information about the Olympic movement's organizational structure, and about traditional efforts of the IOC and the national Olympic committees to dissociate themselves from governmental manipulation, was the degree of importance attached by the White House to its lobbying of state leaders. While the Soviet Union recognized the credence that many Olympic committees, particularly those in the West, gave to Rule 24C of the IOC Charter, which stated, "National Olympic Committees must be autonomous and must resist all pressure of any kind whatsoever, whether of a political, religious or economic nature," [15] the White House overlooked this fact. Accordingly, the Kremlin focused its efforts primarily upon national Olympic officials, while Carter and his aides concentrated upon governmental leaders. [16]

This U.S. preoccupation with influencing foreign governments, rather than national Olympic officials, despite the fact that many Olympic committees acted without fear of state intervention and thus were responsible for reaching their own decisions, resulted in a misallocation of resources and a diminished degree of success. The State Department and the White House were forced into the untenable position of citing support for the boycott from governments who either had no formal Olympic committee or whose committees had defied their wishes and elected to send teams to Moscow. [17] Lloyd Cutler echoed the persistent refrain that the United States had succeeded in winning its allies' support, only to have been abandoned by various Olympic committees, when he lamented, "We are disappointed with the European teams who went against their governments, but this shouldn't be portrayed as our allies deserting us because we did get support from the governments." [18]

That a top administration official could assess the shortcomings of the boycott in such terms becomes more understandable if we realize that the president himself revealed no knowledge of the marked distinctions that existed between a number of Olympic committees and their respective governments concerning the decision-making process. Carter appeared unaware that there was any difference between these two bodies when he characterized as equally definitive both "a decision . . . by a nation's government or a nation's Olympic committee." [19] Such conceptual confusion prompted the White House to misdirect its efforts at persuasion and to be misled as to its degree of success. Diplomatic campaigns can be won only if the appropriate targets are identified; this never occurred.

That the White House pursued its Olympic policy without the benefit of sufficient expertise was revealed in a candid statement by Dr. Robert Berenson, a member of the White House staff. In response to queries by potential U.S. Olympians about the apparent confusion surrounding the boycott campaign Berenson admitted, "Look, we don't have anyone in the White House who works on sports. When all this started, I was the only one there who even knew anyone on the U.S. Olympic Committee. We were listing countries who would boycott that didn't even have Olympic teams. We've learned an awful lot lately." [20] Berenson's observations were substantiated by numerous incidents. There were the government's repeated assertions that Taiwan and Iran would boycott Moscow—this despite the fact that neither country had fulfilled all of the requirements for competition demanded by the IOC and had not received invitations to participate[21]—as well as Carter's alleged cable to South Africa requesting its support, although that country had been out of the Olympic movement for ten years.[22] Perhaps most revealing were remarks made by administration officials before a meeting of the heads of twenty-one national athletic organizations at which the government spokesmen were accused of "talking about kids' sports, like softball—which is not even an Olympic sport."[23]

From all levels of the bureaucracy, the State Department, and the White House, there existed no consistent, informed source of advice on the most expedient means of implementing the boycott. As a result, the administration's approach was misdirected and needlessly ineffectual. The requirement for quick, decisive action demanded a thorough understanding of the basics of the situation, but mitigated against a more deliberate, carefully executed plan of action that would have provided such a foundation for those involved with the issue. As with many similar political dilemmas, this one was decided in favor of immediate action. The White House perceived that although it would make mistakes in the process, it was better to move without delay, unsure of the terrain, than to wait for a more informed approach to be developed and be accused of not responding to the Soviet challenge. The administration's gamble proved costly.

DIPLOMATIC ERRORS

In addition to suffering from the ignorance of those charged with its implementation, the boycott was also marred by several diplomatic errors. These generated unnecessary, counterproductive results. A heightened awareness of the needs and sensibilities of the actors which the United States sought to influence could have minimized resentment toward Washington's policy, while also achieving increased levels of foreign support.

One major diplomatic miscalculation was the decision to employ Muhammad Ali, the former world heavyweight boxing champion, as Carter's primary emissary to five African states, including the key countries of Kenya and Nigeria. Ali was selected for the delicate mission both because he was a black Muslim and because it might elicit popular support in the United States. However, Ali was not trained as a diplomat, and had achieved considerable notoriety for his outspoken candor and refusal to compromise his views on controversial subjects.

When Ali was confronted by Tanzanian reporters with the assertion that the Soviet Union supported national liberation movements, in contrast to U.S. policy, he was shaken and forced to plead ignorance. Ali eventually composed himself and expressed his continued belief that the Soviet invasion should be opposed; however, he promised to "challenge" any U.S. action with which he disagreed.[24] By the time he reached his next stop, Kenya, Ali freely assailed what he found to be the numerous faults of U.S. foreign policy. He now called his trip a "fact-finding mission,"[25] and said that the real thrust of his efforts was to forestall a nuclear war between the superpowers. He reasoned, the United States and the Soviet Union were "the baddest two white men in history. . . . If these two white men start fighting, all us little black folks are going to be caught in the middle." [26]

Accusing Carter of sending him "around the world to take the whipping" over U.S. actions, Ali distanced himself from his original task and admonished African athletes to "do what you want" on the issue of the boycott. [27] Not to be silenced once he became aware of further U.S. faults, Ali flatly declared that he was "not selling America and all her policies," and that had he known the "whole history of America and South Africa," he would have declined to make the trip. [28] Although he subsequently claimed he was "here on a peace mission for Carter" and had no intention of embarrassing the president, [29] his outspoken candor did not win additional African support.

Even had Ali performed his role precisely as the White House had hoped, his mission as such would have been negatively received. Selecting a sports hero to represent the U.S. government's position to the African people, while such top administration officials as Zbigniew Brzezinski and Clark Clifford worked on behalf of the boycott in the Middle East and India, was perceived as a racial insult and as an indication that Carter attached little importance to receiving the backing of the African states. One Tanzanian official aptly questioned, "Would you send Chris Evert to negotiate with London?" [30] Presidents Julius Nyerere of Tanzania and Alhaji Shehu Shagari of Nigeria refused to meet with Ali because he was not an official diplomatic envoy and because to do so would appear to denigrate their positions of authority. [31]

A second example of diplomatic ineptitude was the confrontational approach adopted by the White House toward the IOC during the period when the administration hoped to persuade the International Committee either to move, postpone, or cancel the Moscow Games. Carter attempted to "browbeat" the IOC in a manner similar to that employed in dealings with the U.S. Olympic Committee. Such an approach was destined to produce only resentment and disaffection toward U.S. efforts. [32]

Secretary of State Cyrus Vance, in an address to the executive board of the IOC prior to the Lake Placid Games, ignored tradition and made a blatantly political speech. Castigating the Soviet Union as an "invading nation," he implored the IOC to take immediate action to preserve the integrity of the Olympic ideal. [33] The response by IOC members was uniformly negative. [34] Monique Berlioux, director of the committee, expressed "shock" and anger that the traditionally ceremonial opening of the session had been perverted for political purposes. Julian Roosevelt, one of the U.S. members of the committee, reacted in a similar fashion: "I'm sure Mr. Vance's speech will have an unhappy effect on the membership. . . . I was unhappy and embarrassed with what he said, and I thought it was unnecessary. He forgot what he was there to do—open the session." [35]

As if enough animosity toward U.S. efforts to exert pressure on the IOC had not been generated by the Vance speech, White House aide Joseph Onek's threat to destroy the Olympic movement if the IOC did not support Carter's policies became public at nearly the same time. Although Onek subsequently retracted the remark and apologized to the president of the USOC, the furor generated over the matter had a lasting impact.[36]

Even though the prospect of the IOC accepting the U.S. proposals was never promising, the disregard for the sensibilities of the committee displayed by U.S. officials insured that the government's requests would never receive fair consideration.[37] An organization such as the IOC derived immense pride from its independence and from its refusal to succumb to political pressure. When coercive tactics were applied indiscreetly to try to influence the committee's actions, no positive response could have been expected; for the IOC to accept U.S. initiatives under such circumstances would be tantamount to conceding that its self-image had been a mere illusion. Only through subtle, behind-the-scenes bargaining could the United States have hoped to affect the committee's policies. Instead, the tactics adopted simply insured the IOC's intransigent opposition.

One final instance in which the White House exhibited poor diplomatic judgment related to the failure of Carter to keep the European allies abreast of his boycott plans. Carter neglected to inform the Europeans as to the probable U.S. response should the IOC refuse to take action against the Moscow Games. When he revealed his February 20 deadline for the withdrawal of Soviet troops, Carter surprised and dismayed many foreign leaders. West German officials in particular were upset at being misled about the timing of the boycott deadline.[38] It was doubtful that Carter stood to gain significantly by adhering to a secretive style of action, while he sacrificed a measure of trust by failing to consult fully with the allies in all phases of the Olympic/Afghanistan crisis.

Errors in judgment concerning questions of diplomatic strategy clearly hurt the boycott campaign. Ali's appointment as special African emissary created friction and misunderstanding, and may well have lost the United States a degree of support; he certainly made no positive contribution. The mishandling of the IOC was absolute, and, while it may have had little impact on the eventual decision of the committee, it revealed to all interested parties the insensitivity and lack of subtlety that characterized U.S. diplomacy. Finally, the initial failure of the Carter administration to develop an Olympic policy in close cooperation with the Europeans precluded the achievement of fully integrated action in the later stages of the boycott campaign. Diplomatic efforts failed to enhance U.S. objectives, and in several instances had a decidedly negative impact.

BOYCOTT DEADLINE PREMATURE AND INFLEXIBLE

A White House decision that may be assessed as counterproductive was the setting of a February 20 deadline for the complete withdrawal of Soviet troops from Afghanistan as a prerequisite for U.S. participation at the Moscow Games. In mid-January, Secretary of State Vance intimated that the Soviets had until the middle of February to disengage their troops or face the likelihood of a U.S. boycott. The following week Carter reaffirmed the administration's decision to set an early deadline for Soviet withdrawal and established the date of the ultimatum as February 20.[39] As the deadline approached, the White House reiterated its commitment to a boycott should the Soviets fail to respond.[40] The deadline would not be extended, nor would partial withdrawal or a phony Soviet "peace offensive" be accepted. Should the Soviets act *after* February 20, Carter indicated that the United States would still refuse to participate at Moscow. Once the deadline arrived, the White House declared the "final and irrevocable" nature of its decision, saying that any Soviet action now would have no bearing on the prospects of a U.S. team competing in the Summer Games.[41] Throughout the ensuing months, the administration's commitment to a boycott remained unwavering; the White House was not to back down.

Although Carter claimed the decision to give Moscow a rigid ultimatum was reached after careful deliberation and was in no way premature, it appeared that he settled on such an approach very early. In his memoirs the president stated:

Before making a decision, I held many meetings with my advisers and consulted closely with other heads of state and with sports leaders in our country. . . . It was not an easy decision; we had been hoping our dilemma could be resolved by a firm commitment from the Soviet leaders to withdraw their military forces. However, Ambassador Dobrynin had not brought back any messages from Moscow other than repetitions of the same specious arguments.[42]

As noted previously, however, Carter's "consultations" with U.S. Olympic officials were minimal and one-sided in nature, while discussions with foreign leaders were in a preliminary state at the time Vance first broached the February deadline.

Even if it is accepted that the deadline was not an overzealous, emotional response, how does one explain the inflexible posture adopted by the White House in regard to any possible compromise? Carter's steadfast refusal after the deadline had passed to offer the Soviets an incentive to withdraw their troops, in return for a renunciation of the boycott, made little sense. As Robert Kane of the USOC observed, "Only the foolish and the dead say anything is irrevocable."[43] In the ever-changing arena in which international affairs is conducted, such a statement is especially pertinent; after all, from February to mid-July is an eternity in the minds of statesmen.

Reasons for the Deadline

Carter's Thinking Tended Toward Moral Considerations. Before we attempt to assess the negative results of the rigid February deadline, we should analyze

the possible reasons why it was adopted. First among these was Carter's predilection toward emphasizing strong action on issues of moral concern. The
president's human rights policy was based on the belief that there were certain
universal standards of human behavior that must be respected by all governments. Failure to ensure the observance of such norms was viewed as grounds
for the reduction or elimination of U.S. military and/or economic aid. While
human rights was only one criterion to be factored into the decision-making
process, it was one never before explicitly recognized. Carter's moral outlook
was the basis for such a departure from past "realist" foreign policy emphasis,
and likewise informed his response to the Soviet invasion.

The attempted subjugation of the Afghan people truly appalled Carter and
elicited a response couched in terms of "right" and "wrong," "honorable"
and "deplorable." The president set the tone for the boycott campaign when
he stated, "I believe that going to the Soviet Union is, in effect, an endorsement of the invasion and an endorsement of the violation of morality, human
decency, and international law."[44] That Carter was "trying to rally the free
world to make participation in the 1980 Olympics a true moral equivalent of
war" was evident by his insistence that the United States was prepared to act
unilaterally and without regard for the losses it would be forced to incur.[45]
During an interview on January 20, Carter indicated that, "Regardless of what
other nations might do, I would not favor the sending of an American Olympic
team to Moscow while the Soviet invasion troops are in Afghanistan."[46] In an
interview several months later, the president again implied that the moral imperative concerning Afghanistan was so overwhelming as to obviate any considerations pertaining to the necessity of securing extensive foreign support
prior to taking action: "We make our position very clear, and it's predicated
not on what other nations might do but on our own decision. If all of the
nations go to the Moscow Olympics, we will still not go."[47] While Carter
overstated the single-minded resolution with which the United States was prepared to act,[48] his conviction that a boycott was required to maintain the honor
and ideals of the American people was deeply rooted. Carter hoped that a
boycott would "reverberate around the globe [and would] deter future aggression,"[49] but he felt that, regardless of these eventualities, such a measure was
needed as a reaffirmation of the American people's commitment to that which
is "right."

Only at the risk of misinterpretation can the moralistic impetus behind the
boycott be dismissed. This factor also contributed to the particular style with
which the White House sought to secure the boycott's implementation. An
early deadline, and one which admitted to no compromise, was the primary
manifestation of this approach. It was a device that allowed the United States
to make an unambiguous statement of its resolve, while ostensibly permitting
the Soviets an opportunity to make amends for their behavior in Afghanistan.
Should Moscow refuse to respond, the United States could claim to have provided a reasonable chance to act. Any Soviet overtures after the deadline's

expiration could be dismissed as insincere. Finally, assuming the United States had no illusions as to a possible Soviet withdrawal, the absolute nature of the boycott deadline enabled Carter to present the appearance that his administration would not compromise on a moral issue, while also permitting him the opportunity to satisfy his personal sense of outrage in a manner suited to his moralistic nature.

The Impact of U.S. Public Opinion. While an early and inflexible boycott deadline was compatible with Carter's personal preferences, there are indications that from a policy standpoint he would have preferred a later, although similarly rigid, deadline. On January 2, only two weeks prior to Secretary of State Vance's public commitment to a mid-February deadline, the president's diary entry reflected upon the available options with which to respond to the Soviet invasion: "We had a long discussion about the 1980 Olympics. We will make a statement saying that this issue is in doubt, but not make a decision yet about whether to participate. This one [of the possible responses] would cause me the most trouble, and also would be the most severe blow to the Soviet Union." [50]

What prompted Carter to abandon his caution in employing the Olympics as a primary tool to counter Soviet advances, and indeed to commit the United States to what many viewed as a premature deadline? One answer may be found in the mood of the American people. Carter's popular support had been dwindling, and, faced with a difficult battle to win reelection, he had to be especially attuned to public opinion. When the country so warmly embraced the possibility of punishing the Soviets by means of the Olympic Games, this relieved Carter of a major potential difficulty. However, when the initial, tentative support of the public began to escalate into increasingly vocal and adamant calls for a boycott,[51] the White House was faced with a situation in which it no longer shaped popular opinion, but was in a position of being overwhelmed by it.

In order to cope with this paradoxical situation of "the people" demanding a policy the government itself advocated, but doing so with a vehemence considered potentially harmful by state leaders, the White House accelerated its decision-making process;[52] hopefully control could be reestablished over a constituency considered to be over-mobilized and unmanageable. The outcome of the perceived need for quick action was the decision to announce immediately a boycott ultimatum that would elapse in only four weeks. Such a policy would satiate public opinion, while also effecting the administration's ultimate goals.

However, this solution should be recognized as one which was accepted with a degree of trepidation. Carter was aware that ideally the decision should not have been made at such an early date, and that it placed the United States in a position of heightened vulnerability. Once the deadline was announced, the integrity and credibility of the Carter administration was at stake. Should the United States renege on the deadline, or should it be left with few supporters in its boycott effort, Carter's image and standing among the statesmen of the world would be irreparably damaged. Carter probably would have preferred a somewhat later deadline but was prompted by the force of public opinion to adopt an earlier date.

Demonstration of U.S. Resolve. There was one further factor that prompted the White House to adopt the February 20 deadline. It concerned the lack of conviction among many foreign leaders regarding the reliability of the United States in adhering to its international commitments and treaty obligations.[53] Many questioned whether the United States, and specifically the Carter administration, possessed the resolve necessary to assume a position of leadership on a controversial issue and adhere to it regardless of the consequences. Such skepticism was not easily dispelled, and presented a major obstacle to achieving a worldwide Olympic boycott under the aegis of the Carter White House.

The mid-February deadline was one mechanism by which Carter could attempt to establish the earnestness of his intentions. Such an inflexible ultimatum, and one which gave the Soviets so little time in which to respond, was seen by the White House as conveying a clear signal to the statesmen of the world that the United States had staked out its position and meant to fight for it to the bitter end; Washington would neither waver nor compromise on the boycott issue. Assuming that the White House entertained no illusions as to the Soviet Union withdrawing its troops prior to the Olympics, and that the United States had decided upon taking the leading role in orchestrating a boycott, there was every incentive to act early and decisively. While this entailed certain risks, it also presented an opportunity to establish a "take charge" attitude that could inspire confidence abroad. One can lead only from the front, and the mid-February deadline was one mechanism by which to achieve that position.

Summary. A combination of factors motivated the White House to adopt the confrontational tactic represented by the February 20 boycott deadline. The unyielding tenor of the deadline reflected Carter's personal inclinations, while it also helped to satisfy domestic public opinion and convince foreign nations of the resolve behind the administration's policies. The timing of the ultimatum similarly reflected both domestic and international concerns. The degree of popular indignation manifested by the American people over the Afghanistan invasion demanded that some action be taken by the government. When the prospect of utilizing the Olympic Games as the primary focus of the U.S. response was seized upon with such enthusiasm, Carter opted to act sooner than planned. The early deadline provided a focus for restless sentiment, while enabling Carter to capture the fervor of the moment for possible political advantage. Such a deadline was not without its advantages in Washington's quest to secure broad foreign support for its action. It demonstrated Carter's willingness to take risks and assume a strong position of leadership, and helped to dispel pervasive doubts that existed about the administration's character in times of crisis.

Although, as we shall see in the following section, the deadline produced largely counterproductive results, it is important that we understand the genesis of the decision and the rationale behind its adoption. For the Carter administra-

tion, the allure of the tactic assumed precedence over its role in effecting ultimate objectives. Thus, the deadline was embraced because it symbolized
American morality and willingness to fight for a cause, rather than because it
would inflict the most serious punishment upon the Soviet Union. Carter's vision focused within parameters delimited by a preoccupation with means, rather
than with ends, resulting in a circumscribed perspective that was exploited by
Moscow in order to minimize its losses.

Results of Deadline

Increased Effectiveness of Soviet Propaganda. Early intimations that the United
States was seriously considering utilizing the Olympics as part of a coordinated
response to the Soviet invasion sent waves of shock through the Kremlin's
propaganda apparatus. The years of preparation and the enormous investment
in manpower, money, and prestige were placed in jeopardy. That the events in
Afghanistan could disrupt the smooth operation of the Moscow Games caught
Soviet leaders unprepared; it was several days before the Kremlin reacted, and
even longer before a concerted response was formulated by the propaganda
machinery.[54] The decision by the Carter administration to announce officially
its intention to boycott Moscow should the Kremlin fail to withdraw its troops
before February 20, and to make such an ultimatum scarcely three weeks after
the invasion occurred, and over six months before the opening of the Games
itself, eased the difficult task faced by Soviet propaganda instruments.

By quickly issuing a boycott deadline, and by imbuing it with an air of self-
righteous opposition, the White House exposed itself to charges of seeking to
undermine international sport and the Olympic movement through its failure to
seek a nonconfrontational, diplomatic resolution of the conflict. Prior to the
announcement by Secretary Vance of the mid-February deadline, the leading
sports paper of the Soviet Union had already begun to develop such a theme.
It castigated any possible U.S. action in decisive terms:

Intending to use sport as an instrument of political blackmail, the President, without
taking realistic account of the international situation, decided to cast doubt on whether
American athletes would participate in the Olympic Games in Moscow. . . . But the
plans of the forces of belligerent reaction met with a powerful rebuff. . . . A tidal
wave of support for the 1980 Olympics is rising and sweeping away all barriers raised
by the foes of the Olympic movement and the enemies of peace and détente.[55]

Once the deadline was made official, Soviet propaganda became more focused, identifying U.S. efforts as aimed at splitting the Olympic movement
through a "hostile campaign . . . against mutural [*sic*] understanding and
friendship among nations."[56] The White House was accused of exerting "unprecedented pressure and blackmail" upon the USOC to enforce compliance

with the boycott,[57] and of using similar "blackmail and threats" in dealings with other states.[58]

Nonetheless, Moscow argued that despite such attempts the boycott was an "obvious failure,"[59] and that the United States was reduced to resorting to efforts by the Central Intelligence Agency to undermine the Games.[60] Carter was accused of being so determined to destroy the Olympic Games, while concurrently helping his chances for reelection,[61] that he was willing to permit the CIA to conduct acts of psychological warfare, subversion, and sabotage against the Moscow Olympics.[62] Soviet citizens were warned to beware of such endeavors.

Confronted with this "evidence" of extreme "anti-Olympic" machinations by the United States, Soviet propaganda concluded that those concerned with the preservation of the Olympic ideal should turn to the true guardians of the Olympic movement, the Soviet Union.[63] The Soviet people were said to recognize that the Olympic Games was not fit for political manipulation,[64] but rather was a vehicle best suited to enhancing mutual understanding and respect among the peoples of the world. Conveniently deleting the passage from the Soviet handbook for Party members that had stated, "The view popular in the West that 'sport is outside politics' finds no support in the U.S.S.R.,"[65] the Kremlin staunchly maintained that there was an absolute separation between politics and international sport.[66] One Soviet official declared, "Politicians cannot exploit sports for their own benefit,"[67] while others emphasized Moscow's commitment to an Olympic movement untarnished by political interference.[68] The president of the Soviet Olympic Committee professed such a view when he observed, "We don't want to boycott anyone and we don't want to destroy the Olympic movement . . . [because] everybody who loves sports and the ideals of the Olympic movement" feels a boycott would destroy the Games as they now exist.[69]

Attempting to establish credibility for this position, the Soviets' coverage of the Lake Placid Games avoided polemics while praising the U.S. hockey team and the star U.S. speedskater, Eric Heiden.[70] Moscow sought to convey the image that it appreciated sporting excellence for its own sake, regardless of the national or political overtones attached to it by other states. That the Soviets were above such pettiness was supposedly evidenced by their readiness to attend the 1984 Los Angeles Olympics. In reply to a query as to whether the U.S.S.R. would indeed compete in 1984, the head of the Moscow Olympic Organizing Committee expressed his assurance that "we will take part with pleasure if we are invited. We would like to be present, . . . and we will try to, unlike the Americans."[71] Soviet propaganda relentlessly pursued this supposed dichotomy whereby the United States, under the dictates of the "warmongering" Carter, sought to destroy the Olympic movement and all that it represented, while the Kremlin fought a mighty battle to protect the Olympics from those who sought its demise.[72]

In addition to being guilty of seeking to subvert the Olympic Games, the

United States was also accused of attempting "to disrupt détente and undermine peaceful cooperation among peoples."[73] Indicating that "The Soviet people will not be intimidated" by a U.S. "campaign of blackmail, slander and threats," Carter was denounced for reviving the Cold War and for using athletes as "soldiers" in such a capacity.[74] Various polls were released by the Soviet Institutes which claimed that an overwhelming proportion of the Soviet citizenry felt that the Moscow Games would strengthen peace and cooperation and that Carter's actions were "warmongering" and dangerous.[75] Prominent Soviet athletes, as well as potential Olympians with similar views from numerous other countries, were quoted repeatedly in the Soviet press in support of the official Party line.[76] The United States was portrayed as the instigator of unrest and as the actor determined to pursue a confrontational policy; the Kremlin, in contrast, sought only to pursue peace and was open to all offers aimed at a negotiated compromise.

Finally, Soviet propaganda claimed that the U.S. boycott stemmed in part from a desire to shield U.S. athletes from the prospect of yet another loss to their Soviet counterparts. The chairman of the Moscow Olympic Organizing Committee alluded to the prowess of his country's sportsmen when he observed:

Moscow received the right to hold the 22nd Olympic Games above all because it is the capital of a country whose athletes, in the historically short span of time that they have participated in the Olympic movement, have made an important contribution to its development, a country in which sports have assumed a truly massive scale.[77]

Sovetsky Sport was more direct when it declared that "Americans lost their leadership in world sports long ago. . . ."[78] However, it was Bill Rodgers, the star U.S. marathon runner, who perhaps provided the Soviets with their most powerful tool in establishing U.S. sporting inferiority as a primary impetus for the boycott when he stated, "Moscow has earned the right to host the Olympic Games, because the Soviet Union is the number one nation in sports."[79]

How did the U.S. boycott deadline facilitate such distortions by the Soviet propaganda apparatus? First, the speed with which the deadline was announced, coupled with its unyielding nature, permitted the Kremlin to contend more plausibly that the United States was not truly interested in resolving the crisis, but rather in seeking to score a diplomatic victory in its contest with Moscow, regardless of the consequent effects on world peace and the Olympic movement. The Soviet Union, meanwhile, claimed to seek a moderate compromise consistent with its desire to safeguard détente and with its commitment to the Olympic ideal.

A second way in which Soviet propaganda benefited from the deadline was that its early announcement placed the United States in an isolated position. The early deadline allowed Moscow to argue that, in addition to being bent on destroying the Olympics, Carter was responsible for forcing other states to join the boycott.[80] These states' nonparticipation was said to result not from their own feelings toward Moscow, but rather from coercive pressure applied by the White House.[81] This enabled the Kremlin to absolve the vast majority of non-competing states from responsibility, and thereby to diminish the apparent scope of the boycott's appeal.[82]

Finally, the U.S. decision to place the Soviets under an immediate ultimatum removed any ambiguity from the U.S. position. The Kremlin, regardless of how distasteful it found the prospect of a boycott, took consolation from the fact that it was given more than adequate time to assess its options and was relatively certain that once it acted, the fundamental assumptions underlying its policies would not be overturned by a radical departure in U.S. policy. The White House graciously revealed its plan of action for the ensuing six months once Vance announced the deadline, thereby enabling Moscow to identify and develop themes for dissemination by its propaganda organs with a degree of deliberateness and certainty it otherwise would have lacked.

Reduced Flexibility of U.S. Position. The manner in which the boycott deadline was announced and the qualities imparted to it by the White House left Washington with little maneuverability on the issue.[83] This self-imposed inflexibility was not attractive to other states. Most countries sought to keep options open, and thus preferred to avoid firm commitments until circumstances absolutely required them. The inherently fluid nature of international politics was not a medium in which a rigid ultimatum would likely find significant support.

That Carter was somewhat naive in his appraisal of the potential allure of the mid-February deadline was obvious. He later reflected, ''I knew the decision [to set the February 20 deadline] was controversial, but I had no idea at the time how difficult it would be for me to implement it or to convince other nations to join us.''[84] Had Carter secured a broad commitment from other national Olympic committees and governments prior to imposing the deadline, or had the administration not elected to announce such a strident ultimatum, other states might have been more inclined to support Washington's policy. Foreign leaders sought to avoid an absolute commitment both to prevent political isolation and to permit themselves the alternative of reversing their decision, should the Soviets withdraw, without suffering a loss of credibility. Not until the end of March did the administration indicate any willingness to reconsider its position should the Soviets depart,[85] although most nations expected that should such a development occur, the United States would indeed respond affirmatively. Other countries feared that adherence to the boycott deadline would preclude a relatively easy change of policy; the United States had placed itself in a situation whereby a renunciation of the boycott, whether warranted or not, would result in serious political costs being borne by the White House.

Carter's decision to announce the boycott deadline in mid-January proved to have little positive influence on other nations. Most European Olympic committees remained uncommitted well into May,[86] while several other committees that had earlier voted to boycott expressed a readiness to reconsider should conditions change.[87] Most Olympic committees and state leaders appeared to share the opinion of Donald Miller, executive director of the USOC, that "The international situation is fluid. . . . I don't see why we can't put off our decision until mid-May."[88] The boycott ultimatum gained the White House few supporters, and may have instilled a degree of reticence in those otherwise inclined toward adopting such a policy.

Reduced Boycott's Impact on Games. Perhaps the most counterproductive result of the early boycott deadline was that it enabled the Soviets to take concerted action to minimize the impact of any disruption of the Olympic Games.[89] Whereas the threat of a last-minute boycott would have confronted the Kremlin with a host of uncertainties, the mid-February deadline permitted Moscow to act in deliberate fashion to thwart the U.S. action. Not only was the thrust of Olympic propaganda effectively reoriented, but the Kremlin was also given adequate time to lobby Third World states for their support. The intensity of this effort produced considerable results. Nearly half of the eighty-six teams competing at Moscow received Soviet monetary assistance ranging from 50 to 100 percent of the expenses needed to attend the Games; the Kremlin provided support to twenty-nine nations from the Western Hemisphere.[90] Such financial inducements doubtless swayed the decisions of many of these states.[91]

Had the United States avoided its early boycott deadline, Moscow would not have been prevented from taking similar countermeasures. However, it would have been forced to act without definite knowledge of its adversary's intentions. Preemptive actions on the scale of those conducted in the Third World might have engendered internal opposition; such measures required extensive diplomatic efforts, in addition to further monetary expenditures. It is doubtful that, had the boycott been imposed just prior to the opening of the Games, the Soviets would have acted with the degree of effort and with such preemptive foresight as in fact they did. Moscow probably would have responded in a more disjointed and ineffective fashion had the United States forced it to react through a concealed, delayed play of action, rather than allow it to assume the initiative in a well-conceived counter-boycott effort.

Summary. While the boycott deadline was predicated on several assumptions, ranging from its moral sanctity to its domestic appeal to its demonstration of U.S. resolve, in the final analysis it did not inflict political costs upon the Soviet Union. It enabled the Soviets to respond with great effectiveness to the boycott campaign by presenting them with a clear statement of intended U.S. policy nearly six months prior to the Games. Moscow was able to plan its countermeasures, confident that the United States would not suddenly shift gears and present it with an altered set of circumstances. The Kremlin thus was able to develop a detailed propaganda attack, in addition to taking substantive measures to diminish the scope of the anticipated boycott by enticing nonaligned states to participate in the Summer Games. Finally, the boycott deadline aided the Soviet cause by presenting the United States in an uncompromising and dogmatic light. Foreign leaders were wary of expressing solidarity with Washington because they feared such a commitment would be interpreted by others as absolute, in accord with the nature of the boycott deadline. This would commit these leaders to a position they might in the near future find untenable as a result of changed circumstances; extrication from a boycott position perceived to be unconditional could be accomplished, but only at the risk of losing credibility in the eyes of other nations.

Thus, the premature, inflexible boycott deadline impacted negatively on the achievement of the primary goal of the U.S. initiative, that of forcing the Soviet Union to incur the greatest possible political liabilities consequent to its invasion. That such a paradoxical result could occur was testament to the lack of thorough planning by the White House, and to Carter's losing sight of the boycott's ultimate objective because of his preoccupation with the attractiveness of a specific tactical option.

CONCLUSION

The implementation of the Olympic boycott proved to be more difficult than anyone at the White House had envisioned. The administration's own shortcomings—in conjunction with certain endemic political, logistical, historical, philosophical, and circumstantial obstacles—made the effectuation of the boycott extremely problematic. The White House lacked adequate knowledge of the structure of the international sporting establishment, and thus was at a loss as to how to target most effectively its efforts. A misallocation of time and resources resulted, whereby foreign governments, rather than national Olympic committees, received the overwhelming amount of attention. This created a false impression of success, while contributing little to securing increased commitments of support. The White House also exhibited a paucity of diplomatic skill and political wherewithal. It created resentment and hostility toward its efforts through ill-conceived, insensitive attempts at persuasion (most notably the Ali mission to Africa), while engendering distrust and defiance among allies because of its failure to develop adequate avenues of communication that would create the basis for meaningful cooperation. Finally, Carter's tactical acuity was highly suspect. The decision to announce unilaterally a mid-February boycott deadline of an irrevocable nature may have bolstered the country's confidence in the ability of the White House to act forcefully against the Soviet Union, but in fact it did little to inflict real punishment. The administration doubtless believed itself "tough"; Moscow knew otherwise. The deadline only permitted the Soviets to adjust with greater ease and effectiveness to the boycott, thereby diminishing its detrimental impact.

The White House must be forced to accept a significant degree of responsibility for the limited success of the Olympic boycott. While there existed enormous obstacles to such an effort regardless of Carter's political shortcomings, both because of the scope of the endeavor and because it was an *American* attempt to manipulate the Olympic Games for political advantage, the White House cannot be absolved from a commensurate measure of blame. Its inadequacies and miscalculations exacerbated the inherently problematic nature of its task. While one may be tempted to attribute such failings to the size of the effort and to the short period of time within which it had to be accomplished, it should be remembered that Carter was under no compulsion to adopt such a course of action. It was *his* decision to focus American retaliatory efforts on the Olympic Games, despite the existence of other options. As such, the president must acknowledge that a crucial policy decision was adopted despite a fundamental ignorance as to whether or not it was possible to implement, or how it was to be done.

8

Evaluation of the Use
of the Boycott

The United States-sponsored boycott of the 1980 Moscow Summer Olympics was a unique attempt to wield international sport in a politically punitive fashion. Nonetheless, certain lessons can be gleaned from the campaign that could be relevant to similar efforts in the future. State leaders should be cognizant both of the potential gains and probable risks inherent in the manipulation of sport for political advantage. Such awareness is a prerequisite for the adoption of appropriate policies capable of effective implementation.

NATURE OF INTERNATIONAL SPORT

The first factor that must be considered prior to any political utilization of international sport is the compatibility of a projected plan of action with the political and structural characteristics of sport itself. The U.S. boycott demonstrated that the politically peripheral nature of international sport enabled it to be utilized in a relatively low cost fashion. Carter could label the Soviet invasion "the most serious [crisis] since the last World War,"[1] yet feel that the boycott was an adequate response. Short of violent countermeasures, an Olympic boycott was recognized as one of the more punitive actions that could be taken. Not only would the Soviets be adversely affected, the White House would not expose itself to undue domestic or foreign risks. Only the athletes and certain businesses were forced to sacrifice directly, a fact that minimized internal political repercussions. Internationally, failure to win the support of a particular nation was damaging to the perceived capacity of Washington to demand, and be accorded, solidarity on an issue of global concern, but did not damage intergovernmental relations per se.

Sport can be imbued with great symbolic importance, yet intrinsically it has no political content, whereas disagreements among allies over nuclear strategy or trade barriers may imply wide-ranging philosophical discord, while creating serious substantive difficulties. Conflicts over sport are normally confined to the realm of the symbolic. The capacity of sport to perform political functions without the risks attendant upon other modes of action makes it attractive to state leaders. Employed appropriately, international sport can produce significant results with minimum cost.

From a structural perspective, however, international sport is not as appealing to government leaders. The fierce independence of the IOC, as well as that of many national Olympic committees, creates serious difficulties for states seeking to capitalize politically through the manipulation of sport. The various administrative organs comprising the international sports establishment are fraught with internecine quarrels, but have demonstrated an ability and willingness to band together in defense of their freedom from government encroachment.[2] The steadfast persistence of those national Olympic committees which had a degree of real independence in asserting their exclusive right to decide all Olympic-related questions was displayed by the U.S. Olympic Committee. Despite the enormous governmental pressure to which it was subjected, and which it realized would prevail in this instance, the USOC refused to admit in principal to any deprecation of its sovereignty. Robert Kane, president of the committee, captured the essence of such conviction when he declared, "That we seem to have adopted partially the point of view of the government doesn't mean that we've capitulated."[3]

Athletes exhibited a similar refusal to succumb to state coercion. One U.S. competitor was willing to take the U.S. Committee to court for its supposed violation of federal law and of its incorporating charter once it voted to accept the government's position.[4] An Irish competitor defiantly concluded, "No athletes are going to boycott an Olympics. It's the governments who will boycott and governments have no power. As far as I'm concerned, I'm going to Moscow and so will everybody else."[5] Such sentiment, while not "realistic," nonetheless indicated the deep convictions held by a significant majority of the Olympic community that the domain of sports was their own, and should be so preserved regardless of the power wielded by those seeking their own measure of influence. Such proud defense of their independence by athletes, Olympic officials and administrative bodies forced many governments, most notably that of Margaret Thatcher's in Great Britain, to admit defeat. While any government could have enforced its decision upon its national Olympic body, if willing to resort to extreme measures, most democratic leaders were reluctant to take such steps for fear of creating a domestic political backlash.

Statesmen were also forced to cope with a complex, multidimensional administrative structure when dealing with questions of international sport, and were often unsure of the appropriate target for their persuasive efforts. The variegated, nonnational composition of the Olympic apparatus presented the further problem that government leaders frequently found it difficult to predict the behavior of particular organs of the Olympic movement. Since "IOC members are not representatives of their states to the Olympic body; rather they are . . . ambassadors of the Olympic ideal to their homelands,"[6] governments had no direct conduit through which to exert influence over the IOC itself, nor to assess the likely direction in which that body would move. Similarly, state leaders in Western nations had little confidence that they could predict the course of action to be taken by their national Olympic committees. Thus, while governmental manipulation of international sport presented significant opportunities for political gain, the structural diversity and independence characterizing the organization of sport posed countervailing obstacles.

SYMBOLIC IMPORTANCE OF OLYMPICS

While the suitability of *any* government action regarding international sport must be evaluated with great care and expertise, efforts focused upon the Olympic Games must be scrutinized far more thoroughly.[7] Since the symbolic importance of the Olympics is universally acknowledged, and the mass media has succeeded to such an extent in instantaneously transmitting events to a global audience, the temptation to intervene politically in the Games has increased dramatically. Yet, while statesmen may feel the allure of utilizing the Olympics as a "quick-fix" to a myriad of political problems, they must realize that the same symbolic significance that has made the Games attractive for political purposes has fostered a strong reservoir of world sentiment that the Olympics should be excluded from the "petty," "transient" concerns of international politics.

Although statesmen may be inclined to dismiss those who revere the Olympics regardless of its shortcomings, and who seek to minimize the political intrusions foisted upon the Games, as mere "idealists" who have lost touch with "reality," they are at peril to do so. While the Olympic Games has always been highly political, and, far from demonstrably increasing international goodwill and understanding—indeed they may be only "war minus the shooting"[8]—many cling fervently to an Olympic ideal divorced from such reality. These individuals reject what "is" in favor of what could be. As the executive producer of NBC sports typically surmised, "Tell me that even in ancient Greece the Games were shot with politics and commercialism and competitors cheated, that still doesn't alter the ideal."[9] Such attachment to the Olympic ideal became translated into a political force of considerable importance, primarily in the Western states;[10] "reality" did not exist for national leaders as an "objective" entity, but rather was imbued with irrational aspects of human emotion.

Thus, although one U.S. athlete correctly evaluated his role in the boycott as that of a "pawn," and attempted to put the boycott into perspective by stating, "There shouldn't be politics in the Olympic Games. . . . But we have to be realistic . . . the perfect political tool to hurt somebody culturally, politically, or economically is a boycott. . . . So that's how it is," [11] he failed to recognize the potential power of "idealist" sentiment. Western leaders could not disregard such feeling if it achieved widespread currency; rather, they had to overcome idealist apprehension prior to any boycott effort. This was often attempted by stressing the values most cherished by Olympic defenders. Edmund Muskie appealed to the notion that only by abstaining from competition could the integrity of the Olympics be maintained when he categorized the Soviet invasion as being "180 degrees opposed to the Olympic ideal." [12] Carter likewise adhered to such thinking when he declared, "I believe in the desirability of keeping Government policy out of the Olympics, but deeper issues are at stake." [13] The administration implicitly admitted the strength and significance of idealist opinion by the tenacious manner in which it sought to portray the boycott as the ultimate expression of loyalty to the Olympic ideal. Realist political leaders confronted idealist sentiment by characterizing their own actions in terms most amenable to their opponents; cooptation through an apparent affinity of objectives was a dominant strategy employed, especially in view of the improbability that idealists would alter their fundamental value orientation.

The symbolic significance of the Olympic Games attracts the attention of national leaders in search of alternative solutions to political problems. The globalization of the Games affords a worldwide forum in which to act, and offers the cunning, and successful, statesman a unique opportunity to develop international sympathy and support for his cause. Yet, the refusal of considerable segments of the global community to forfeit their intuitive commitment to the "Olympic ideal" creates serious difficulties for those attempting to tamper politically with the Olympic Games. Western statesmen in particular must neutralize, or coopt, the idealist "faction" before an Olympic-related boycott policy may be broached with any hope of success. The fate of attempts to manipulate the Olympics politically is predicated to a great extent upon the degree to which the symbolic meaning attached to the Games can be channeled in support of, rather than in opposition to, a state's efforts.

POLITICAL DIFFICULTIES AND RISKS OF ORGANIZING A BOYCOTT

A final factor that must be considered by statesmen prior to the attempted implementation of a boycott-type policy is the broad political difficulties endemic to any large-scale action of that kind. [14] National leaders must recognize the problematic nature of seeking to effect a coordinated policy among regimes of the most diverse and/or antagonistic orientations. [15] Not only must countries be convinced that a proposed initiative warrants consideration, they must also be reconciled to acting in conjunction with those not normally perceived as friends or allies. In addition, the erosion of a rigidly bipolar world order, and the concomitant move toward a more bipolycentric or multipolar structure, has undermined the cohesiveness of international alliance systems. Thus, all statesmen face serious obstacles in efforts to develop a global policy vis-à-vis the Olympic Games.

Should national leaders choose to pursue political action through the medium of the Olympics, they must be aware that less than complete success will involve significant costs. Both the State Department and the White House realized that any inability on their part to develop a broadly based initiative, in addition to securing the allegiance of their primary allies, would be interpreted as an indication of U.S. ineffectuality and lack of influence.[16] Since the boycott clearly placed the prestige of the Carter presidency on the line, it was crucial that the White House receive at least the support of the Western allies. In an effort to exert pressure in that direction, Washington identified its initiative as being merely one facet of general allied policy.[17] The NATO countries were to be enlisted in the boycott as part of a "package" response to the Afghanistan invasion. Such efforts at cooptation made it all the more imperative that the White House succeed.

The failure of Western Europe, with the exception of West Germany,[18] to join the U.S. boycott presented Washington with a serious threat to its already shaky sense of self-confidence and to its world image. The United States appeared isolated from its allies, and unable to forge a united Western coalition. Washington could claim that it had received governmental support from France, Italy, and Britain, but the fact was that these nations did not adopt Carter's boycott.[19] Moscow was free to exploit the apparent discord in the West and to transform it into an effective propaganda instrument. Malcolm Fraser, prime minister of Australia, identified a possible result of the failure of the White House to enlist European backing when he observed, as previously quoted, "I pray that the Soviet Union will not interpret this [the failure of Australia's national Olympic committee to boycott] and other decisions of Olympic federations around the world as a weakening of Western will as Nazi Germany did in 1936."[20] Yet, could it be expected that the Kremlin would draw any other conclusion?

Not only does an endeavor of the magnitude of an Olympic boycott present enormous challenges for the most consummate of politicians, but, once such an action is initiated, it is imperative that it be perceived as successful. Any lesser result jeopardizes the credibility and esteem of the sponsor government and impairs its ability to act effectively in the future. Since a boycott requires a total commitment by its primary advocate in order to have any hope of success, and failure portends such adverse consequences, it should be only with the utmost of caution that government leaders identify themselves too closely with this type of action.

CONCLUSION

While any individual study has limited applicability, the 1980 U.S. Olympic boycott is an illustrative example of the use of international sport as an instrument of power politics. The decision to utilize the Olympics as a vehicle to inflict political damage revealed the particular allure such a tactic held for government leaders. The Olympic Games was the quintessence of sporting competition among nations and embodied to a heightened extent the political potentialities inherent in sport. Of a politically peripheral nature and capable of being utilized with little risk, international sport appeared as an ideal tool of national policy. Since the Olympics was imbued with such symbolic importance and received enormous media attention, its attraction was compelling.

However, the U.S. boycott also demonstrated the potential pitfalls of any governmental attempt to manipulate the Olympic Games. Although certain difficulties faced by the Carter administration were unique to its effort, another body of problems would exist for any similar endeavor regardless of the nature of the sponsor regime. The independence of the administrative apparatus of the Olympic movement, coupled with its complex organization, posed one set of obstacles for state leaders,[21] while the need to enlist support from the most diverse of nations presented yet another. Such endemic problems would certainly be compounded by a host of others particular to any given situation. Finally, since the world is directed by individuals forced to act without the benefit of hindsight or the luxury of careful deliberation, not to mention by those often manifesting a lack of political acumen, one must expect the commission of serious errors in the process of policy implementation.[22] These human foibles would only serve to exacerbate the difficulties inherent in such a policy decision.

The Olympic Games, now more than ever before, have a political component that *demands* recognition. National leaders must be cognizant of the opportunities offered by the Games for the pursuit of state objectives, especially in a world that many argue has increasingly abjured the use of force in favor of alternative, nonmilitary tactics.[23] Statesmen would be remiss should they be unaware of all possible avenues to further the cause of their constituencies. However, with the political utility of international sport acknowledged, it should also be emphasized that the effective pursuit of policy objectives through a vehicle such as the Olympic Games remains a problematic task fraught with numerous obstacles. Failure to achieve stated goals entails significant consequences which, although short of war, can involve serious political liabilities. While the political exploitation of international sport is a viable policy option, it is one which should not be pursued without an appropriate measure of caution.

Notes

PREFACE

1. Although there had been opposition to Moscow's hosting of the 1980 Olympics soon after the International Olympic Committee's (IOC's) decision in 1974 in favor of the Soviet entry (see Lord Killanin's comments in *My Olympic Years*, [New York: William Morrow and Company, 1983], 173), the trial of Soviet scientist and dissident Anatoly Shcharansky in 1978 renewed the debate and first brought the idea of a boycott to the American public's attention. President Carter opted against such a policy (David B. Kanin, *A Political History of the Olympic Games* [Boulder, Colorado: Westview Press, 1981], 116 [hereafter cited as *Political History*]). Despite accusations in *Pravda* that Carter had shown himself opposed to the Moscow Games both at the time of the Shcharansky trial in 1978 and during the furor over the presence of Soviet troops in Cuba in 1979 (*Current Digest of the Soviet Press*, Apr. 16, 1980, 7–8 [hereafter cited as *Soviet Press*]), Carter never put forth the idea of an Olympic boycott prior to the unfolding of events in Afghanistan.

2. See David B. Kanin, "The Role of Sport in International Relations" (Ph.D. diss., The Fletcher School of Law and Diplomacy, 1976 [hereafter cited as "Role of Sport"]).

3. John Vinocur, *New York Times*, 2 Jan. 1980, A12 (hereafter cited as *NYT*).

4. Jimmy Carter, *Keeping Faith: Memoirs of a President* (Toronto: Bantam Books, 1982), 473 (hereafter cited as *Memoirs*).

5. Allan Mayer et al., *Newsweek*, 28 Jan. 1980, 20–28.

6. *NYT*, 5 Jan. 1980, A6.

7. This is not to argue that morality has no place in international relations. Charles Beitz makes a persuasive argument that indeed "There are no reasons of basic principle for exempting the internal affairs of states from external moral scrutiny." However, Beitz acknowledges the concerns raised by theorists such as George Kennan about mo-

rality as a determinant of foreign policy behavior and thus stresses the need to recognize both "normative and empirical" considerations in applying "principles to practice" (Charles R. Beitz, *Political Theory and International Relations* [Princeton: Princeton University Press, 1979], 181–83 [hereafter cited as *Political Theory*]). Thus, President Carter's attempt to promote his own vision of international morality may not have been ill-advised per se, but rather because of a failure to assess accurately the "empirical considerations" alluded to by Beitz that could have impacted negatively upon his efforts.

CHAPTER 1

1. Roger Rosenblatt, *Time*, 4 Aug. 1980, 67–68.
2. Jeffrey Segrave and Donald Chu, ed., *Olympism* (Champaign, Illinois: Human Kinetics, 1981), 106.
3. Kanin, "Role of Sport," 16–17.
4. Peter J. Beck, *History Today*, July 1980, 7–9; Kanin, "Role of Sport," 43.
5. While Switzerland initially decided to boycott the 1956 Games to protest the Soviet invasion of Hungary, the Swiss National Olympic Committee, led by Swiss IOC member Albert Mayer, eventually reversed its position and opted to compete. Although the Swiss team in fact failed to take part in Melbourne, this was because the final decision had been reached too late to allow for transportation to be arranged to the Games (at least according to Mayer). Ramadhan Ali, *Africa at the Olympics* (London: Africa Books, 1976), 20 (hereafter cited as *Africa*); Allen Guttman, *The Games Must Go On: Avery Brundage and the Olympic Movement* (New York: Columbia University Press, 1984), 162 (hereafter cited as *Brundage*).
6. Dennis A. Williams, *Newsweek*, 28 Jan. 1980, 24.
7. Never before had nonstate actors sought to utilize so extensively the enormous propaganda potential of the Games, nor had the athletes themselves ever been the subject of coercive, life-threatening political actions.
8. Neil Amdur, *NYT*, 6 Jan. 1980, sec. 5, 1, 8.
9. Segrave and Chu, *Olympism*, 120.
10. Ali, *Africa*, 17.
11. Ibid., 18.
12. Segrave and Chu, *Olympism*, 110.
13. Ibid.
14. Ibid., 111.
15. Red Smith, *NYT*, 4 Jan. 1980, A16.
16. Guttman, *Brundage*, 161.
17. Guttman, *Brundage*, 162; Red Smith, *NYT*, 4 Jan. 1980, A6.
18. Guttman, *Brundage*, 254.
19. Ibid., 184.
20. Lord Killanin, *My Olympic Years*, 172.
21. Ibid., 173.
22. Ibid., 172.
23. Ibid., 183. Killanin drew almost verbatim from the ideas expressed by former IOC President Baillet-Latour in the 1930s.
24. Ibid., 12, 143.
25. Segrave and Chu, *Olympism*, 124.

26. Ibid., 120.

27. Guttman, *Brundage*, 162; Segrave and Chu, *Olympism*, 113.

28. Segrave and Chu, *Olympism*, 108.

29. Ron Fimrite, *Sports Illustrated*, 4 Feb. 1980, 18–22 (hereafter cited as *SI*); Segrave and Chu, *Olympism*, 113. This is currently Rule 24C of the IOC rules.

30. Segrave and Chu, *Olympism*, 113.

31. Kanin, *Political History*, 5.

32. Puerto Rico is one such example.

33. Kanin, *Political History*, 5.

34. Steven R. Weisman, *NYT*, 17 Apr. 1980, 13.

35. *NYT*, 11 June 1980, 4.

36. Kanin, *Political History*, 5.

37. Segrave and Chu, *Olympism*, 112.

38. Guttman, *Brundage*, 162.

39. Killanin, *My Olympic Years*, 10.

40. Red Smith, *NYT*, 16 Jan. 1980, A20.

41. Kanin, *Political History*, 6.

42. *NYT*, 21 Jan. 1980, A4.

43. Anthony Austin, *NYT*, 27 Jan. 1980, sec. 4, 2; Vadim Medish, *The Soviet Union*, 4th ed. (Englewood Cliffs, NJ: Prentice–Hall, 1990), 373.

44. Craig R. Whitney, *NYT*, 14 July 1980, A7.

45. Amdur, *NYT*, 22 Jan. 1980, A8.

46. Killanin, *My Olympic Years*, 151.

47. U.S. Department of State, *Department of State Bulletin*, vol. 80., Mar. 1980, 51 (hereafter cited as *Bulletin*); U.S. Department of State, *Bulletin*, vol. 80., May 1980, 14.

48. Although in certain wars, perhaps the most notable being World War II, definitive resolutions are achieved, these are a rarity. While war is the most extreme form of international relations, it seldom produces clear results. If unambiguous results rarely emerge from violent confrontation, they are even less likely to occur through intercourse conducted on a diplomatic or economic plane. See Hulme, "The Viability of International Sport as a Political Weapon: The 1980 U.S. Olympic Boycott" (Ann Arbor, Michigan: University Microfilms International, 1989) [hereafter cited as "U.S. Olympic Boycott"], 28, n. 51., for further analysis.

49. Kanin, "Role of Sport," 8.

50. Ibid., ii, iii.

51. See Robert Keohane and Joseph Nye, *Power and Interdependence: World Politics in Transition* (Boston: Little, Brown, 1977) [hereafter cited as *Power and Interdependence*], Chap. 2 for a cogent discussion of realist conceptions of international politics. The tenets of complex interdependence are then presented as a contrasting perspective, and as descriptive of the international environment to an increasing extent.

52. *NYT*, 1 Mar. 1980, A15.

53. *NYT*, 12 Mar. 1980, sec. 2, 4; *NYT*, 29 Feb. 1980, sec. 4, 13.

54. *NYT*, 25 June 1980, A17; E. M. Swift, *SI*, 22–29 Dec. 1980, 30–38.

55. Weisman, *NYT*, 26 Feb. 1980, A1.

56. Robert McG. Thomas, Jr., *NYT*, 5 Mar. 1980, sec. 2, 3.

57. *NYT*, 26 Feb. 1980, C12. Emphasis added to demonstrate the significance of the feeling that the Winter Olympians performed a true service for the American people

that deserved to be rewarded in a manner reminiscent of that normally reserved for the heroes of war.

58. Salye Stein, *NYT*, 2 Mar. 1980, sec. 4, 20.

59. Such feelings arose in part from the taking of U.S. hostages by Iranian "students," in part from the latest increase in energy prices stemming from the 1979 Iranian Revolution, and in part from a general reluctance to accept that the American hegemony of the 1950s and early 1960s was a thing of the past and that U.S. power would be challenged relentlessly in the years to come from heretofore unlikely sources.

60. Mayer et al., *Newsweek*, 28 Jan. 1980, 20–28.

61. *Time*, 28 Jan. 1980, 16.

62. See Ali, *Africa*, 19–20.

63. See Hans J. Morgenthau, revised by Kenneth W. Thompson, *Politics Among Nations: The Struggle For Power and Peace*, 6th. ed. (New York: Alfred A. Knopf, 1985), 86–92, for a relevant analysis of the policy of prestige and its implications for national power.

64. Killanin, *My Olympic Years*, 208.

65. Kanin, *Political History*, 5. Puerto Rico could be cited as an appropriate example.

66. Ali, *Africa*, 20.

67. Austin, *NYT*, 27 Jan. 1980, sec. 4, 2.

68. "Reactionaries Left in Isolation," *Soviet Press*, 25 June 1980, 6 (condensed in *Sovetsky Sport*, 22 May 1980, 3).

69. Kanin, "Role of Sport," 8.

70. Ibid., 301.

71. Ibid., iii.

72. R. W. Apple, Jr., *NYT*, 26 Jan. 1980, A4. Killanin perhaps overstated the predominance of the United States and USSR in the political use of sport. While the United States and the Soviet Union have concentrated—at least prior to 1980—on the demonstration of superiority through athletic achievement, African states waged a protracted political struggle against both South Africa and Rhodesia through the vehicle of international sport that lasted from 1966 through the 1976 Montreal boycott.

73. Joseph Brodsky, *Atlantic Monthly*, June 1980, 35–39. The process by which the Soviet Union was finally awarded the 1980 Olympic Games began as early as June 4, 1962 when Moscow first hosted a session of the IOC. Lord Killanin later referred to this event as "an important step towards their bid to stage the Games." (See Killanin, *My Olympic Years*, 169.) In 1970, Soviet Olympic officials submitted their first official bid to host the Games. Although rejected in favor of Montreal, the Soviet leadership remained determined to prevail and redoubled its lobbying efforts within the IOC. Four years later, the International Committee, meeting in Vienna to determine the site of the 1980 Games, rewarded Soviet efforts. In a nearly unanimous decision (see Killanin, *My Olympic Years*, 172), Moscow prevailed over Los Angeles and was selected to host the twenty-second Olympiad.

74. Reston, *NYT*, 6 Apr. 1980, sec. 4, 17.

75. See Baruch Hazan, *Olympic Sports and Propaganda Games: Moscow 1980* (New Brunswick, N.J.: Transaction Books, 1982 [hereafter cited as *Propaganda Games*]).

76. Austin, *NYT*, 27 Jan. 1980, sec. 4, 2.

77. Whitney, *NYT*, 14 July 1980, A7.

78. U.S. Department of State, *Bulletin*, vol. 80, Mar. 1980, 50; Anthony Lewis, *NYT*, 11 Feb. 1980, A19.

79. Melinda Beck and William E. Schmidt, *Newsweek*, 28 Jan. 1980, 22.

80. Peter Beck, *History Today*, July 1980, 9.

81. Weisman, *NYT*, 26 Feb. 1980, C11.

82. *NYT*, 20 Jan. 1980, sec. 5, 2.

CHAPTER 2

1. Fimrite, *SI*, 4 Feb. 1980, 18–22.

2. *NYT*, 14 Feb. 1980, A16.

3. U.S. Department of State, *Bulletin*, vol. 80, Mar. 1980, 50.

4. Gwertzman, *NYT*, 16 Jan. 1980, A1.

5. Although forced by U.S. actions to withdraw Soviet missiles from Cuba in 1962, Khrushchev obtained an American pledge not to invade Cuba, and an implicit promise by Kennedy that U.S. missiles in Turkey would be withdrawn after the crisis had passed. (Even so, the missile crisis was one cause behind Khrushchev's ouster in 1964.) See Graham T. Allison, *Essence of Decision: Explaining the Cuban Missile Crisis* (Boston: Little, Brown and Company, 1971) [hereafter cited as *Essence of Decision*]. The U.S. boycott ultimatum, however, offered no face-saving solution for Kremlin officials.

6. Jane Gross, *NYT*, 26 Jan. 1980, A4.

7. Amdur, *NYT*, 27 Jan. 1980, A1.

8. *NYT*, 8 Jan. 1980, 18.

9. U.S. Department of State, *Bulletin*, vol. 80, Mar. 1980, 52.

10. U.S. Department of State, *Bulletin*, vol. 80, May 1980, 14.

11. U.S. Department of State, *Bulletin*, vol. 80, June 1980, 16.

12. Carter, *Memoirs*, 474.

13. Frank J. Prial, *NYT*, 18 Mar. 1980, A3.

CHAPTER 3

1. Amdur, *NYT*, 26 May 1980, A8.

2. In 1955, IOC rules stated for the first time that "NOC's [*sic*] must be completely independent and autonomous and entirely removed from political, religious or commercial influence" (Segrave and Chu, *Olympism*, 113). In 1980, the rules similarly required that national committees "must be autonomous and must resist all pressures of any kind whatsoever, whether of a political, religious or economic nature" (Amdur, *NYT*, 22 Jan. 1980, 8).

3. Steve Cady, *NYT*, 16 Jan. 1980, A14.

4. A. O. Sulzberger, Jr., *NYT*, 31 Jan. 1980, A6.

5. Gross, *NYT*, 17 Jan. 1980, A14.

6. Kane similarly believed that the United States should refrain from attempting to move, postpone, or cancel the Games. He felt that a U.S. boycott was appropriate only under extreme circumstances:

If there's a serious problem at the site of the games, then I believe that the United States ought to consider pulling out of the games for that year. In other words, if the situation worsens in the Persian Gulf, and if Moscow becomes a dangerous place and lives could conceivably be placed in jeopardy, then I think that either the International Olympic Committee ought to call off the games or the United States, for the protection of its own athletes, should consider staying out of the games for that year. That's a far different thing from a boycott. That would be a matter of security, not politics (*U.S. News and World Report*, 21 Jan. 1980, 27–28).

7. Weisman, *NYT*, 19 Jan. 1980, A1.

8. Cady, *NYT*, 16 Jan. 1980, A14.

9. Weisman, *NYT*, 19 Jan. 1980, A1, 8.

10. Ibid., 8.

11. *NYT*, 21 Jan. 1980, A4.

12. Terence Smith, *NYT*, 21 Jan. 1980, A1; *NYT*, 21 Jan. 1980, A4.

13. Gross, *NYT*, 17 Jan. 1980, A14.

14. Gross, *NYT*, 21 Jan. 1980, A1.

15. Amdur, *NYT*, 27 Jan. 1980, A14.

16. Cady, *NYT*, 16 Jan. 1980, A14.

17. Fimrite, *SI*, 4 Feb. 1980, 18–22.

18. *NYT*, 12 Feb. 1980, A6.

19. Red Smith, *NYT*, 3 Feb. 1980, sec. 5, 5.

20. Amdur, *NYT*, 9 Feb. 1980, A4. That Kane was not presenting "his" proposals with enthusiasm was apparent to Lord Killanin, who noted, "it seemed that Kane was putting forward his government's case without any heart." Also, in a meeting with Kane and Miller the previous week, Killanin was told by the two USOC leaders that "on hearing the president's request [to present a proposal to the IOC to either move, postpone, or cancel the Games] . . . they had protested against the interference by the federal government in the affairs of the USOC. They said that under Olympic rules their committee must be autonomous and resist political pressure." Killanin felt that Kane and Miller had "made it quite clear . . . that they had to appear, as instructed by their government, in front of the IOC session to present the government's view" (Killanin, *My Olympic Years*, 185, 178–79). The two USOC officials did nothing to cast doubt upon Killanin's impressions. Kane repeatedly questioned the wisdom of politically manipulating the Games, observing, "I don't think it would be conducive to the continuance of the games if boycotts become common practice. There are always differences between nations, and if there were a boycott every time this happened, there would never be Olympic Games." He continued, "It becomes a never-ending thing when we use the Olympics as a tool on political issues." Finally, in response to questions about the possibility of the IOC adopting the policies proffered by the Carter administration, and reluctantly conveyed to the International Committee by the USOC, Kane responded, "There would be at least three alternatives: If the situation does not worsen, the games could go on as planned. If the situation worsens, the games could be canceled or they could be awarded to another site in another country. However, it's so late now that a change in site would not be possible until 1981" (*U.S. News and World Report*, 28 Jan. 1980, 27–28). With such a lack of personal conviction about their government's position, it was highly unlikely that USOC officials would persuade a hostile IOC to abandon its commitment to the Moscow Olympics.

21. Amdur, *NYT*, 13 Feb. 1980, A1, 8.

22. Ibid., 9.

23. Amdur, *NYT*, 15 Feb. 1980, A6.

24. *NYT*, 21 Feb. 1980, A12.

25. *NYT*, 22 Feb. 1980, A10.

26. *Soviet Press*, 16 Apr. 1980, 8.

27. Weisman, *NYT*, 3 Apr. 1980, A13.

28. Weisman, *NYT*, 4 Apr. 1980, A3.

29. Weisman, *NYT*, 5 Apr. 1980, A3.

30. *NYT*, 9 Apr. 1980, A13.

31. Ibid.

32. Kenny Moore, *SI*, 21 Apr. 1980, 30–33.

33. Weisman, *NYT*, 13 Apr. 1980, A1.

34. U.S. Department of State, *Bulletin*, vol. 80, May 1980, 14.

35. Ibid., 15.

36. Weisman, *NYT*, 13 Apr. 1980, A1.

37. Amdur, *NYT*, 19 June 1980, B7.

38. Ibid.

39. Gwertzman, *NYT*, 16 Jan. 1980, A1.

40. U.S. Department of State, *Bulletin*, vol. 80, Apr. 1980, 46.

41. *Weekly Compilation of Presidential Documents* 16:520–21, 21 Mar. 1980 (hereafter cited as *Presidential Documents*).

42. U.S. Department of State, *Bulletin*, vol. 80, May 1980, 14, 15.

43. Peter A. Young, *NYT*, 1 Mar. 1980, A20; *NYT*, 8 July 1980, A16.

44. Marvin Stone, *U.S. News and World Report*, 21 Apr. 1980, 96.

45. *NYT*, 28 May 1980, sec. 2, 3.

46. Amdur, *NYT*, 6 Jan. 1980, sec. 5, 1, 8.

47. Weisman, *NYT*, 19 Jan. 1980, A1.

48. Martin Tolchin, *NYT*, 24 Jan. 1980, A6.

49. Weisman, *NYT*, 13 Apr. 1980, A1.

50. Amdur, *NYT*, 27 Jan. 1980, A1.

51. Sulzberger, Jr., *NYT*, 30 Jan. 1980, A12; Sulzberger, Jr., *NYT*, 31 Jan. 1980, A6; *NYT*, 22 Feb. 1980, A6.

52. Weisman, *NYT*, 26 Feb. 1980, A1.

53. Amdur, *NYT*, 28 Jan. 1980, A5.

54. Sulzberger, Jr., *NYT*, 31 Jan. 1980, A6.

55. Amdur, *NYT*, 15 Feb. 1980, A6; Amdur, *NYT*, 6 Apr. 1980, sec. 5, 6.

56. Weisman, *NYT*, 13 Apr. 1980, A1, 18.

57. Craig Neff, *SI*, 28 July 1980, 18–19.

58. U.S. Department of State, *Bulletin*, vol. 80, Apr. 1980, 46.

59. Weisman, *NYT*, 13 Apr. 1980, A1.

60. *U.S. News and World Report*, 11 Aug. 1980, 8.

61. Weisman, *NYT*, 26 May 1980, 8.

62. *NYT*, 4 July 1980, A9.

63. *NYT*, 31 July 1980, sec. 4, 20.

64. Red Smith, *NYT*, 27 Apr. 1980, sec. 5, 5; Amdur, *NYT*, 15 June 1980, sec. 1, 1; *U.S. News and World Report*, 11 Aug. 1980, 8.

65. Edwin McDowell, *NYT*, 13 Jan. 1980, C1.

66. Amdur, *NYT*, 18 Jan. 1980, C16.

67. *NYT*, 17 Oct. 1980, B6.

68. As Lord Killanin noted, the 1978 Amateur Athletic Act virtually made the USOC the official governing body of all amateur sports in the United States and thereby reduced the committee's independence. He claimed that "through the act it [the USOC]

is answerable in some ways to the government'' (Killanin, *My Olympic Years*, 179).

69. Robert Kane betrayed an awareness of the committee's susceptibility to adverse congressional action when, in response to a question about whether the USOC was "bound to obey" congressional sentiment on the boycott issue, he stated: "No, it would not be bound to obey, because the U.S. Olympic Committee is a private organization. But we would, of course, be receptive to any admonition from our government'' (*U.S. News and World Report*, 21 Jan. 1980, 27–28). Any such "receptivity" by the USOC may be adjudged to stem largely from fear of congressional and/or executive reprisal.

70. Amdur, *NYT*, 6 Jan. 1980, sec. 5, 1, 8.

71. *NYT*, 16 Jan. 1980, A14.

72. Terence Smith, *NYT*, 21 Jan. 1980, A4.

73. *NYT*, 26 Jan. 1980, A4.

74. *Time*, 4 Feb. 1980, 20ff.

75. Amdur, *NYT*, 27 Jan. 1980, A14.

76. *Time*, 4 Feb. 1980, 20ff. Emphasis added to stress that, while Carter had for the moment chosen not to adopt compulsory measures to enforce a U.S. boycott, he refused to dismiss completely the possibility of such an action in the future and instead chose to brandish this option in a manner designed to instill fear into the U.S. Olympic Committee.

77. Barbara Basler, *NYT*, 8 Feb. 1980, B2.

78. Moore, *SI*, 31 Mar. 1980, 16–17.

79. Frank Litsky, *NYT*, 22 Mar. 1980, A1.

80. Moore, *SI*, 31 Mar. 1980, 16–17.

81. Litsky, *NYT*, 22 Mar. 1980, A19.

82. Weisman, *NYT*, 4 Apr. 1980, A3.

83. Ibid.

84. *NYT*, 5 Apr. 1980, A30.

85. Weisman, *NYT*, 10 Apr. 1980, A18.

86. Ibid.

87. Moore, *SI*, 21 Apr. 1980, 30–33.

88. Ibid.

89. John B. Treaster, *NYT*, 12 Jan. 1980, A1.

90. Mayer et al., *Newsweek*, 28 Jan. 1980, 20–21f.

91. Gross, *NYT*, 21 Jan. 1980, A1.

92. Amdur, *NYT*, 25 Jan. 1980, A10.

93. Weisman, *NYT*, 21 Feb. 1980, A1.

94. Television network news was also a factor in influencing public opinion, although it remains debatable in what direction viewers were led. Between January and April 1980, the three major networks presented 151 in-depth stories concerning the boycott issue on the nightly news. Over 20 percent of these stories focused on debate within the USOC and IOC over the proposed boycott, while 12 percent dealt with the reactions of U.S. athletes and coaches to White House efforts. Thus, approximately one-third of the stories could be expected to focus on those opposed to U.S. policy. Twenty percent of the reports analyzed the actions of the president, the State Department, and Congress, and therefore probably reflected pro-boycott sentiment, while another 30 percent of the coverage dealt with the status of U.S. allies on the boycott proposal and thus could be classified as a mixture of conflicting viewpoints. Although

the newscasts also covered separately the ongoing developments in Afghanistan, and thereby contributed to general anti-Soviet feeling, the networks on the whole appeared to act in a balanced fashion. An analyst contended that "NBC provided a high degree of balance in its reporting. . . . CBS was somewhat skeptical [of the boycott], . . . [while] ABC broadcast a more international perspective, providing news about concerns and frustrations of American allies as well as Soviet planners" (Laurence Barton, "The American Olympic Boycott of 1980: The Amalgam of Diplomacy and Propaganda in Influencing Public Opinion" [Ann Arbor, Michigan: University Microfilms International, 1983], 133, 100–02 [hereafter cited as *Diplomacy and Propaganda*]). (See Hulme, "U.S. Olympic Boycott," 94–95, n. 94, for criticism of Barton's interpretation of his admittedly useful data.) These assertions suggest that network television did little to promote the boycott, and indeed may have acted to moderate an increasingly vocal anti-Moscow, pro-boycott public opinion.

95. Red Smith, *NYT*, 29 Feb. 1980, A22.

96. Red Smith, *NYT*, 16 Jan. 1980, A20.

97. Jerry Kirshenbaum, *SI*, 28 Jan. 1980, 7–8.

98. Red Smith, *NYT*, 16 Jan. 1980, A20.

99. Donald P. Doane, *U.S. News and World Report*, 3 Mar. 1980, 51–52. The AFL-CIO also attempted to reinvigorate the issue of convicted Soviet dissident Anatoly Shcharansky in an effort to broaden the appeal of anti-Olympic actions (Kanin, *Political History*, 118).

100. *NYT*, 31 Jan. 1980, A6.

101. *NYT*, 24 Jan. 1980, A18; Arthur Langer, *NYT*, 20 Jan. 1980, sec. 4, 18; Arthur Howe, *NYT*, 7 Mar. 1980, A26; Christy Mathes, *NYT*, 10 Feb. 1980, sec. 4, 20; *NYT*, 11 Apr. 1980, A26; Ernest Boehm, *NYT*, 27 July 1980, sec. 4, 20 (emphasis in original).

102. Republican Congressman Edward J. Derwinski, one of the more vocal supporters of a proposed boycott, elaborated a well-conceived agenda of issues designed to increase the public appeal of Carter's efforts. Taking the Afghanistan invasion simply as the culmination of objectionable Soviet behavior, Derwinski proceeded to review the full range of threatening actions and policy decisions undertaken by the Kremlin:

On top of the Afghanistan invasion, you have to look at the Soviets' propaganda role against the U.S. in Iran and throughout the Middle East, the buildup of Soviet military forces and the threat this poses to the North Atlantic Treaty Organization, and the Soviet military buildup in the islands north of Japan. You get a picture of an aggressive, belligerent power. In these circumstances, I don't think the Soviet Union is the proper host for the Olympics.

In addition to political and military transgressions, Soviet officials were accused of manipulating sport for the benefit of the ruling regime, an activity said to be rejected by US statesmen: "We [the U.S.] keep politics out of the Olympics. They [the USSR] don't. There's a dual standard, and we're on the short end of it. The battle lines should have been drawn a long time ago. They were not. But at this point, given the worldwide reaction to their Afghanistan invasion, we have an issue we can use against the Soviets." Finally, Moscow was indicted for encouraging the "professionalization" of their amateur athletes in violation of IOC guidelines: "Even if there weren't an Afghanistan crisis, I think one could make a very good case against Soviet sponsorship based on their noncompliance with Olympic rules limiting competition to nonprofessionals." He urged "The Olympic Committee [of the U.S.] . . . be much more energetic in defending the rights of real amateurs against what I consider the professionals of the Soviet Union, East Germany and a few of the other bloc countries." Confident in his analysis, the Illinois representative dismissed concerns over the opposition of athletes and predicted, "if our government reached a decision—in concert with the U.S. Olympic Committee and others, of course—to institute a boycott of the Olympics, then U.S. public opinion, and therefore the cooperation of our athletes, would obviously follow" (*U.S. News and World Report*, 21 Jan. 1980, 27–28).

103. Treaster, *NYT*, 12 Jan. 1980, A1.

104. *NYT*, 20 Jan. 1980, A13.

105. Warren Weaver, Jr., *NYT*, 20 Jan. 1980, A19.

106. Irvin Molotsky, *NYT*, 27 Jan. 1980, A14.

107. Tolchin, *NYT*, 24 Jan. 1980, A6; Marjorie Hunter, *NYT*, 25 Jan. 1980, A1.

108. Hunter, *NYT*, 25 Jan. 1980, A1; Sulzberger, Jr., *NYT*, 29 Jan. 1980, A8; Sulzberger, Jr., *NYT*, 30 Jan. 1980, A12.

109. Clyde H. Farnsworth, *NYT*, 29 Mar. 1980, A31.

110. Treaster, *NYT*, 12 Jan. 1980, A1; Kirshenbaum, *SI*, 21 Jan. 1980, 7ff.

111. Treaster, *NYT*, 12 Jan. 1980, A1.

112. Terence Smith, *NYT*, 21 Jan. 1980, A4.

113. *NYT*, 15 Jan. 1980, A9; Tolchin, *NYT*, 24 Jan. 1980, A6.

114. In a March 21 speech to representatives of U.S. athletes, Carter, after declaring unequivocally that the United States would not send a team to Moscow, underscored the foundation upon which such a decision was based when he observed, "The American people are convinced that we should not go to the Summer Olympics. The Congress has voted overwhelmingly, almost unanimously, which is a very rare thing, that we will not go." Although Carter also expressed the mistaken belief that "our major allies, particularly those democratic countries who believe in freedom, will not go," (*Presidential Documents* 16:518–19, 21 Mar. 1980) he clearly was correct in his evaluation of public opinion and congressional sentiment.

115. Farnsworth, *NYT*, 13 Mar. 1980, sec. 4, 1.

116. Farnsworth, *NYT*, 29 Mar. 1980, A31.

117. Dierdre Carmody, *NYT*, 10 Apr. 1980, A12.

118. Amdur, *NYT*, 6 Jan. 1980, sec. 5, 1, 8.

CHAPTER 4

1. *Time*, 4 Feb. 1980, 20ff.

2. Weisman, *NYT*, 21 Feb. 1980, A1.

3. Kirshenbaum, *SI*, 28 Jan. 1980, 7–8.

4. U.S. Department of State, *Bulletin*, vol. 80, May 1980, 14.

5. *Business Week*, 4 Feb. 1980, 30–31.

6. U.S. Department of State, *Bulletin*, vol. 80, May 1980, 14.

7. Gwertzman, *NYT*, 22 Jan. 1980, A1.

8. R. W. Apple, Jr., *NYT*, 18 Jan. 1980, A8.

9. Liechtenstein, Monoco, and Norway were the other European countries that chose to boycott (*Soviet Press*, 25 June 1980, 6).

10. U.S. Department of State, *Bulletin*, vol. 80, June 1980, 14–15.

11. *NYT*, 1 Feb. 1980, A8.

12. Ibid.

13. Pranay B. Gupte, *NYT*, 6 Feb. 1980, A8.

14. Robert Tucker identified the source of African resentment at the Ali mission when he noted, "The new egalitarianism [of Third World states] expresses above all the desire of the elites of the new states to achieve a collective status that will insure their recognition as equals" (Robert Tucker, *The Inequality of Nations* [New York: Basic Books, 1977], 63).

15. *NYT*, 8 Feb. 1980, B2; Dave Anderson, *NYT*, 5 Feb. 1980, C21.

16. Robert Keohane's analysis of collective action provides an interesting means of evaluating Carter's rationale concerning U.S. sponsorship of an alternate sporting event. Reflecting on the problem of encouraging collective action on a grand scale, Keohane reasons that, in order to overcome the "free-rider" dilemma, certain incentives need to be offered to prospective participants. These incentives differentiate between active and passive members of a generalized collective by rewarding active players with an additional product or service not available to noncontributors. He explains, "the success of certain large groups relying on a diffuse membership to provide public goods was explained by their provision of private goods as a by-product of membership" (Robert O. Keohane, *After Hegemony: Cooperation and Discord in the World Political Economy* [Princeton, N.J.: Princeton University Press, 1984], 77 [hereafter cited as *After Hegemony*]). The "public good" to be provided by the White House was a condemnation of Soviet aggression in Afghanistan through the imposition of political and economic sanctions effected through an Olympic boycott. Carter attempted to realize his goal at least partially by offering an alternate sports competition for those countries who elected to boycott. However, in addition to the fact that such an event had little intrinsic appeal, it was eventually decided that the proposed competition was to be open to all countries. Thus, Keohane's observation on the need to privatize certain goods as a "by-product of membership" was ignored; the "free-rider" problem remained. Even those states which valued a non-Olympic international sports festival had nothing to gain by supporting a boycott.

17. Terence Smith, *NYT*, 2 Feb. 1980, A13.

18. Kirshenbaum, *SI*, 28 Jan. 1980, 7–8.

19. Amdur, *NYT*, 2 Feb. 1980, A13.

20. Weisman, *NYT*, 21 Feb. 1980, A1.

21. In an effort to gain African support for an alternate international event, the United States stated that South Africa would be barred from the competition.

22. *NYT*, 15 Mar. 1980, A4.

23. *NYT*, 19 Mar. 1980, A3.

24. Lord Killanin claimed that pressure was applied through various U.S. embassies to IOC members and to the international sports federations to move or postpone the Moscow Games. (Killanin, *My Olympic Years*, 192.)

25. Rule 54 of the IOC Charter required that the Olympics be held during "the last year of the Olympiad which they are to celebrate. . . . In no circumstances . . . may they be postponed for another year" (Fimrite, *SI*, 4 Feb. 1980, 18–22). Although the White House may have felt that they could persuade the IOC to circumvent its charter, the greater likelihood is that administration officials and those connected with formulating Olympic policy were unaware of such a provision, and perhaps of the content of the charter as a whole (see Chapter 7, section entitled "Lack of Understanding of the International Sports Structure").

26. Amdur, *NYT*, 10 Feb. 1980, A8.

27. Vance labeled the Soviets as an "invading nation" in order to establish the basis for U.S. nonparticipation at Moscow, and as a means of applying pressure to the IOC to adopt the U.S. position. He presented his views by stating, "Let me make my government's position clear—we will oppose the participation of an American team in the Olympic Games in the capital of an invading nation. This position is firm. It reflects the deep conviction of the United States Congress and American people" (Killanin, *My Olympic Years*, 184).

28. Amdur, *NYT*, 10 Feb. 1980, A8.

29. Killanin, *My Olympic Years*, 181, 182.

30. Basler, *NYT*, 8 Feb. 1980, B2.

31. Amdur, *NYT*, 10 Feb. 1980, A8.

32. Amdur, *NYT*, 13 Feb. 1980, 13; Killanin, *My Olympic Years*, 188; Amdur, *NYT*, 26 May 1980, 8.

33. Amdur, *NYT*, 13 Feb. 1980, 12. See Killanin, *My Olympic Years*, 187, for a summary of the full text of the IOC statement.

34. Lord Killanin (statement), *NYT*, 13 Feb. 1980, A13. Lord Killanin implored the governments involved in the controversy to come together and resolve their differences. Although he stressed that the IOC could not surmount the political problems of the world, he vowed that he, "as President of the IOC, and all members will do everything in our power to assist in this so that the Games of the XXII Olympiad can take place in the right atmosphere" (Killanin, *My Olympic Years*, 188).

35. Killanin, *My Olympic Years*, 187–88.

36. Amdur, *NYT*, 13 Feb. 1980, A1.

37. Weisman, *NYT*, 13 Feb. 1980, A1. One reason the White House may have clung to its optimistic evaluation was that the IOC had never taken an actual vote on the USOC proposal. They had simply reaffirmed Moscow as the site of the Games.

38. For instance, in early May the USOC discreetly attempted to get the thirty-five-member Pan American Sports Federation to adopt a resolution calling for a one-year postponement of the Games. While it has not been definitively established that the White House initiated the USOC effort, it is unlikely that such an endeavor would have occurred independent of government sponsorship. It should be noted that the federation rejected the USOC proposal and adopted instead a resolution calling for the IOC to reduce the nationalistic elements of the Games. (Killanin, *My Olympic Years*, 188; Amdur, *NYT*, 26 May 1980, 8.)

39. Killanin, *My Olympic Years*, 196, 213, 214.

40. However, Carter did indicate an interest in establishing a permanent site in Greece for the Summer Games and said that the United States would support such a change. Lord Killanin viewed the president's "interest" with skepticism, "the governments that endeavored to prevent their athletes competing in Moscow were among the greatest supporters of a permanent site in Greece, e.g., the United States, Britain, and West Germany. This created a diversion" (Killanin, *My Olympic Years*, 213).

41. Killanin's reflections on the meeting illustrated the inflexibility of both parties' positions. The IOC president assessed Carter as "a weak president" who, "anxious for a postponement of the Olympic Games," even at this late date. This would indicate either that Carter still sought to alter the position of the IOC or that he simply was trying to generate favorable publicity by meeting with Killanin despite no hope of a positive outcome. That the IOC had no intention of compromising was indicated by Killanin's observation, "I reiterated our position [to Carter] and said there was no

way of reneging on the contract with Moscow" (Killanin, *My Olympic Years*, 212–13).

42. Weisman, *NYT*, 17 May 1980, A6. Former IOC president Avery Brundage had also employed such rhetoric on several occasions. In response to protests prior to the opening of the 1968 Olympics in Mexico City, the fiery Brundage stated, "The Mexico Games will take place, even if I have to be there alone with five South Africans" (Ali, *Africa*, 54). Similarly, speaking in the wake of the attack on Israeli athletes at the 1972 Munich Games, he declared, "The Games must go on . . . ," a sentiment obviously shared by his successor, Lord Killanin (Guttman, *Brundage*, 254).

43. Western Europe is unique in the sense that, through the European Economic Community, it has achieved remarkably high levels of economic cooperation and policy integration. In addition, tentative steps have been taken in the political realm to effect similar results; the European Parliament is one manifestation of such efforts.

44. Terence Smith, *NYT*, 21 Jan. 1980, A1.

45. Weisman, *NYT*, 2 Mar. 1980, sec. 4, 4.

46. Kanin, *Political History*, 123.

47. Ibid., 127.

48. Ibid., 135.

49. Paul Lewis, *NYT*, 6 Feb. 1980, A10. This was premised on the position advocated by West German Foreign Minister Genscher that called on the Kremlin to "create" the conditions necessary for the Games to occur. (Kanin, *Political History*, 135.)

50. The European Parliament was first elected in 1979. It is largely ceremonial and its members are elected by direct multinational European suffrage. (Kanin, *Political History*, 135.)

51. Robert D. Hershey, Jr., *NYT*, 16 Feb. 1980, A7. It also voted to ban sales of surplus commodities to the Soviet Union. (Kanin, *Political History*, 135.)

52. Kanin, *Political History*, 135.

53. Vance met with West German Foreign Minister Genscher and then traveled to London and Paris for discussions with Genscher's British and French counterparts. (Kanin, *Political History*, 135–36.)

54. Prial, *NYT*, 4 Feb. A2; Paul Lewis, *NYT*, 6 Feb. 1980, A10.

55. Paul Lewis, *NYT*, 20 Feb. 1980, A8.

56. Since the West European governments were not liable to withhold passports to enforce a boycott because such an action was contrary to their political traditions, the final decision was likely to be reserved for the national Olympic committees.

57. By late May, most Western European governments had decided to support a boycott, albeit with varying degrees of enthusiasm. (Kanin, *Political History*, 137.) However, the delay in reaching such a position, and the tenuous nature of the consensus, negated the impact a united governmental stance would have had on national Olympic committees.

58. Treaster, *NYT*, 2 Feb. 1980, A1.

59. Moore, *SI*, 31 Mar. 1980, 16–17. West Germany, Switzerland, Turkey, and the Netherlands deferred decisions until government sports officials could be consulted. (Kanin, *Political History*, 136.)

60. West Germany was also perceived as a crucial country in affecting the momentum of the boycott.

61. Raoul Mollet, president of the Belgian Olympic Committee and spokesman for

a group of fifteen Western European Olympic committees, asked the IOC to adopt an antinationalism amendment that would ban national flags, anthems, and remaining traces of nationalism. In addition, Mollet asked the IOC to declare explicitly that participation in the Olympics involved no political statement on the part of competitors. (Vinocur, *NYT*, 22 Apr. 1980, 14.) Meeting in Lausanne in late April the IOC partially adopted the proposals of the European committees. It stated: 1) Each national Olympic committee could use its own rather than its country's name at the Games. 2) The national Olympic committee's flag or the flag of the IOC could be substituted for the country's flag during the opening and closing ceremonies. 3) Only one person had to parade in the opening and closing procession. 4) At victory ceremonies either the country's flag, the national Olympic committee's flag, or the Olympic flag could be flown, and the Olympic hymn could be substituted for the country's national anthem. (Killanin, *My Olympic Years*, 200.)

62. In early May, eighteen West European national Olympic committees met in Rome and agreed to permit their athletes to travel to Moscow if they could refuse ceremonial displays such as the wearing of national uniforms, the use of national flags and anthems, and full participation in the opening ceremonies. (Kanin, *Political History*, 137.)

63. Liechtenstein, Monoco, and Norway also boycotted. If one wishes to consider Turkey as Western European because of its membership in NATO, it should be added to this list. It should be noted that individual boycotts by federations and athletes in Western Europe were significant and effectively destroyed the equestrian, field hockey, yachting, and shooting competitions. (Kanin, *Political History*, 138.)

64. Red Smith, *NYT*, 4 Jan. 1980, A16.

65. Vinocur, *NYT*, 4 Jan. 1980, A7; Cady, *NYT*, 14 Jan. 1980, A14.

66. Apple, Jr., *NYT*, 18 Jan. 1980, A8.

67. David Bird, *NYT*, 23 Jan. 1980, A8.

68. William Borders, *NYT*, 25 Jan. 1980, A3.

69. Prial, *NYT*, 4 Feb. 1980, A2.

70. *NYT*, 15 Feb. 1980, A6.

71. As early as January 21, the British Olympic Association said it would compete at Moscow regardless of the government's position. (Kanin, *Political History*, 124.) *Sovetsky Sport* quoted Denis Fellows, chairman of the association, as being adamantly opposed to a boycott: "We [the British Olympic Association] take the strongest possible stand against any attempt by a government to interfere with our participation in the Games. Politicians are using the Olympic movement as a whipping boy" (*Soviet Press*, 13 Feb. 1980, 9).

72. Vinocur, *NYT*, 22 Jan. 1980, A8.

73. Hershey, Jr., *NYT*, 16 Feb. 1980, A7.

74. Apple, Jr., *NYT*, 4 Mar. 1980, A3.

75. Kanin, *Political History*, 131; Apple, Jr., *NYT*, 14 Mar. 1980, A10.

76. *NYT*, 18 Mar. 1980, A3. The vote in the House of Commons was 315 to 147 in favor of a boycott. However, since one-quarter of the MPs abstained, the pro-boycott measure was denied a majority. (Kanin, *Political History*, 132.)

77. The British Olympic team thereby became the first West European team to accept an invitation to Moscow. While the French Olympic Committee had accepted the Soviet invitation to compete the day after it was received, it did not vote formally to attend the Games until May 13. (Kanin, *Political History*, 132, 137.)

78. Apple, Jr., *NYT*, 26 Mar. 1980, A10.

79. Weisman, *NYT*, 26 May 1980, A1.

80. Vinocur, *NYT*, 2 Jan. 1980, A12.

81. Vinocur, *NYT*, 7 Jan. 1980, A6. *Sovetsky Sport* quoted Baum's reaction to a potential boycott in greater detail, "It's totally absurd to use boycotts of this sort to resolve political problems; if this were done, before long there wouldn't be any competitions taking place anywhere in the world" (*Soviet Press*, 13 Feb. 1980, 10). Baum also indicated his concern with the difficulty of securing the compliance of independent sports officials with government wishes. He said the government would not employ financial or travel restrictions to pressure the Olympic Committee. (Kanin, *Political History*, 125.)

82. Terence Smith, *NYT*, 21 Jan. 1980, A4.

83. *NYT*, 26 Jan. 1980, A4. Genscher was the head of the junior party in the coalition government—the Free Democratic Party—and was more supportive of a boycott than Chancellor Schmidt.

84. Willy Brandt was one of those highly critical of the Carter boycott proposal. (Kanin, *Political History*, 125.)

85. Of particular importance was normalized relations with East Germany. (Kanin, *Political History*, 124.)

86. Kanin, *Political History*, 128. It appears that Schmidt personally opposed a boycott but was forced into accepting it.

87. Terence Smith, *NYT*, 21 Jan. 1980, A1.

88. Treaster, *NYT*, 2 Feb. 1980, A13; Hershey, Jr., *NYT*, 16 Feb. 1980, A7.

89. Hershey, Jr., *NYT*, 16 Feb. 1980, A7; In a poll conducted by *Der Spiegel*, 52 percent of those expressing an opinion were in favor of a boycott while 44 percent were opposed.

90. Ibid.

91. Kanin, *Political History*, 129; *NYT*, 21 Mar. 1980, A3.

92. This was prior to Daume's final reversal of position on May 10 and to his strong appeal to the Olympic Committee Praesidium to participate at Moscow. (Kanin, *Political History*, 137.)

93. *NYT*, 24 Apr. 1980, A10.

94. *NYT*, 20 May 1980, A4.

95. Vinocur, *NYT*, 16 May 1980, A10.

96. Vinocur, *NYT*, 25 Jan. 1980, A10.

97. *NYT*, 11 Feb. 1980, A12.

98. Vinocur, *NYT*, 25 Jan. 1980, A10. An article in *Pravda* warned Bonn of the implications of a pro-boycott policy, "The FRG government's 'recommendation' on nonparticipation in the Moscow Olympics is an obvious cold war relapse in West German policy. This is exactly how it is being understood and assessed" (*Soviet Press*, 28 May 1980, 13–14).

99. Kanin, *Political History*, 129.

100. On May 14, one day prior to the final vote by the full West German Olympic Committee on participation at Moscow, Manfred Ewald, one of the leaders of the East German Olympic Committee, spoke to West German sports officials about the boycott. The incident received extensive publicity and generated intense resentment among the Federal Republic's Olympic contingent. (Kanin, *Political History*, 138.)

101. Both IOC President Killanin and Soviet Chairman Brezhnev believed that the

rest of Europe would follow the position that the Federal Republic eventually chose to take. Brezhnev told Killanin that he hoped to use the occasion of Tito's funeral to speak to Schmidt about the boycott. He intimated that his "requests [to Schmidt] were to be that pressure should not be put by Schmidt's government on the West German NOC so the athletes could take part in the Games" (Killanin, *My Olympic Years*, 208).

102. Vinocur, *NYT*, 4 Jan. 1980, A7. The same minister said on January 26—several weeks later—that France would go to Moscow. (Kanin, *Political History*, 130.)

103. Vinocur, *NYT*, 22 Jan. 1980, A8; Paul Lewis, *NYT*, 6 Feb. 1980, A10.

104. *NYT*, 24 Jan. 1980, A6.

105. Graham Hovey, *NYT*, 22 Feb. 1980, A10.

106. Paul Lewis, *NYT*, 20 Feb. 1980, A8.

107. Flora Lewis, *NYT*, 24 Mar. 1980, A8.

108. Fimrite, *SI*, 4 Feb. 1980, 18–22.

109. Even after the Sakharov exile, nearly three-quarters of all Frenchmen were opposed to a boycott. However, elite intellectual opinion—as reflected by the editorial positions of leading French publications—was affected by the exile of the Soviet dissident. The conservative newspapers *Le Figaro* and *L'Aurore*, as well as the leftist newspaper *Le Matin*, urged French athletes to boycott. *Le Monde* adhered to its anti-boycott position for an additional two months, yet it too eventually endorsed a boycott. (Kanin, *Political History*, 129–30.)

110. Hershey, Jr., *NYT*, 16 Feb. 1980, A7; French public opinion polls revealed the increasing disfavor with which the boycott initiative was received in that country. In a January survey, 65 percent of those interviewed were against a boycott. A mid-February poll indicated that opposition had increased to 75 percent.

111. The timing of the decision may have been related to the May 9 announcement by West German Olympic Committee President Willi Daume that he had changed his position and now strongly recommended participation at the Moscow Games. (Kanin, *Political History*, 137.)

112. Paul Lewis, *NYT*, 14 May 1980, A1.

113. *NYT*, 1 May 1980, A2. See Hulme, "U.S. Olympic Boycott," 161, n. 128, for an enumeration of the seven steps the French Olympic Committee sought the Soviet Union to adopt in order to "de-nationalize" the Games. Assuming those conditions were met, the French Committee declared that it was the duty of all IOC member states to permit participation, which it stated to be "even more important in a period of tension and international conflict" than in a time of peace and normalcy.

114. Weisman, *NYT*, 26 May 1980, A1; Although the French Olympic Committee decided to participate, the equestrian, yachting, fencing, and shooting teams chose to boycott.

115. Flora Lewis, *NYT*, 15 May 1980, A10.

116. Liechtenstein, Monoco, and Norway did not reply to the invitations to compete in the Olympics by the original May 24 deadline; they eventually chose to boycott. See Kanin, *Political History*, 127, 133, 136, for elaboration, particularly upon the Norwegian Olympic Committee's repeated reversals of position.

117. In the wake of the Sakharov exile, Prime Minister Van Agt added his voice to those supporting a boycott. (Kanin, *Political History*, 127.)

118. Treaster, *NYT*, 12 Jan. 1980, A1; *Time*, 28 Jan 1980, 15–16; Hershey, Jr., *NYT*, 16 Feb. 1980, A7; *NYT*, 20 May 1980, A8. (The vote by the Netherlands Olympic Committee to attend the Games was 49 in favor, 19 against.)

119. The Belgian Olympic Committee acted despite the prime minister's belief that all of the European Community states would boycott the Games. (Kanin, *Political History*, 136.)

120. *NYT*, 29 Jan. 1980, A8.

121. *NYT*, 29 Jan. 1980, A8; Fimrite, *SI*, 4 Feb. 1980, 21.

122. Foreign Minister Ruffini, while refusing to act decisively, declared that his government "was at Washington's side." However, that the government was not prepared to assume an active leadership role on the boycott question was evident when Ruffini, in conjunction with his West German counterpart, issued a joint statement on February 24 saying that no governmental decision would be made until May 24, the final date for accepting invitations to compete at Moscow. (Kanin, *Political History*, 131.)

123. *Time*, 9 June 1980, 66.

124. Henry Tanner, *NYT*, 21 May 1980, A14.

125. The Spanish government sought to maintain a cautious profile on the boycott issue because of concern lest the Olympic debate either disrupt the November meeting in Madrid of the Conference on Security and Cooperation in Europe convened to review the Helsinki Final Act or impair its efforts to join NATO and the European Community. (Kanin, *Political History*, 133.)

126. *NYT*, 24 May 1980, A3.

127. *NYT*, 8 Feb. 1980, B2; *NYT*, 20 May 1980, A8. Historically, Sweden's policy has been to participate only in those sanctions backed by the United Nations.

128. *NYT*, 16 May 1980, A10; *NYT*, 20 May 1980, A8. The Irish Olympic Committee voted 19 to 1 in favor of attending the Moscow Games.

129. *NYT*, 11 May 1980, A6. The Swiss Olympic Committee voted 24 to 22 (with 2 abstentions) to participate.

130. *NYT*, 30 Jan. 1980, A12.

131. *NYT*, 20 May 1980, A8; Fimrite, *SI*, 4 Feb. 1980, 18–22; *NYT*, 3 Feb. 1980, A10.

132. Amdur, *NYT*, 6 Apr. 1980, sec. 5, 6.

133. Ibid.

134. The response of the West German public to a proposed boycott was an exception to the anti-boycott sentiment manifested in most European states. See p. 58.

135. Treaster, *NYT*, 12 Jan. 1980, A1; *NYT*, 27 Jan. 1980, A14.

136. Henry Giniger, *NYT*, 21 Feb. 1980, A11.

137. Giniger, *NYT*, 23 Apr. 1980, A3.

138. Fimrite, *SI*, 4 Feb. 1980, 18–22.

139. Amdur, *NYT*, 4 Apr. 1980, sec. 5, 6.

140. Ibid.

141. Andrew H. Malcolm, *NYT*, 15 Mar. 1980, A4.

142. *NYT*, 14 Apr. 1980, A9.

143. *NYT*, 27 Apr. 1980, A4.

144. *NYT*, 27 Apr. 1980, A4. This was the same formula regarding participation originally posited by West German Foreign Minister Genscher.

145. Seventeen Asian states joined the Olympic boycott. These included China and Japan, both with high quality teams. (*NYT*, 25 May 1980, Sec. 1, 8).

146. Henry Scott Stokes, *NYT*, 6 Jan. 1980, A12.

147. Treaster, *NYT*, 2 Feb. 1980, A13. It was after the Sakharov issue had ostensibly solidified Europe in favor of a boycott that the Japanese government announced it would

make a nonbinding decision on February 10; it was intimated that such a decision would favor the U.S. initiative. (Kanin, *Political History*, 134.)

148. *NYT*, 27 Mar. 1980, A6. The secretary added that the government would change its position should the Soviets withdraw from Afghanistan. (Kanin, *Political History*, 134.)

149. *NYT*, 16 Apr. 1980, A13.

150. Vinocur, *NYT*, 4 Jan. 1980, A7.

151. *NYT*, 16 Apr. 1980, A13.

152. The vote in favor of a boycott was 29 to 13. The national Olympic committee also refused to permit seven national federations to compete individually (the IOC Executive Board had authorized such participation, subject to approval by the federation's respective Olympic committee). The decision by the Japanese Committee to accede to the government's wishes was opposed by most Japanese. (Kanin, *Political History*, 134, 138; *Soviet Press*, 25 June 1980, 6.)

153. Bird, *NYT*, 23 Jan. 1980, A8.

154. *NYT*, 26 Jan. 1980, A4.

155. Basler, *NYT*, 31 Jan. 1980, A1.

156. Treaster, *NYT*, 2 Feb. 1980, A13.

157. *NYT*, 25 Apr. 1980, A12.

158. Vinocur, *NYT*, 4 Jan. 1980, A7.

159. James P. Sterba, *NYT*, 26 Jan. 1980, A1. Indeed, Pakistan had pushed the conference to endorse a boycott. (Kanin, *Political History*, 141.)

160. *NYT*, 10 May 1980, A4.

161. *NYT*, 24 May 1980, A3.

162. *NYT*, 7 Jan. 1980, C4.

163. Indira Gandhi had recently been reelected as the leader of the Indian government and was in a powerful domestic position. She reaffirmed her country's commitment to the Moscow Games—in an attempt to reinstate a special relationship with the Soviet Union—soon after the boycott initiative was launched by the United States. In addition to India, Vietnam, Laos, Kampuchea, Syria, and, after considerable uncertainty, Burma, chose to attend the Games. (Kanin, *Political History*, 141, 142.)

164. These states included Thailand, Indonesia, Malaysia, Singapore, and the Philippines. However, such states as Saudi Arabia, Djibouti, Qatar, and Oman, "none of which had Olympic teams in the first place, immediately supported the Olympic boycott" (Kanin, *Political History*, 140–42). Thus, the boycott "counted" among its adherents states lacking the capacity to compete.

165. Kanin, *Political History*, 141. The Saudis were particularly concerned with any matter of general Muslim interest because Arabia was the homeland of Islam and the Saud family the guardians of the holy cities of Mecca and Medina. Should the Saudis fail to act decisively on a matter of such import as the Soviet invasion of Afghanistan, they would put themselves in jeopardy of forfeiting their position of leadership within the Islamic world. If this occurred, the basis of legitimacy of the Saud family would be undermined. Thus, the Saudi government, despite having indicated that it would not participate at Moscow *prior* to the Afghanistan invasion, sought to portray itself as having acted in defense of its Islamic brother. In addition, Malaysia and Indonesia used the Islamic Conference to attack the Moscow Olympics, while other Muslim states such as Djibouti, Qatar, and Oman supported a boycott because of their religious identification.

166. Sterba, *NYT*, 29 Jan. 1980, A1.

167. *NYT*, 22 Jan. 1980, A3. Emphasis added to demonstrate the significance of religious concerns as a motivating force behind the decisions of many Asian countries to boycott Moscow.

168. Kanin, *Political History*, 142.

169. None of these countries changed their previously stated positions as a result of Ali's tour.

170. Moscow gave these states travel expenses, coaches, and equipment as incentives to participate in the Games.

171. Gupte, *NYT*, 13 July 1980, sec. 5, 1. Seventeen black African countries voted to boycott; nineteen states elected to compete. It should be noted that only thirty-six out of forty-nine African countries were IOC members in good standing.

172. Kenya had boycotted the 1976 Montreal Olympics because the IOC refused to bar the New Zealand team. Kenya objected to the presence of the New Zealanders because that country's rugby team had competed in South Africa.

173. Kanin, *Political History*, 142.

174. *NYT*, 3 Feb. 1980, A10.

175. Kanin, *Political History*, 142.

176. Ibid. The Supreme Council was a highly effective organization whose responsibilities included coordination of any political actions involving the Olympics.

177. President Shagari, preserving policy flexibility, said that his country would attend the Games unless the Supreme Council for Sport in Africa reconsidered its decision to oppose a boycott. (Kanin, *Political History*, 143.)

178. *NYT*, 8 Feb. 1980, B2.

179. Ibid. Nigerian President Alhaji Shehu Shagari refused even to meet with Ali.

180. *NYT*, 29 Jan. 1980, A8.

181. *NYT*, 23 Apr. 1980, A10.

182. Robert D. McFadden, *NYT*, 25 May 1980, A1. The military coup was carried out by those seeking improved relations with the Soviet Union. (Kanin, *Political History*, 143.)

183. *NYT*, 26 Jan. 1980, A4.

184. Despite the council's efforts to stress the nonaligned character of African states, many countries were intensely concerned with their superpower relations and acted accordingly. For instance, both Liberia, a traditional U.S. ally, and Zaire, heavily dependent upon Western aid, predictably supported the boycott. (Kanin, *Political History*, 142.)

185. Gupte, *NYT*, 13 July 1980, sec. 5, 1.

186. Such domestic factors may also be cited in connection with Zimbabwe's decision to apply for admission to the Games. Seeking to gain support from a sports-loving white population in order to forge a degree of national unity, black leader Robert Mugabe sought to capitalize on participation at Moscow. In addition, he sought to use the Games as a demonstration of his country's international legitimacy. (Kanin, *Political History*, 142.)

187. Ibid., 144; Argentina originally supported competing at Moscow; its eventual decision to boycott may have resulted partially from the West German government's action in favor of a boycott.

188. Peru was vocal in its anti-boycott stance, while Chile was the only Latin Amer-

ican country to support immediately Carter's boycott initiative. (Kanin, *Political History*, 144; *NYT*, 10 May 1980, A4.)

189. Kanin, *Political History*, 144.

190. One obvious exception was Cuba, whose anti-boycott stance was predicated primarily upon its intimate ties to the Soviet government. In addition, certain states may have been affected by U.S. power and influence in the hemisphere, a concern that, because of geographic circumstances, was not manifest relative to the Soviet Union. (Kanin, *Political History*, 143–44.)

191. David Bird, *NYT*, 23 Jan. 1980, A8.

192. Ibid.

193. *NYT*, 24 May 1980, A3.

194. Ibid.

195. Ibid. The Australian Labour party offered to finance the athletes should the government withdraw its support. (Kanin, *Political History*, 134.)

196. *NYT*, 29 May 1980, A8.

197. *NYT*, 16 June 1980, A5. (The *New York Times* said that 126 out of the original 218 members of the Australian Olympic team still planned to compete at Moscow.); *Time*, 9 June 1980, 66. (*Time* said that 75 percent of the original team members would still participate.)

198. *NYT*, 7 June 1980, A16.

199. *NYT*, 20 Apr. 1980, A18.

200. Eastern Europe adhered to the Soviet Union's position. Even Rumania, noted for its opposition to Soviet interventionism, chose to participate. (Kanin, *Political History*, 123.) This was significant considering its refusal to follow Moscow's boycott of the 1984 Los Angeles Olympics.

201. Fimrite, *SI*, 28 July 1980, 10–17.

202. Robert Martin, *U.S. News and World Report*, 11 Aug. 1980, 43; Whitney, *NYT*, 20 July 1980, A1. (Forms of symbolic protest included avoiding the opening ceremony and using the Olympic flag or national Olympic committee flag instead of the national flag.)

203. *NYT*, 24 May 1980, A22.

204. U.S. Department of State, *Bulletin*, vol. 80, July 1980, 30. Seventy-one percent of all the medals won by athletes outside of the Soviet bloc at the 1976 Montreal Olympics were won by national teams and sports federations not participating at Moscow.

205. *NYT*, 28 May 1980, A10.

206. U.S. Department of State, *Bulletin*, vol. 80, July 1980, 30.

207. McFadden, *NYT*, 25 May 1980, A1.

208. *NYT*, 14 July 1980, sec. 3, 4.

209. One analyst observed a similar disregard for the actions of Western Europe, noting, "most third world states ignored West European decisions in making their own" (Kanin, *Political History*, 140).

210. For instance, U.S. vehemence precluded the French government from openly espousing a boycott. This ultimately proved disastrous to White House hopes for French support.

211. After all, the United Nations General Assembly had overwhelmingly condemned the Soviet invasion.

CHAPTER 5

1. In fact, Soviet leaders had probably hoped to host the Olympics soon after they had first participated in 1952. However, recognizing both the Soviet Union's lack of proper physical facilities and the conservative bias of the IOC, no overtures were made until 1962. In June of that year, the IOC held an important session in Moscow; this was a crucial step in Soviet efforts aimed at eventually hosting the Games. (Killanin, *My Olympic Years*, 169.) Thus, although Soviet Olympic officials initially applied to host the Olympics in 1970, consideration was accorded such a goal many years before.

2. For a comprehensive analysis of Moscow's Olympic propaganda effort, see Hazan, *Propaganda Games*.

3. Hazan, *Propaganda Games*.

4. Ibid. Evidence for the shock that the boycott produced was the prolonged period of time that the Soviet propaganda apparatus took to adjust to White House intimations about the possibility of a boycott.

5. Ibid. It remains unclear to what extent Soviet assistance was offered to Third World countries prior to the Afghan invasion, and thus according to precedent (e.g., Munich provided similar subsidies to bolster attendance), and to what degree Soviet overtures were solely in response to the boycott initiative. Lord Killanin supported the first interpretation:

Prior to Afghanistan the Soviets had always said they would do this [offer subsidies] for certain Third World delegations. They had asked Olympic Solidarity [a fund to help underfinanced national Olympic committees] to assist certain NOCs to travel to airports where Aeroflot had pickup rights, then they would be flown to Moscow free. At the time of the Moscow Games, this proposal was misquoted and misused by political sections of the Western press as if it were a last-minute decision to try to save the Games. I do not believe any NOC received subsidies from Moscow unless they had agreed to assistance prior to the Afghanistan situation.

As a slight caveat, Killanin added, "We [the IOC] did agree there could be further assistance in what is always subsidised, accomodation in the Olympic village" (Killanin, *My Olympic Years*, 202). Baruch Hazan emphasized the latter interpretation.

6. Austin, *NYT*, 4 Aug. 1980, sec. 3, 1.

7. *U.S. News and World Report*, 4 Aug. 1980, 20–21; William Oscar Johnson, *SI*, 4 Aug. 1980, 42. Japan televised the Games for thirty minutes at 7:20 A.M. and 11:20 P.M.; the ratings were only 4 percent of the audience. West Germany televised thirty minutes of the Games per day. In the United States, NBC-TV televised eight to nine minutes on the "Today Show" in the mornings and several minutes on the nightly news program; ABC-TV and CBS-TV were restricted by IOC rules to six minutes of coverage per day (IOC regulations limited film coverage to two minutes, three times a day for all networks without a contract to televise the Games). *NYT*, 18 June 1980, C31.

8. Mayer et al., *Newsweek*, 28 Jan. 1980, 20–28.

9. Although Soviet Olympic leaders attempted to dispel the anxieties of IOC officials concerning the sentiments expressed in the *Book of the Party Activist*, their protestations that the manual was "only a minor problem" and was strictly "an internal document for . . . work inside . . . [the] party" were unconvincing in the context of Brezhnev's position. The Soviet Chairman, in response to Lord Killanin's recitation of the relevant passages from the handbook, queried, "What's wrong with that?" Despite Killanin's firm reply that "everything was wrong" since the Games were awarded not

on a political but rather on a sporting basis, the Soviet leader clearly thought otherwise. (Killanin, *My Olympic Years*, 209.)

10. Mayer et al., *Newsweek*, 28 Jan. 1980, 20–21.

11. The 1976 Olympics left the city of Montreal nearly $1 billion in debt.

12. *Time*, 9 June 1980, 66.

13. Whitney, *NYT*, 20 July 1980, A1.

14. Whitney, *NYT*, 14 July 1980, A7. For instance, a West German film on the relationship between politics and sports was not allowed to be transmitted from the Soviet communication center handling coverage of the Moscow Olympics.

15. *Time*, 4 Aug. 1980, 28–33.

16. Whitney, *NYT*, 20 July 1980, A1.

17. E. J. Kahn, Jr., *New Yorker*, 18 Aug. 1980, 58–60f.

18. Yuri Brohlin, *NYT*, 12 Feb. 1980, A23.

19. U.S. Department of State, *Bulletin*, vol. 80, Mar. 1980, 51.

20. U.S. Department of State, *Bulletin*, vol. 80, June 1980, 15.

21. See Hazan, *Propaganda Games*.

22. *NYT*, 9 Feb. 1980, A4.

23. Stephen Smith, as reported by Bruce Nelan, *Time*, 21 July 1980, 68–69.

24. Flora Lewis, *NYT*, 22 July 1980, A19.

25. Michael T. Harrigan, *NYT*, 12 Jan. 1980, A19.

26. Harrison E. Salisbury, *NYT*, 31 Jan. 1980, A23.

27. Harrigan, *NYT*, 12 Jan. 1980, A19.

28. Salisbury, *NYT*, 31 Jan. 1980, A23.

29. Gwertzman, *NYT*, 21 May 1980, A16; Secretary of State Muskie, among others, made the claim that the boycott reduced the Moscow Olympics to a mere "athletic event."

30. McFadden, *NYT*, 25 May 1980, A8.

31. Weisman, *NYT*, 26 May 1980, A7n.

32. The boycott also inflicted losses upon several major corporations, as well as on numerous small businesses. For further discussion of the economic consequences of the boycott, see the following section.

33. McDowell, *NYT*, 27 Jan. 1980, sec. 3, 19.

34. *Business Week*, 4 Feb. 1980, 30–31.

35. Whitney, *NYT*, 7 June 1980, A16; Of the foreign tourists expected to attend the Olympics, 1,300 out of 20,000 Japanese went, 2,000 out of 7,500 British, 400 out of 4,500 Australians, and between 3,000 and 6,000 out of an estimated 12,000 West Germans.

36. *Time*, 4 Aug. 1980, 28–33.

37. Ray Rowan, *Fortune*, 25 Feb. 1980, 90–93; NBC-TV's contract with Moscow called for payment of $87 million. This included $50 million to Gostelradio for technical services, $35 million for television rights ($22.3 million to the Moscow Olympic Organizing Committee and $12.7 million to the IOC), and $2 million to Gostelradio for "unspecified technical services." According to the *Wall Street Journal*, $52 million of NBC's money was earmarked by Soviet Olympic officials to facilitate construction of a $300 million television complex in Moscow which would handle coverage of the Games. (Cooney, *Wall Street Journal*, 6 Feb. 1980, 1.)

38. By the beginning of February, NBC technicians in Moscow had already received

forty-five tons of sophisticated TV equipment to be used in the network's coverage. (Cooney, *Wall Street Journal*, 6 Feb. 1980, 1.)

39. Rowan, *Fortune*, 25 Feb. 1980, 90–93. (Lothar Bock was the chief negotiator for NBC-TV in its successful effort to win the contract to cover the Moscow Games.); Les Brown, *NYT*, 12 Jan. 1980, A43.

40. *Time*, 19 May 1980, 82.

41. Les Brown, *NYT*, 12 Jan. 1980, A43; *NYT*, 29 Jan. 1980, D16. (Typical prime-time advertising on NBC-TV for the summer season sold for $75,000 per minute. Advertising for the Olympics sold for $165,000 per minute and advertisers were forced to buy a minimum of $1,000,000 worth of time; they were not allowed to pick the time of day their commercials would run. NBC reserved the right to spread an advertiser's commercial minutes throughout the day.); The *Wall Street Journal* estimated NBC's profits from Olympic commercial advertising at $20–25 million. This was contrasted to the $12–14 million expected from summer reruns. (Cooney, *Wall Street Journal*, 6 Feb. 1980, 1.)

42. One TV executive accurately assessed NBC's loss when he observed, "It isn't losing the extra profit that will hurt NBC as much as the loss of prestige. . . . It reinforces NBC's image as the lackluster network that can't get anything right." (Cooney, *Wall Street Journal*, 6 Feb. 1980, 1.)

43. *Time*, 19 May 1980, 82. The Soviet position on NBC's contractual obligations was firm, "The contract [between NBC-TV and the Moscow Olympic Organizing Committee] did not cover the possibility that the US team would not participate. Thus, NBC is obligated to pay the whole sum, no matter what (except for $3 million), before the Games begin." (*Soviet Press*, 14 May 1980, 6.)

44. Peter Funt, *NYT*, 17 Feb. 1980, sec. 2, 37.

45. Les Brown, *NYT*, 12 Jan. 1980, A43.

46. McFadden, *NYT*, 25 Jan. 1980, A10.

47. The first vice chairman of the Moscow Olympic Organizing Committee was quoted in *Sovetsky Sport* as stating, "Tours have been sold, tickets have been sold. . . . The only thing we can guarantee the American tourist agency Russian Travel Bureau . . . is that we are holding these tours and tickets for them" (*Soviet Press*, 14 May 1980, 23).

48. Jill Smolowe, *NYT*, 17 Apr. 1980, A17.

49. *NYT*, 18 June 1980, A3.

50. Whitney, *NYT*, 8 Aug. 1980, A7.

51. The Soviets eventually agreed to a settlement in which they retained $5 million of payments previously received from RTB, while returning the remainder to American tourists who had booked trips to Moscow with the American travel agency. (Barton, "Diplomacy and Propaganda," 116–17.) While individual tourists succeeded in recouping most of their down payments, travel agents in the United States lost approximately $4 million in commissions from Olympic tour cancellations. (Cooney, *Wall Street Journal*, 195:1, 6 Feb. 1980.)

52. McDowell, *NYT*, 13 Jan. 1980, C1; McDowell, *NYT*, 27 Jan. 1980, sec. 3, 19.

53. Levi-Strauss paid considerably for this role. It cost them $270,000 for the rights to supply the official uniforms for U.S. teams to the 1980 Lake Placid Winter Olmpics, the 1980 Moscow Summer Olympics, and the 1979 Pan-American Games. (Cooney, *Wall Street Journal*, 6 Feb. 1980, 1.)

54. *NYT*, 22 Feb. 1980, sec. 4, 4. It was also hoped that the Olympics would provide

an impetus for the successful conclusion of negotiations for a jeans manufacturing facility in the Soviet Union. (Cooney, *Wall Street Journal*, 6 Feb. 1980, 1.)

55. *Time*, 28 Jan. 1980, 15-16.

56. *NYT*, 15 June 1980, A33.

57. The boycott's effect on the number of states and athletes at the Games was also significant. Lord Killanin observed, "The organising committee had originally hoped for over 120 [teams], while I had felt we would have somewhere around the 100-minus mark . . . under normal conditions" (Killanin, *My Olympic Years*, 208). The eighty-one states and 5,900 athletes who competed was the smallest field since the 1964 Games in Tokyo. (Robert P. Martin, *U.S. News and World Report*, 11 Aug. 1980, 43.)

58. Amdur, *NYT*, 15 June 1980, sec. 5, 1; Thirty-nine percent of the men ranked in the top ten in the world in their events in 1979 were absent from the track competitions at Moscow.

59. Robert P. Martin, *U.S. News and World Report*, 11 Aug. 1980, 43; Stephen Smith, as reported by Bruce Nelan, *Time*, 21 July 1980, 68-69.

60. Amdur, *NYT*, 15 June 1980, sec. 5, 1.

61. Whitney, *NYT*, 25 May 1980, A7.

62. *NYT*, 24 May 1980, A22.

63. Juan Antonio Samaranch, Lord Killanin's newly elected successor to the presidency of the IOC, also attempted to portray the effects of the boycott in a positive vein. He argued, albeit unconvincingly, "The Olympic movement has come out *stronger* and *more united* than ever from one of the most serious trials it has ever experienced" (emphasis added, *NYT*, 30 Sept. 1980, D25).

64. U.S. Department of State, *Bulletin*, vol. 80, May 1980, 15.

65. Tolchin, *NYT*, 24 Jan. 1980, A6.

66. Whitney, *NYT*, 21 Jan. 1980, A5; Whitney, *NYT*, 16 July 1980, sec. 2, 6.

67. Tolchin, *NYT*, 24 Jan. 1980, A6.

68. Only the Soviet Union and East Germany have had success comparable to the United States in the most recent Olympiads.

69. Lord Killanin, writing several years after the boycott, had predicted a much different course of events. He observed, "There is no doubt that all the tensions and pressures [of the boycott] left some scars and divisions in certain NOCs, but I believe these were less than the unity that was created for the future" (Killanin, *My Olympic Years*, 204-5).

70. Lance Morrow, *Time*, 11 Feb. 1980, 72.

71. *NYT*, 28 Mar. 1980, A34; *NYT*, 17 Jan. 1980, A22.

72. U.S. Department of State, *Bulletin*, vol. 80, Mar. 1980, 50-51.

73. Serge B. Hadji, *NYT*, 27 Jan. 1980, sec. 5, 2.

74. While both superpowers, as well as their respective "blocs," had competed in the Olympics between 1952 and 1976, the Games had lacked universality. The Peoples' Republic of China, Africa, and much of the Third World either had not competed at all or had done so only periodically.

CHAPTER 6

1. Robert Keohane's analysis of the difficulties of achieving collective action in a "Prisoner's Dilemma"-type environment is instructive. He points to the fact that in such a situation, however desirable the production of a collective good, it either "will not be

produced, or will be underproduced, despite the fact that its value to the group is greater than its cost'' (Keohane, *After Hegemony*, 68-69). For further consideration of Keohane's arguments, see Hulme, ''U.S. Olympic Boycott,'' 240, n. 1.

2. Keohane emphasizes the significance of the systemic level of analysis in evaluating state behavior. He argues that such '''third image' . . . models . . . draw our attention to ways in which barriers to information and communication in world politics can impede cooperation and create discord even when common interests exist'' (emphasis added, Keohane, *After Hegemony*, 69).

3. See R. Keohane and J. Nye, *Power and Interdependence*, Chapters 1 and 2.

4. Ibid.

5. Tony Smith captures the significance of Third World efforts to forge a de facto independence when he observes,

[T]he dynamics of international affairs [during the last 35 years] have in large measure been the result of the relationship between American imperialism and Third World nationalism. . . . The point . . . is to insist on the reality of Third World nationalism as a potent force in world politics since 1945; a force that is neither the willing puppet of northern commercial interests (as a host of leftist theorists have alleged) nor the spineless pawn of the dominant parties in international affairs (as more right-wing writers, who see southern countries as mere counters in the contest between East and West, frequently suppose) (Tony Smith, *The Pattern of Imperialism: The United States, Great Britain, and the late-industrializing world since 1815* [New York: Cambridge University Press, 1981], 139 [hereafter cited as *Imperialism*]).

6. That the developed Northern states have exhibited no absolute identity of interests has been accepted by most analysts in recent years. However, there has been a tendency to exaggerate the homogeneity of Third World goals, perspectives, and policies. Several theorists, including Tony Smith and Robert Tucker, have argued strongly against such tendencies, attempting to portray a more complex, differentiated ''Third World'' (Tony Smith, *Imperialism*, 7–9; Tucker, *The Inequality of Nations*, 58, 89.)

7. One need only examine the lack of concerted response to Japan's seizure of Manchuria in 1931 and to Mussolini's invasion of Ethiopia in 1935 to find examples of failures to respond decisively to acts of aggression.

8. U.S. Department of State, *Bulletin*, vol. 80, May 1980, 14.

9. U.S. Department of State, *Bulletin*, vol. 80, Mar. 1980, 50.

10. Whitney, *NYT*, 8 Feb. 1980, A6.

11. Prial, *NYT*, 4 Feb. 1980, 2.

12. Stokes, *NYT*, 17 Jan. 1980, A9.

13. As the representative component of, and principal spokesman for, the international sporting establishment, the IOC has consistently expressed the idealistic sentiments of the athletic community. It has pronounced the Olympic movement to ''nonpolitical,'' has implored its supporters to continue efforts to keep the Games, ''clean, pure and honest,'' and has stated that it never ''started to make political judgements, [because] it would be the end of the Games'' (Segrave and Chu, *Olympism*, 113; Guttman, *Brundage*, 254; Fimrite, *SI*, 4 Feb 1980, 18-22). Consecutive presidents of the committee voiced similar beliefs. Speaking at a meeting in 1969 between the IOC executive board and representatives of various national Olympic committees, Avery Brundage placed the Olympics on a transcendent plane removed from the lowly concerns of international politics. He declared, ''Empires dissolve, governments disappear, kingdoms vanish, but the ancient Olympic Games lasted twelve centuries and they were not based on temporal power. And so will the modern Games survive if we stick together

and adhere to the lofty ideals laid down by the Baron de Coubertin'' (Guttman, *Brundage*, 184). Brundage's successor, Lord Killanin, echoed such convictions when, at the height of the boycott crisis, he offered to put himself ''at anyone's disposal in order to assist the situation'' since, as president of the IOC, he felt ''neutral and above politics'' (Killanin, *My Olympic Years*, 208).

14. However, there are certain national Olympic committees that do not represent an independent country. Puerto Rico is one of the few examples where the Olympic committee structure does not reflect international boundaries.

15. *NYT*, 21 Apr. 1980, A11; Kanin, *Political History*, 3-4.

16. A cursory description of the structure of the IOC should enable us better to understand the delimitation of authority within that organization. The president of the International Committee is elected initially to an eight-year term and can be reelected for four year intervals. The nine members of the executive board are elected for four year terms and serve under the direction of the president and three vice presidents. (Kanin, *Political History*, 5.) The executive director, while not an IOC member, assists in organizational and logistical functions. Membership in the IOC is by invitation only and has been restricted by the current membership to include nationals from fewer than half of the world's countries. Members receive no monetary compensation for their duties. Since the entire IOC meets only once a year in non-Olympic years, twice during the Olympiad, the daily implementation of policy is delegated to the president. Policy decisions are reserved for the executive board which convenes two or three times annually. Barring exceptional circumstances, however, ultimate authority resides in the individual members who can, although such occasions are rare, overturn the decisions of both the president and the executive board. (Killanin, *My Olympic Years*, 208, 13, 165, 16; Vinocur, *NYT*, 23 Apr. 1980, 3.) Once a final decision is reached, IOC members are bound by an oath of allegiance that requires them to abide by official policy. This stipulates that ''Once the IOC has taken a decision, all members are bound to implement and report it within their own area and outside that area if they are invited to speak officially and with the approval of the president of the IOC. In this they are fulfilling the role of an ambassador, who may not personally agree with a policy but must abide by his government's decision'' (Killanin, *My Olympic Years*, 165).

17. *NYT*, 1 Feb. 1980, A8.

18. Governments may impair the autonomy of national Olympic committees by exerting control directly through the actions of state officials and/or by providing significant funds to the committees which can then be manipulated to gain influence over committee decisions. (Kanin, *Political History*, 5; Amdur, *NYT*, 22 Jan. 1980, 8.)

19. Weisman, *NYT*, 17 Jan. 1980, A14.

20. Harrigan, *NYT*, 12 Jan. 1980, A19; Amdur, *NYT*, 6 Jan. 1980, sec. 5, 1, 8.

21. Vinocur, *NYT*, 22 Jan. 1980, A8.

22. Bird, *NYT*, 23 Jan. 1980, A8; *NYT*, 6 Feb. 1980, A10. The Olympic committees represented at the council were: Mexico, Sweden, New Zealand, Great Britain, Nigeria, Kuwait, the Bahamas, the Dutch Antilles, Puerto Rico, Bulgaria, Liechtenstein, the Sudan, Cameroon, Ethiopia, India, Malaysia, Japan, Australia, and Fiji.

23. *NYT*, 4 May 1980, A1.

24. *NYT*, 20 May 1980, A8; *NYT*, 24 May 1980, A3; Weisman, *NYT*, 3 Apr. 1980, A13.

25. The international federations are responsible for the technical aspects of the Games. (Killanin, *My Olympic Years*, 187.)

26. As Lord Killanin accurately noted, "The IFs agree . . . not to hold major competitions just before or during the period of the Games. None would have sanctioned alternative meetings and thus national federations would not be able to compete" (Killanin, *My Olympic Years*, 192). Killanin's certainty regarding the position of the international federations was premised on the fact that all international governing associations were bound by the Olympic Charter not to sanction rival competitions that could undermine the Olympic Games. (Phillip Shinnick, *NYT*, 16 Mar. 1980, E2.) All of the federations fulfilled Killanin's expectation and lent their support to the Moscow Games. (Killanin, *My Olympic Years*, 198.)

27. Shinnick, *NYT*, 16 Mar. 1980, sec. 5, 2.

28. Amdur, *NYT*, 2 Mar. 1980, sec. 5, 12.

29. When he commented on the USOC decision to boycott Moscow, Lord Killanin indicated that Olympic committees which elected to boycott the Games could face difficulties in their relations with the IOC: "In view of what was happening in the United States that figure of 797 [the vote in favor of a boycott was 1,604 to 797] surprised and delighted me. At least if we were to lose the United States in Moscow there would still be people who could maintain the Olympic cause from a position of loyalty" (Killanin, *My Olympic Years*, 194-95). Although this statement appeared to proffer the possibility of favorable relations between the IOC and those who had resisted the pressure to boycott, Killanin's position soon hardened. Despite the USOC being told that no decision would be made about possible sanctions for its action until the conclusion of the Moscow Games, the IOC president stated, "I must admit my own feeling was that prior to Colorado Springs [where the USOC voted to boycott] the members of the USOC, individually, had done everything to resist government interference in accordance with our rules, but when it had become a matter of national security they had succumbed to pressures and could be in breach of the Olympic Charter, as our lawyer advised" (Killanin, *My Olympic Years*, 196). The IOC membership had a long memory and could be very unforgiving.

30. Lord Killanin revealed the conviction of the IOC that it was an organization independent of external forces when he declared, "no agency, organisation, person, or government instructs anyone to appear before the IOC. That is the prerogative of the IOC and we do not instruct, we invite." The IOC president continued, "The power of the International Olympic Committee rests in its autonomy. As a trusteeship it is answerable to none . . . " (Killanin, *My Olympic Years*, 179, 71).

31. In *Transnational Relations and World Politics*, Robert Keohane and Joseph Nye examine the phenomenon of transnational relations. They define transnational relations as contacts occurring "across state boundaries that are not controlled by the central foreign policy organs of governments." Among the primary effects of transnational organizations, two have particular relevance. The first is that such organizations promote "international pluralism" by facilitating the linkage of national interest groups. Thus, the IOC, both through its oversight and its coordinating functions, creates bonds among national Olympic committees (i.e., among national groups concerned with a common interest: international sport and the Olympic Games). Although many, if not most, of the world's national Olympic committees have a restricted degree of autonomy and thus are not completely independent of central government control, Western Olympic committees generally conform to the requirements for transnational actors. The second significant effect is that autonomous actors may emerge that pursue private foreign policies which may deliberately conflict with state policies. See Robert O. Keohane and Joseph

S. Nye, eds., *Transnational Relations and World Politics* (Cambridge, Massachusetts: Harvard University Press, 1972), iv-xxix, 371-98 [hereafter cited as *Transnational Relations*]. National Olympic committees, especially Western Olympic committees, often act contrary to their governments' wishes. This was evidenced repeatedly by the failure of West European Olympic groups to respect their governments' calls to boycott. Also, the IOC, acting as an autonomous decision maker, stubbornly pursued an independent foreign policy throughout the boycott crisis. Thus, the existence of transnational national interest groups, for example, national Olympic committees, organized by a central, coordinating transnational actor, the IOC, presents formidable obstacles to governments seeking to influence Olympic policy on a national or international level.

32. Carter, *Memoirs*, 476.

33. Mayer et al., *Newsweek*, 28 Jan. 1980, 20-21.

34. Sulzberger, Jr., *NYT*, 30 Jan. 1980, A12. Kennedy was quoted in the Soviet press as stating, "Grain sales and Olympic Games cannot be elements of American foreign policy" (*Soviet Press*, 20 Feb. 1980, 19).

35. James Reston, *NYT*, 6 Apr. 1980, sec. 4, 17; *NYT*, 1 Apr. 1980, B10; Howell Raines, *NYT*, 11 Apr. 1980, D14.

36. Raines, *NYT*, 11 Apr. 1980, D14.

37. Articles in the Soviet press relentlessly attacked the U.S. boycott initiative as "a policy subservient to President Carter's reelection considerations" and as an effort "dictated by the short-term plans of Carter['s] election headquarters." (*Soviet Press*, 7 May 1980, 18-19; *Soviet Press*, 16 Apr. 1980, 7-8.)

38. Vinocur, *NYT*, 22 Jan. 1980, A8.

39. Paul Lewis, *NYT*, 20 Feb. 1980, A8.

40. Apple, Jr., *NYT*, 14 Mar. 1980, A10.

41. Amdur, *NYT*, 7 Feb. 1980, B7. With a persistence matched only by Soviet spokesmen, Lord Killanin continually emphasized the alleged domestic political motives of the Carter administration in its pursuit of the boycott. He characterized administration efforts as "the campaign of a president trying to squirm his way out of an electoral defeat already firmly written ten months before the election by the American voters," and told Carter he wished the U.S. Constitution could be changed "so that the primary and presidential elections did not coincide with the Olympic Games." The IOC president also analyzed both the actual and potential effects of the boycott in terms of Carter's quest for electoral success. He stated, "Whatever the rights and wrongs of the Afghanistan affair, the judgement of one man, already scrambling for his political life in the American presidential election campaign, which occurs in the Olympic year, had turned the Olympic arena into what was to be its own battleground." Killanin added that, had the boycott been successful, the "Olympic Movement might have been wrecked—on the altar of American political expediency" (Killanin, *My Olympic Years*, 183, 214, 178).

42. Amdur, *NYT*, 7 Feb. 1980, B7.

43. See p. 130, n. 5 of the Introduction for a discussion of the circumstances surrounding the nonparticipation of the Swiss team.

44. Both the Soviet press and the president of the IOC stressed that the Olympic Games had proceeded as usual throughout the lengthy U.S. involvement in Southeast Asia. An article in *Izvestia* noted, "F. M. Carrasquilla, Chairman of the Colombian National Olympic Committee, makes the sensible point that the Olympic Games were

held as usual when the United States was waging a war of aggression against the peoples of Indochina'' (*Soviet Press*, 5 Mar. 1980, 7). Lord Killanin made a similar observation:

In the context of sport and of the Olympic Games in particular, the invocation of a country's political misdeeds to justify reprisals is always double-edged. The Soviets claim they were ''invited'' into Afghanistan; the 1976 Winter Games were allotted to Denver (which, however, later resigned its claim) in 1970, in the middle of America's involvement in the Far East. Killanin added that such involvement ''was never raised as an issue.'' (Killanin, *My Olympic Years*, 10-11, 182).

45. Stephen Daly, *NYT*, 9 Mar. 1980, sec. 22, 1.

46. U.S. Department of State, *Bulletin*, vol. 80, Mar. 1980, 50.

47. Ibid., 52.

48. The editorials were taken from the *New York Times* during the period 12 January 1980 to 29 June 1980.

49. Such an ''idealist'' perspective stands in stark contrast to the Hobbesian state of nature where, in the absence of a common power to enforce the laws of nature (i.e., a government), each individual acts only to further his own position and where, accordingly, ''the life of man [is] solitary, poor, nasty, brutish, and short.'' Thomas Hobbes, *Leviathan* (1651) (Indianapolis, Indiana: Bobbs-Merrill Educational Publishing, 1958), 107.

50. James Riordan, *NYT*, 29 June 1980, sec. 4, 19; Harold Howe, II, *NYT*, 8 Feb. 1980, 30; *NYT*, 17 Jan. 1980, A22; These editorials expressed similar ideas.

51. Julius Levine, *NYT*, 20 Jan. 1980, sec. 4, 18.

52. Stephen E. Taylor, *NYT*, 29 Jan. 1980, A18; Joseph Veach Noble, *NYT*, 31 Jan. 1980, A22.

53. Irving Dardik, *NYT*, 10 Feb. 1980, sec. 5, 2.

54. Morrow, *Time*, 11 Feb. 1980, 72.

55. David K. Crossen, *NYT*, 2 Mar. 1980, sec. 4, 20; Harrigan, *NYT*, 12 Jan. 1980, A19; James Brudish, *NYT*, 21 Jan. 1980, A22.

56. *NYT*, 20 Jan. 1980, sec. 5, 2.

57. Guttman, *Brundage*, 254. Brundage had, on several previous occasions, voiced similar objections to efforts aimed at disrupting the Olympics for political causes. In 1956, the IOC president argued, ''Every civilized person recoils in horror at the savage slaughter in Hungary [in reference to the Soviet invasion], but that is no reason for destroying the nucleus of international cooperation and goodwill we have in the Olympic Movement.'' Twelve years later, Brundage chose nearly the same words when he issued a statement condemning political attempts to influence the Games, ''The world, alas, is full of injustice, aggression, violence and warfare, against which all civilized persons rebel, but this is no reason to destroy the nucleus of international cooperation and good will we have in the Olympic Movement'' (Guttman, *Brundage*, 162, 241).

58. Austin, *NYT*, 4 Aug. 1980, sec. 3, 1.

59. Whitney, *NYT*, 15 July 1980, B12.

60. Vinocur, *NYT*, 22 Apr. 1980, A14; *Time*, 28 Jan. 1980, 15.

61. Paul Lewis, *NYT*, 14 May 1980, A1; Vinocur, *NYT*, 4 Jan. 1980, A7.

62. Tanner, *NYT*, 21 May 1980, A14; *NYT*, 30 June 1980, A7; Vinocur, *NYT*, 4 Jan. 1980, A7.

63. Moore, *SI*, 21 Apr. 1980, 30-33 (emphasis in original).

CHAPTER 7

1. Amdur, *NYT*, 19 July 1980, A3.

2. Red Smith, *NYT*, 21 July 1980, C7. The outspoken IOC president made repeated accusations that the White House formulated and implemented its Olympic policy without the benefit of proper advice. Killanin reflected that "many of the statements from the White House [at the beginning of the campaign] indicated to me that Washington was not conversant with the Olympic structure. The glib ideas about moving the Games were neither politic nor desirable, and the idea of postponing events for a year took no account of the complexity of the international sporting programme or the strict IOC rule that the Games take place in the last year of the Olympiad." Recalling a February 2 meeting with White House counsel Lloyd Cutler, Killanin noted, "Cutler told me to my surprise that under Olympic rules the Games could only be held with an international truce in effect and this rule should be invoked." Dismissing such a recommendation as premised not on the modern, but rather on the ancient, Olympic Games, the president of the IOC added, "Our conversation showed too that Cutler did not realise IOC members were not their country's representatives to the committee, nor did he understand the rules of the international federations and their independence, and neither, I suspect, did he understand the position of the national Olympic committees. As the meeting went on I became more and more concerned about the ignorance of Olympic matters at the White House." Killanin applauded his own ability to maintain "a calm in the face of all this ignorance." Killanin, *My Olympic Years*, 175, 177.

3. See Chapter 6 for a comprehensive discussion of the nature of the international sporting establishment.

4. The IOC was originally conceived as having no substantive affiliation with any member of the international state system and has sought to perpetuate this position throughout its existence. See Hulme, "U.S. Olympic Boycott," 285, n. 69, for further analysis of the nature of the IOC's development in terms of Keohane and Nye's theoretical framework.

5. The failure of the White House to appreciate the significance of this fact had serious ramifications. According to Keohane and Nye, transnational organizations may produce certain effects. One of these is additional constraints on state behavior as a consequence of increases in dependence or interdependence in the international arena. The authors stress that "Perceptions of transnational relations by governmental elites are . . . a crucial link between dependence or interdependence, on the one hand, and state policies on the other." Since Carter and his aides did not identify the nongovernmental, transnational character of the IOC, inappropriate policies were formulated that ignored systemic constraints imposed upon state actions as a result of the changing character of the international system. A second potential effect of transnational organizations identified by Keohane and Nye is a heightened capacity of more powerful states located at the center of transnational networks to exert influence over other states. Such influence is exercised through governmental control of, or alliance with, a particular transnational organization. (Keohane and Nye, *Transnational Relations*, iv-xxix.) In the case of the boycott, however, the belief of the White House in its ability to persuade other states to support its initiative, at least partially because of its influence over the IOC, proved mistaken. The geocentric nature of the International Committee (i.e., the fact that it had no unique relationship to one or two specific states) precluded the pos-

sibility of U.S. government policy being exported to other countries via a pliable transnational organization. White House efforts in such a direction produced few results.

6. Kanin, "Role of Sport," 40–41; Red Smith, *NYT*, 21 July 1980, sec. 3, 7.

7. *NYT*, 24 Mar. 1980, A8.

8. Tolchin, *NYT*, 24 Jan. 1980, A6; Treaster, *NYT*, 2 Feb. 1980, A1.

9. Moore, *SI*, 31 Mar. 1980, 16–17.

10. Amdur, *NYT*, 15 Feb. 1980, A6.

11. Lord Killanin remarked, "What they [the United States and Britain] did not understand was that without the cooperation of the international federations no such [alternative] competition would be possible" (Killanin, *My Olympic Years*, 192). Concurring with the IOC president's analysis, political historian David Kanin observed, "The administration vastly underestimated the problems [logistical and with the international federations] of . . . [alternative] games." He further reasoned that concentrating on "alternative games distracted U.S. officials from other strategies, such as approaches to individual federations designed to remove individual sports and components of national teams from Moscow" (Kanin, *Political History*, 119, 120).

12. *NYT*, 19 Mar. 1980, A3.

13. Anne Marden, *NYT*, 28 Mar. 1980, A34.

14. Fimrite, *SI*, 4 Feb. 1980, 18–22.

15. Ibid.

16. *U.S. News and World Report*, 28 Apr. 1980, 7.

17. U.S. Department of State, *Bulletin*, vol. 80, July 1980, 30; McFadden, *NYT*, 25 May 1980, A1.

18. Weisman, *NYT*, 26 May 1980, A7.

19. U.S. Department of State, *Bulletin*, vol. 80, June 1980, 15.

20. Weisman, *NYT*, 13 Apr. 1980, A19.

21. *NYT*, 28 May 1980, A10.

22. Kirshenbaum, *SI*, 3 Mar. 1980, 11. South Africa's Olympic Committee was expelled from the movement in 1970; South Africa had not participated in an Olympic Games since 1960.

23. David M. Alpern, *Newsweek*, 21 Apr. 1980, 41–42.

24. *NYT*, 4 Feb. 1980, A10.

25. Dave Anderson, *NYT*, 5 Feb. 1980, C21.

26. *NYT*, 5 Feb. 1980, A14.

27. Ibid.

28. Ibid.; Gupte, *NYT*, 6 Feb. 1980, A8.

29. Gupte, *NYT*, 6 Feb. 1980, A8.

30. *Time*, 18 Feb. 1980, 34, 37.

31. Dave Anderson, *NYT*, 5 Feb. 1980, C21; *NYT*, 8 Feb. 1980, B2.

32. One manifestation of such results was the sentiment voiced by Lord Killanin when he recalled a February 2 meeting with Lloyd Cutler in Dublin. The IOC president observed, "I discovered that Cutler had not flown in from Washington to discuss, but rather to instruct. It was not a question of examining the problem from all its aspects. There was only one position, the political one, as far as he was concerned." Killanin continued,

he [Cutler] had come with a demand from the president of the United States that the International Olympic Committee either postpone or cancel the Games. I was rather angry. Here again was the American attitude of bringing out the bulldozer to save someone from an awful fate, or what

America thought was an awful fate. It was this sense of arrogance, not personally shown by Cutler but evident in the high-handed approach of the White House, that raised my hackles. . . . He [Cutler] told me that the USOC was to request a full session of the IOC on the instructions of the president of the United States to cancel or postpone the Games. I was angered at this request. . . . here we had the world's most powerful democracy crushing that treasured independence [between governments and national Olympic committees] in one simple statement (Killanin, *My Olympic Years*, 176, 178).

33. Amdur, *NYT*, 10 Feb. 1980, A8.

34. Writing several years later, Lord Killanin felt the impact of Vance's speech to have been profound:

Vance's speech was greeted in absolute silence by everybody. . . . Some of my members were so incensed they did not attend the reception given later by Vance . . . Vance's speech had drawn the IOC membership together as though someone had lassoed them with an enormous rope. On every side . . . there were words of disgust at what the United States government was doing and the way it was going about it (Killanin, *My Olympic Years*, 184).

35. Amdur, *NYT*, 11 Feb. 1980, A3. In fact, according to IOC President Killanin, Vance never officially opened the session. (Killanin, *My Olympic Years*, 184.)

36. Amdur, *NYT*, 10 Feb. 1980, A8.

37. In order to appreciate the full impact of Vance's speech upon the IOC, one need only note the hostility it aroused in the former president of that organization two years after the event. In preparing his book, *My Olympic Years*, Lord Killanin devoted numerous pages to a discussion of the secretary's address before the International Committee. Fearing Vance's possible actions, Killanin claimed to have briefed Lloyd Cutler several days before the meeting on the nature of an appropriate opening address for a pre-Olympic IOC session, "The function is usually purely ceremonial and I made this point since, with so much ignorance, I did not want Vance to suffer the embarrassment of making a political speech in the wrong place at the wrong time." When U.S. officials then failed to provide the IOC with a copy of Vance's speech until a half hour prior to the opening of the IOC session, and when the IOC president was initially forced to evaluate the address from excerpts he could gather from its prior distribution, the situation worsened. Killanin recalled, "it [Vance's speech] was on the desks of the news editors around the world, but not on the desk of the president of the IOC." He reflected that after Vance and Cutler had finally arrived to show him a copy of the speech, "I immediately demanded to know why I had not received a copy of . . . [the] speech although it had been issued to the media." Characterizing the speech as "outrageously political," Killanin said he was told by Vance that, nonetheless, "That is what I believe and that is what I am going to say." Referring to the content of the secretary's address, Killanin commented on the difficulties of Vance's main proposals "to transfer the Games from Moscow to another site, or multiple sites, this summer." Refuting the U.S. official's assertions that the "practical difficulties . . . could be overcome," and that, in addition to there being "a precedent for canceling the Games . . . it would be possible, with a simple change of rules, to postpone the Games for a year or more," Killanin declared, " 'A simple change of rules' is not as simple as might be thought, as it would tend to split the Olympic Movement and international sports throughout the world." He concluded by noting that the speech "was the depth of insensitivity before an audience whose lives had encompassed the propagation of the Olympic Movement for many years," and that, "in order to correct any mistakes and have the last word," the presi-

dent of the IOC now speaks last at pre-Olympic opening sessions of the committee. (In the past, the president of the host country's national Olympic committee had made a welcoming speech, followed by the IOC president, and finally by the host government's head of state or designated representative.) (Killanin, *My Olympic Years*, 180–84, 144–45.)

38. Amdur, *NYT*, 6 Apr. 1980, sec. 5, 6; Kirshenbaum, *SI*, 3 Mar. 1980, 11.

39. Gwertzman, *NYT*, 16 Jan. 1980, A1; Gwertzman, *NYT*, 22 Jan. 1980, A1.

40. The State Department adopted an even more rigid position about the U.S. ultimatum than did the White House. (Kanin, *Political History*, 120–21.)

41. Weisman, *NYT*, 13 Feb. 1980, A9; Amdur, *NYT*, 15 Feb. 1980, A6; Weisman, *NYT*, 21 Feb. 1980, A1.

42. Carter, *Memoirs*, 481.

43. Donald P. Doane, *U.S. News and World Report*, 3 Mar. 1980, 51–52.

44. U.S. Department of State, *Bulletin*, vol. 80, June 1980, 15.

45. Mayer et al., *Newsweek*, 28 Jan. 1980, 20–28. The potential costs the United States would incur as a result of a unilateral boycott action included the losses businesses would face consequent to the mandatory embargo of March 28 on the shipment of sporting goods and other Olympic-related products to the Soviet Union. Should the United States act alone, numerous other countries could easily step in and supply the embargoed goods, thereby making the U.S. action one of voluntary self-sacrifice.

46. *NYT*, 21 Jan. 1980, A4; Kirshenbaum, *SI*, 28 Jan. 1980, 7–8.

47. U.S. Department of State, *Bulletin*, vol. 80, June 1980, 16.

48. Carter's tendency to overstate the potential willingness of the United States to act alone was discussed in Chapter 1.

49. Terence Smith, *NYT*, 21 Jan. 1980, A1.

50. Carter, *Memoirs*, 474.

51. The surprising rapidity with which the American public moved to support a boycott was discussed in Chapter 3.

52. Kirshenbaum, *SI*, 28 Jan. 1980, 7–8.

53. For instance, the United States was accused by some of "abandoning" Taiwan and South Vietnam despite previous expressions of commitment.

54. See Hazan, *Propaganda Games*.

55. Austin, *NYT*, 14 Jan. 1980, A6. The president of the Olympic movement in Italy was quoted by the Soviet press in evidence of the universal repudiation of the Carter boycott, "all competitions, including the Olympic Games, should serve the ideas of unity and brotherhood among peoples, and in no case should they be used for political purposes" (*Soviet Press*, 13 Feb. 1980, 9).

56. *NYT*, 1 Feb. 1980, A8.

57. *NYT*, 14 Apr. 1980, A9. For instance, an article in *Izvestia* stressed that the USOC voted to boycott only as a result of "brainwashing" by government officials, including Vice President Mondale and General Jones, the chairman of the Joint Chiefs of Staff. The White House was also criticized for threatening the financial solvency of the USOC by pressuring the committee's corporate sponsors and by challenging its tax exempt status. Finally, the article concluded that the USOC "decision" to boycott was reached as a direct consequence of "the President's orders" (*Soviet Press*, 14 May 1980, 5–6).

58. McFadden, *NYT*, 25 May 1980, A8. Gisli Halldorsson, chairman of Iceland's national Olympic committee, was quoted by *Sovetsky Sport* as saying that his committee

elected to participate at Moscow despite intense pressure from the White House, the U.S. embassy, and the local branch of the Coca-Cola Company which refused to provide its customary financial assistance to the Icelandic athletes. (*Soviet Press*, 25 June 1980, 6.)

59. United Press International was quoted by *Sovetsky Sport* as saying that the boycott's effect had changed "from a bomb to no more than a pitiful firecracker" since "apparently more countries will participate in the Moscow Olympics than did in the 1976 Olympic Games in Montreal." Also, the Soviet press noted that "The countries that have decided to boycott the Olympics make a rather curious crew. Among them are fascist Chile, the dictatorial regimes of Haiti, Honduras and Paraguay, South Korea, which is in the grip of huge popular demonstrations against the reactionary clique, China, Israel and Pakistan" (*Soviet Press*, 25 June 1980, 5).

60. *NYT*, 17 Apr. 1980, A13; Whitney, *NYT*, 25 May 1980, A7.

61. Soviet propaganda repeatedly posited a close connection between Carter's domestic concerns and electoral difficulties and his "anti-Olympic" boycott initiative. The White House was accused of seeking "most of all . . . a conflict that would make Americans rally around the current President . . . [in order to] distract them from the internal problems rending the US" (*Soviet Press*, 16 Apr. 1980, 8). One writer concluded, "As far as the American administration's intentions are concerned, one can only say that trying to mix sports and politics is bad enough, but it's even worse when the US President starts to use sports in his election campaign." *Izvestia* quoted a U.S. runner in support of such a position, "President Carter is having a hard time right now, and he's ready to try anything to get himself reelected" (*Soviet Press*, 5 Mar. 1980, 7).

62. *NYT*, 7 July 1980, A2.

63. Various organs of the Soviet propaganda apparatus emphasized Moscow's commitment to the Olympic ideal and determination to adhere without deviation to the Olympic Charter and to the policies of the IOC. *Izvestia* commented that the "Soviet people are preparing for these Games in strict accordance with the Olympic Charter," while *Sovetsky Sport* quoted the president of the Canadian Olympic Committee as observing, "There's no reason to boycott, since the USSR has always respected Olympic rules and continues to do so. Those who are calling for a boycott for this reason ought to be condemned by public opinion and by leaders of the international sport movement" (*Soviet Press*, 5 Mar. 1980, 6; *Soviet Press*, 13 Feb. 1980, 10). Lord Killanin concurred with the ostensible willingness of the Kremlin to support IOC decisions. He noted Soviet acquiescence on measures designed to reduce the nationalistic elements of the Games, as well as Brezhnev's assurance "to do his very best so that the atmosphere might improve" for the holding of the Moscow Games. (*NYT*, 4 May 1980, 1; Killanin, *My Olympic Years*, 214, 210; Vinocur, *NYT*, 24 Apr. 1980, 10.)

64. *Pravda* stressed that "If sports is made the servant of politics, this will mean a death sentence for the Olympic Games and for international sports in general." It was argued that, according to the Olympic Charter, "the participation of an athlete in the Olympic Games does not mean that he supports any particular political ideology or the policy of the country in which the International Olympic Committee organizes the Games." However, in contrast to Soviet policy, the United States and West Germany were accused of "introducing politics into sports and . . . violating the basic provisions of the Olympic Charter" (*Soviet Press*, 16 Apr. 1980, 8; *Soviet Press*, 28 May 1980, 13–14).

65. Whitney, *NYT*, 14 July 1980, A7.

66. Ignati T. Novikov, chairman of the Moscow Olympic Organizing Committee, attempted to downplay the significance of the passage in the Soviet party handbook by charging the Western press with exaggeration and deception:

The so-called "accusations" that we have politicized the Games are based on groundless conjectures or quotations "excerpted" from individual articles or publications. For example, the Western press is making wide use of one or two quotations from information brochures. In such an important matter as the preparations for and holding of the Olympic Games, chicanery and distortion are despicable. We have not followed and are not following such a path, although I cannot help but note that it is not quotations but entire articles in magazines and newspapers published in the US and other capitalist countries that are doing real damage to the international sports movement (*Soviet Press*, 25 June 1980, 5).

67. Basler, *NYT*, 6 Feb. 1980, A10.

68. *Izvestia* observed, "The USSR Olympic Committee, true to the ideals of the Olympic movement, condemns attempts to use sports as a means of political pressure . . . " (*Soviet Press*, 5 Mar. 1980, 6).

69. Basler, *NYT*, 6 Feb. 1980, A10.

70. Whitney, *NYT*, 25 Feb. 1980, A9.

71. Whitney, *NYT*, 16 July 1980, B6.

72. The question of the significance of Afghanistan to the boycott issue and to the position of the two superpowers on the Olympics in general was summarily dismissed by *Pravda*, "The events in Afghanistan have no relation to the Olympic movement. Attempts to artificially link one question with the other are the handiwork of unscrupulous politicians" (*Soviet Press*, 28 May 1980, 14).

73. Austin, *NYT*, 22 Jan. 1980, A9. *Izvestia*, seeking to remind the Western Europeans of their stake in positive relations with the Soviet Union, observed, "The peoples' fundamental interests are indissolubly linked with detente. The Europeans were the first to experience its beneficial results firsthand, and they do not intend to throw its fruits under the feet of those who are ready to trample them" (*Soviet Press*, 5 Mar. 1980, 7).

74. Weisman, *NYT*, 21 Feb. 1980, A1; *NYT*, 21 Feb. 1980, A12; Olga Korbut, *NYT*, 13 Apr. 1980, sec. 4, 18; Whitney, *NYT*, 17 Apr. 1980, A1, 16.

75. Austin, *NYT*, 4 Mar. 1980, A3; Ninety-four percent of those surveyed in Moscow in a supposedly scientific study responded that the Moscow Games would strengthen international peace and cooperation. (Stephen Smith, as reported by Bruce Nelan, *Time*, 21 July 1980, 68–69.)

76. For example, U.S. Olympic champion Rod Milburn was quoted by *Sovetskaya Rossia* as criticizing the White House for making "us hostages in its political game," while Australian Debbie Wells provided potent ammunition against Western anti-Olympic tactics when she declared, "Just a few weeks ago I said I wanted to go to Moscow. But now, after being threatened with death if I go to Moscow, I've stopped talking" (*Soviet Press*, 7 May 1980, 18–19; *Soviet Press*, 25 June 1980, 5).

77. *Soviet Press*, 25 June 1980, 5.

78. Ibid., 6.

79. *Soviet Press*, 5 Mar. 1980, 7.

80. Thus, as Western European governments increasingly expressed support for the boycott, Soviet officials and state propaganda organs imputed such decisions to U.S. coercion. Lord Killanin agreed with the Soviet interpretation, citing the West German Olympic Committee's vote against participation as a notable example. He argued:

The whole affair was orchestrated in a manner that indicated the influence of the United States. The [West German] NOC arranged to have a meeting in Düsseldorf, and the day before West German President Karl Carstens invited all those taking part to a reception to give them the country's position. Then, when the delegates arrived the following morning for their crucial debate, not only did they find it was in public with the press present, but it was televised live (Kanin, *Political History*, 124; Killanin, *My Olympic Years*, 215).

81. For instance, *Sovetsky Sport* lamented, "One can only regret that Washington managed to *drag* onto the 'anti-Olympic team' such countries as Canada and Japan, whose athletes wanted so much to go to the Olympic Games" (emphasis added, *Soviet Press*, 6 June 1980, 6).

82. *Pravda* attacked White House policy along such lines when it declared, "With cynical disregard for the Olympic Charter and the traditions of the Olympic movement, Washington politicians are trying to impose the decision to boycott the 1980 Olympics . . . on other countries at the governmental level and then make the national Olympic committees submit to this decision" (*Soviet Press*, 16 Apr. 1980, 7–8).

83. Lord Killanin accurately assessed the situation when he observed, "President Carter . . . seemed to have rigid ideas and had put himself in a position from which there was nowhere to withdraw . . . " (Killanin, *My Olympic Years*, 211–12).

84. Carter, *Memoirs*, 482.

85. Brzezinski seemingly indicated that a previous refusal by the White House to admit to any possibility of a renunciation of the boycott policy was being reevaluated when he stated, "We certainly will reconsider if they depart, but that seems very, very unlikely" (Moore, *SI*, 31 Mar. 1980, 16–17).

86. Paul Lewis, *NYT*, 14 May 1980, A1.

87. For instance, Pakistan said it would reconsider its decision to boycott should conditions change. Also, the president of the Canadian Olympic Committee stated, "We have voted to reassess this decision [to boycott] if the international situation improves" (*NYT*, 10 May 1980, A4; *NYT*, 27 Apr. 1980, A4).

88. Weisman, *NYT*, 3 Apr. 1980, A13.

89. Keohane and Nye's discussion of sensitivity versus vulnerability interdependence is instructive. The authors distinguish between the two types of interdependence according to the time frame in which events are considered and the capacity and will of the principal actors to alter policies in response to changed circumstances. Sensitivity is defined as the "liability to costly effects imposed from outside before policies are altered to try to change the situation." It attempts to evaluate "how quickly . . . changes in one country bring costly changes in another, and how great are the costly effects?" Vulnerability, on the other hand, considers "an actor's liability to suffer costs imposed by external events even after policies have been altered." The degree of vulnerability is affected by an actor's political will, governmental ability, and resource assets. Thus, should a government possess the necessary attributes, severe sensitivity interdependence need not signify similar vulnerability over the longer term. When applied to the mid-February deadline, these two concepts help illuminate the impact such an ultimatum had on the Soviet government. Since the White House issued its demands for withdrawal six months prior to the opening of the Moscow Olympics, the Kremlin had sufficient time, as well as the will, ability, and resources, to adjust its policies in order to minimize the impact of U.S. actions. Had the Soviet leadership been confronted with a last-minute boycott, such comprehensive adaptation would have been significantly more difficult to achieve because of time constraints, and because of both uncertainties regarding

governmental will to act prior to a firm U.S. decision and governmental ability to thwart U.S. policy clarified at a later date. Thus, the early boycott deadline enabled the Kremlin to reduce its vulnerability, while forfeiting the U.S. capacity to inflict significant costs upon Moscow because of the high degree of Soviet sensitivity interdependence to U.S. policy. As Keohane and Nye note, sensitivity interdependence is the basis for meaningful political influence only when the rules and norms in effect can be taken for granted or when it would be prohibitively costly for dissatisfied actors to alter their policies quickly. For the United States to expect to exert influence through the mechanism of sensitivity interdependence, any boycott deadline would have had to have been issued at a date close enough to the Games itself to render Soviet countermeasures impracticable, thus insuring a continuance of the basic rules in effect prior to the U.S. action. (See Keohane and Nye, *Power and Interdependence*, Chapter 1.)

90. Amdur, *NYT*, 15 June 1980, sec. 5, 1. The Kremlin provided 100 percent assistance to nineteen teams from the Western Hemisphere to attend the Games; it provided 50 percent assistance to another ten teams from the Western Hemisphere for the same purpose. Also, in the wake of the U.S. boycott the IOC expanded the scope of its "Olympic Solidarity" fund to include all Olympic committees deprived of their usual sources of income, particularly government grants. The fund, formerly reserved solely for Third World countries, was budgeted for $1,000,000. (*Time*, 9 June 1980, 66.) The expanded fund was designed to insure that the maximum possible number of states be represented at the Moscow Games, and that no participants be deprived of the opportunity to compete because of financial hardship.

91. The president of the IOC claimed the Soviets had acted to encourage Third World participation prior to the events in Afghanistan, and implied that the counter-boycott efforts of the Kremlin essentially duplicated previous initiatives. Lord Killanin argued that "the Soviets, in their efforts to influence the maximum number of NOCs before the Moscow Olympics, visited certain Third World countries making very generous offers, sometimes publicly, sometimes privately, long before they invaded Afghanistan" (Killanin, *My Olympic Years*, 151). Despite such arguments, the heightened intensity and expanded scope of Soviet overtures to Third World states subsequent to the issuance of the February 20 deadline were significant, and their effects noticeable.

CHAPTER 8

1. John J. Budacovich, *NYT*, 1 Mar. 1980, A20.

2. *NYT*, 21 Apr. 1980, A11. For instance, on April 20 the nine-member IOC executive board met with the Moscow Olympic Organizing Committee, the presidents of all twenty-six Olympic sports federations, and heads of the West European national Olympic committees for three days in Lausanne, Switzerland, in an effort to formulate a concerted plan of action to thwart the U.S. boycott.

3. E. J. Kahn, Jr., *New Yorker*, 10 Mar. 1980, 53–56.

4. Weisman, *NYT*, 10 Apr. 1980, A18.

5. *NYT*, 20 Jan. 1980, sec. 5, 2.

6. Kanin, "Role of Sport," 42.

7. One analyst explained such a necessity with considerable insight:

The IOC's insistence on the political purity of the Games heightens awareness when political interference occurs. When other world class contests are affected, the situation is likely to be treated as an annoying incident, not a major catastrophe. But the Olympics, with its nonpolitical propaganda, draws much more attention and criticism when politics infiltrate the bastion (Segrave and Chu, *Olympism*, 106).

8. Rosenblatt, *Time*, 4 Aug. 1980, 67–68.

9. Red Smith, *NYT*, 26 May 1980, C5.

10. Keohane and Nye provide a means of explaining the mechanism by which popular support for the Olympic movement could become a potent political force through their analysis of transnational actors. Such entities, in this case the IOC as symbolic representative of the entire Olympic movement, are capable of playing significant roles in the international political arena because "men identify themselves and their interests with corporate bodies other than the nation-state." Since man is capable of associating himself with a transnational actor not beholden to any individual state's interests, not only can such an actor focus interests already formulated into a more cohesive body of clearly articulated views, it can also promote ideas consistent with its own orientation. (See Keohane and Nye, *Transnational Relations*, iv-xxix.) Thus, the international sporting "establishment" had the capacity both to orchestrate sympathetic public opinion into a recognizable, effective lobbying vehicle and to cultivate a sporting sensibility among the uncommitted or nominally antagonistic segments of the world community in order to develop their appreciation of the sanctity of the Olympic Games.

11. William Nack, *SI*, 28 Jan. 1980, 48–50.

12. Gwertzman, *NYT*, 21 May 1980, A16.

13. U.S. Department of State, *Bulletin*, vol. 80, Mar. 1980, 51.

14. Robert Keohane's assertion that the dilemmas of collective action that beset contemporary international relations "are rendered less intractable by the small number of states involved" is not applicable for a boycott of the scale envisioned by the White House. Although it is true that "Even in global negotiations, the number of states does not exceed about one hundred and fifty, many of which do not play significant roles," in an effort such as the boycott that sought both quantitative and qualitative levels of cooperation, states with little sporting prowess nonetheless occupied Washington's attention. Therefore, the difficulties of achieving the sought-after degree of collective action were considerable. (See Keohane, *After Hegemony*, 77.)

15. In attempting to distinguish between harmony and cooperation, Keohane indicates potential obstacles for statesmen seeking to effect a global boycott of the Olympic Games. Keohane notes that "Harmony refers to a situation in which actors' policies (pursued in their own self-interest without regard for others) *automatically* facilitate the attainment of others' goals." In order for harmony to exist, "No communication is necessary, and no influence need be exercised"; it is an apolitical relationship. Cooperation, in contrast, "requires that the actions of separate individuals or organizations— which are not in pre-existent harmony—be brought into conformity with one another through a process of negotiation." Since cooperation necessitates the alteration of patterns of behavior, and since cooperation only occurs under "the specter of conflict," Keohane stresses that it is a "highly political" phenomenon. (See Keohane, *After Hegemony*, 51–53.) Thus, statesmen hoping to forge a broadly based coalition for retributive purposes—such as the Olympic boycott—must expect to confront significant political resistance from states functioning in a fundamentally nonharmonious milieu.

16. Kirshenbaum, *SI*, 28 Jan. 1980, 7–8; Weisman, *NYT*, 19 Jan. 1980, A1.

17. U.S. Department of State, *Bulletin*, vol. 80, May 1980, 14. For instance, Vice President Mondale said, "if we and our allies and friends fail to use every single peace-

ful means available to preserve the peace, what hope is there that peace will long be preserved?''

18. As mentioned previously, Norway, Liechtenstein, and Monoco joined the Federal Republic in boycotting Moscow, and thus comprised the entire West European pro-boycott contingent.

19. Weisman, *NYT*, 26 May 1980, A1.

20. *NYT*, 24 May 1980, A3.

21. Keohane and Nye's observation that ''As governments become more ambitious . . . the impact of transnational relations . . . create[s] a 'control gap' between the aspiration for control and the capability to achieve it'' sheds light on the inability of statesmen to dictate policy to the guardians of international sport. (Keohane and Nye, *Transnational Relations*, xxiii.)

22. Graham Allison identifies many significant obstacles to policy implementation that confront decision makers; these include reliance on organizational routine and standard operating procedures, bureaucratic parochialism, and excessive rigidity in unusual or crisis situations. Furthermore, political leaders are constrained in the choice of policy alternatives by similar bureaucratic tendencies. (See Allison, *Essence of Decision*, 93–94, 79, 90, 68, 89 for further elaboration.) Therefore, statesmen contemplating a policy similar to the U.S. boycott initiative should be prepared to receive abnormally biased recommendations from bureaucratic organizations generally unfamiliar with considering international sport as a tool of world politics. In addition, leaders should expect to encounter heightened obstacles to the implementation of their decisions by those same organizations which probably have not developed standard operating procedures to handle such directives.

23. See Keohane and Nye's *Power and Interdependence: World Politics in Transition* for a discussion of the emergence of complexly interdependent relationships between states that have eliminated the use of military force in such situations. Lily Gardner-Feldman's *The Special Relationship between West Germany and Israel* also details circumstances where military recourse is not considered as an option for the resolution of conflicts or disagreements between closely identified states.

Jones, P. M. "Political Battles on Ice." *Senior Scholastic*, 7 February 1980, 7–11.
Kahn, H. "How to Save the Games." *Sport*, April 1980, 9.
Lewis, W. S. *Encore*, May 1980, 50–51.
Macleans, 21 January 1980; 4 February 1980; 3 March 1980; 21 April 1980; 5 May
    1980; 28 July 1980; 4 August 1980.
Nation, 9 February 1980; 22 March 1980; 3 May 1980.
National Review, 22 February 1980; 21 March 1980; 2, 7 May 1980; 8 August 1980.
Newsweek, 28 January 1980; 18 February 1980; 10, 31 March 1980; 21 April 1980; 12
    May 1980; 14, 28 July 1980; 4, 11 August 1980; 22 December 1980.
New Yorker, 10 March 1980; 18 August 1980.
"Olympic Boycott as Political Weapon." *Center Magazine*, May/June 1980, 7–13.
People, 11 February 1980; 14 April 1980.
Reader's Digest, July 1980; August 1980.
Rowan, Ray. *Fortune*, 25 February 1980, 90–93, 96.
Saturday Review, 12 April 1980; May 1980.
Sports Illustrated, 21, 28 January 1980; 4 February 1980; 3, 31 March 1980; 21 April
    1980; 28 July 1980; 4 August 1980; 22–29 December 1980.
Time, 28 January 1980; 4, 11, 18 February 1980; 31 March 1980; 19, 26 May 1980; 9
    June 1980; 7, 21, 28 July 1980; 4, 11 August 1980.
"XXII: The Sad Olympiad." *America*, 2 February 1980, 73–74.
U.S. News and World Report, 21, 28 January 1980; 4, 11, 18, 25 February 1980; 3,
    31 March 1980; 14, 21, 28 April 1980; 26 May 1980; 9 June 1980; 7, 21 July
    1980; 4, 11 August 1980.
Weekly Compilation of Presidential Documents, 21 March 1980, 517–21.
"What a Boycott Cost Moscow." *Business Week*, 4 February 1980, 30–31.
World Press Review, April 1980; June 1980; July 1980.

NEWSPAPERS

Cooney, John E. "Olympic Jitters." *Wall Street Journal*, 6 February 1980, 1, 16.
New York Times, 28 December 1979–1 November 1980.

UNPUBLISHED MATERIALS

Barton, Laurence. "The American Olympic Boycott of 1980: The Amalgam of Diplo-
    macy and Propaganda in Influencing Public Opinion." Ann Arbor, Michigan:
    University Microfilms International, 1983.
Hulme, Derick L., Jr. "The Viability of International Sport as a Political Weapon: The
    1980 US Olympic Boycott." Ann Arbor, Michigan: University Microfilms In-
    ternational, 1989.
Kanin, David B. "The Role of Sport in International Relations." Ph.D. diss., The
    Fletcher School of Law and Diplomacy, 1976.

Selected Bibliography

BOOKS

Ali, Ramadhan. *Africa at the Olympics*. London: Africa Books, 1976.

Guttman, Allen. *The Games Must Go On: Avery Brundage and the Olympic Movement*. New York: Columbia University Press, 1984.

Hazan, Baruch. *Olympic Sports and Propaganda Games: Moscow 1980*. New Brunswick, N.J.: Transaction Books, 1982.

Kanin, David B. *A Political History of the Olympic Games*. Boulder, Co.: Westview Press, 1981.

Killanin, Lord, *My Olympic Years*. New York: William Morrow and Company, 1983.

Segrave, Jeffrey and Donald Chu, editors. *Olympism*. Champaign, Il.: Human Kinetics, 1981.

PERIODICALS

Beck, P. J. "Politics and the Olympics: the Lesson of 1924." *History Today*, July 1980, 7–9.

Black Enterprise, June 1980; July 1980.

Brodsky, Joseph. *Atlantic Monthly*, June 1980, 35–39.

Commonweal, 15 February 1980; 23 May 1980.

Current Digest of the Soviet Press, 13 February 1980; 5 March 1980; 16 April 1980; 7, 14, 28, May 1980; 25 June 1980.

Delloff, L. M. *Christian Century*, 27 February 1980, 221.

Department of State Bulletin, March 1980; April 1980; May 1980; June 1980; July 1980.

Herr, R. "Stillborn Olympics." *New Republic*, 16 February 1980, 12–14.

Index

ABC-TV, 10, 137, 149

Afghanistan invasion: and British history, 101; international response to, 51–52, 56, 67, 89, 127, 146; and Moscow Games, 49, 63, 116; and Soviet Union, 38–40, 45, 47, 66–67, 91, 112, 149; U.S. response to, 18, 36, 78, 80, 95, 103, 129, 137, 163. *See also* Carter, Moscow Games

AFL-CIO, 37, 137

Africa: and Ali, 46, 110, 139; and boycott, 46, 48, 67–69, 72, 77, 92, 97, 103, 139, 147

Ali, Muhammad, 46–47, 68, 109–11, 139, 147

allies, 45, 53, 56, 62, 80, 108, 127

Allison, Graham, 167

alternate event, 29–30, 47–48, 94–95, 107, 139, 159

Amateur Athletic Act, 35, 135–36

Amateur Athletic Board, 55

Amateur Athletic Union (AAU), 30, 36

America: and boycott, 87, 156; international position of, 132; and Lake Placid Games, 10; and multinational competition, 48; public opinion, 38, 40, 62, 78, 87, 114, 138, 140; and South Africa, 46; tourists, 81–83; and Third World, 153

American Broadcasting Corporation. *See* ABC-TV

American Society of Newspaper Editors, 41–42

Andropov, Yuri, 79

Annunzio, Frank, 10

Antilles (Netherlands), 154

Antwerp, 1, 3

ARD, 13

Argentina, 70, 147

Asia, 64–67, 147

Association of National Olympic Committees, 70, 93

Athens, 2, 97

athletes: and alternate event, 47–48, 107; individual, 34, 71, 142; influences upon, 22, 27–29, 31, 73, 95, 124, 138; non-Soviet, 53, 55–56, 58, 60, 69, 71, 100–101, 141–42, 148; perspective of, 32, 98, 100, 124–26, 138, 153, 163; position of, 94, 124; restrictions upon, x, 19, 32, 55, 80, 123; So-

athletes, (*continued*)
  viet, 118, 137; Soviet view of, 118;
    and USOC, 23, 31–32, 124, 134
Australia, 48, 70–71, 94, 127, 148, 150,
  154
Austria, 62
axis powers, 3
Axthelm, Pete, 37

Bahamas, 154
Baillet-Latour, Comte Henri de, 3, 130
Bani-Sadr, Abolhassan, 67
Barcelo, Carlos Romero, 71–72. *See also*
  Puerto Rico
Barton, Laurence, 137
Baum, Gerhart, 57, 143. *See also* West
  Germany
Beitz, Charles, 129–30
Belgium, 3, 53, 61, 94, 96, 144–45
Benaisa, Godfrey L., 69
Berenson, Robert, 26, 108
Berlin, 1, 3, 27, 71, 97, 127
Berlioux, Monique, 49, 106–7, 110. *See
  also* International Olympic Committee
Bock, Lothar, 151
Bolshoi ballet, 77
Book of the Party Activist, 76, 149
Bradley, Bill, 38
Brandt, Willy, 143
Brazil, 70
Brezhnev, Leonid, 143–44, 149, 162
Britain, 48, 52, 53–56, 76, 127, 140,
  150
British Olympic Association, 45, 54–56,
  94, 96, 101, 107, 142, 154
Brooks, Herb, 10
Brown, Harold, 26
Brundage, Avery, 3–4, 6–7, 100–101,
  141, 153–54, 157. *See also* Interna-
  tional Olympic Committee
Brzezinski, Zbigniew, 110, 164
Bulgaria, 154
bureaucracy, 167
Burma, 146
Bush, George, 96
business, 40–41, 81–84, 123, 151, 161
Byrd, Robert C., 26, 35, 38
Byrne, Brendan, 30

Cameroon, 154
Canada, 44, 48, 62–64, 92, 94, 162, 164
Carnes, Jimmy, 14
Carrasquilla, F. M., 156–57
Carrington, Lord, 54–55
Carstens, Karl, 164
Carter, Jimmy: and Afghanistan, ix–x,
  19, 22, 39–40, 45, 103, 113–14, 123;
  and Ali, 46–47, 109–10; and allies,
  45, 53–54, 56–57, 60, 62, 91, 93,
  111, 127, 138; and athletes, 27–28,
  138; criticisms of, xi, 98, 102–3, 107–
  9, 116, 119, 121–22, 139, 158; and
  deadline, 25, 58, 111–12, 114–16,
  119, 121; evaluation of, x, 47, 69, 73,
  111; international efforts of, 25, 43–
  44, 46–47, 70–72, 107, 109, 112–15;
  and IOC, 49–50, 110–11, 134, 140;
  international strategy of, 19–20, 44–
  46, 97–98, 108, 113, 139; and Killanin, 50–51, 96, 105–6, 140; and
  Lake Placid Games, 10, 13–14; and
  moralist policy, 46, 113–14, 130; mo-
  tivations of, ix–xi, 17–20, 40, 45, 96,
  112–15, 138, 156; obstacles to, 11,
  90–98, 101–3; and Olympic movement, 51, 86, 93, 126, 140; and public
  opinion, 38–40, 42, 114–15, 138; and
  reelection, 78, 95–96, 156; results of
  efforts, xi, 18, 23–24, 27, 78–80,
  138; and Soviet Union, 8, 78, 116–19,
  161; and USOC, 18, 22–23, 25–26,
  31, 34–35, 38, 44, 80, 112, 136; U.S.
  strategy of, 21–23, 26–27, 30, 34–36,
  39, 41–42, 87, 95, 136; weaknesses
  of, 19, 36, 105–9. *See also,* United
  States
Carter, Rosalyn, 39
CBS-TV, 37, 137, 149
Central Intelligence Agency (CIA), 117
Central Powers, 3
Chile, 70, 98, 147–48, 162
China (PRC), 65–67, 145, 152, 162. *See
  also* Taiwan
Christian Democratic party (West Germany), 59
Christopher, Warren, 18–29, 25, 35, 40,
  44, 99, 107

Civiletti, Benjamin R., 33–34
Clark, Joe, 62–63
Clifford, Clark, 110
Coca-Cola, 83–84, 162
Coe, Sebastian, 56
Coghlan, William, 101
Cold War, 11, 43, 48, 85, 118, 143
collective action, 89–90, 102, 126–27, 139, 152–53, 166
Commerce Department, 41
common market, 52–53, 59, 80, 94. *See also* European Community
Communist party, 78
complex interdependence, 90, 131, 167. *See also* interdependence
Conference on Security and Cooperation in Europe, 145
Congress, 8, 29–34, 38–40, 47, 136, 138
Congress of Sorbonne, 2, 5
Conservative party, 54
corporations, 32, 35, 81, 84
Costa Rica, 77
counter-Olympics, 30, 47, 94, 107
Cuba, 27, 98, 129, 133, 148
Cutler, Lloyd: and boycott, 17, 23, 33–34, 39, 44, 46–47; and Killanin, 50, 158–60; as spokesperson, 20, 80, 108; and USOC, 24, 26, 160
Czechoslovakia, 13

Daume, Willi, 57–58, 101, 143–44. *See also* West Germany
Davenport, Willie, 34
deadline. *See* boycott
de Coubertin, Baron Pierre, 1–4, 14, 154
De Gaulle, Charles, 61
Democrats, 38, 95
Denmark, 53, 61, 96
Der Spiegel, 143
Derwinski, Edward J., 137–38
D'Estaing, Valery Giscard, 60–61
detente, 4, 58, 80, 91, 116, 118, 163
Djibouti, 146
Dobrynin, Anatoly, 112

Eastern Europe, 44, 84, 96, 148. *See also* Soviet bloc

East Germany (GDR), 12, 14, 59, 138, 143, 152
East-South relations, 52
East-West conflict, 12, 85, 103
Edstrøm, Sigfrid, 6
Edwards, Gene, 18
Egypt, 2
embargo, x, 41–42, 161. *See also* boycott
Ethiopia, 153–54
Europe. *See* Eastern Europe, Western Europe
European Community (EC), 52–53, 141, 145
European Economic Community. *See* common market, European Community
European Parliament, 52, 141
Eurovision, 13
Ewald, Manfred, 143

Fahd, Faisal bin, 66
Far East, 72, 157. *See also* Asia
federal district court, 82
federations. *See* national federations, international federations
Fellows, Denis, 56, 142
Fiji, 154
Finland, 61, 101
Ford, Gerald, 97
foreign policy, 129–30
France: and boycott, 45, 52–54, 59–61, 92, 101, 127, 144; national Olympic committee, 54, 59–60, 92, 94, 101, 107, 142, 144; publications, 60, 144; public opinion, 60; and United States, 60–61, 92, 148
Fraser, Malcolm, 70–71, 127
Free Democratic Party (West Germany), 143
free-rider dilemma, 139. *See also* collective action
"Free World Olympics," 47. *See also* alternate event

Gambia, 68–69
Games. *See* Moscow Games
Gandhi, Indira, 146

Gardner-Feldman, Lily, 167
Genscher, Hans-Dietrich, 57, 59, 141, 143, 145
Germany, 1, 3, 127. *See also* East Germany, West Germany
Gorbachev, Mikhail, 88
Gostelradio, 150
governments: and IOC, 94–95; and NOCs, 48, 65, 73, 93, 154; and sport, 9–10, 14–15, 125; and transnational relations, 156, 158–9
Great Britain. *See* Britain
Greece, 1, 45, 62, 86, 98–99, 125, 140

Haiti, 162
Halldorsson, Gisli, 161–62
Hart, Gary, 31
Hazan, Baruch, 149
Heiden, Eric, 10, 117
Helmick, Robert, 30, 36
Helsinki, 2, 11–12, 149, 152
Helsinki Final Act, 145
Hitler, Adolf, 27, 97
Hobbes, Thomas, 157
Honduras, 162
House of Representatives, 30, 34, 38–39. *See also* Congress
House of Commons: Britain, 54–56, 142; Canada, 63
human rights, 52, 69, 113
Humphrey, Hubert, 13
Hungary, 2, 9, 97, 103, 130, 157

idealist beliefs, 98–103, 125–26, 153–54, 157
Image Factory Sports, Inc., 83
India, 67, 110, 146, 154
Indonesia, 146
interdependence, 164–65
International Athletes Club (Britain), 55
International Emergency Economic Powers Act, 35
international federations, 94, 105–7, 139, 154–55, 159
international law, 86
International Olympic Committee (IOC): and alternate event, 106–107; boycott

response, 50, 165; functioning of, 105, 154; international position, 6, 94, 106–7, 124–25, 140–41, 155–56, 158, 166; and Moscow Games, 44, 49–50, 101, 106–107, 111, 129, 132, 134, 140; and NOCs, 5–6, 22, 72, 93–94, 108, 133, 142, 155; and nationalism, 5, 54, 142; and Olympic Games, 2–7, 86, 88, 142, 147, 153, 165; participation policy of, 3, 5–6, 25, 72, 101; 108–9, 149; philosophy of, 4, 51, 111, 149, 153–54; rules of, 50, 86, 93, 108, 131, 139, 146, 149, 155, 158; and Soviet Union, 50, 132, 137, 140–41, 149, 162; and United States, 22–24, 49–51, 106–7, 110–11, 139–40, 158–60, 165; and USOC, 23–24, 30, 33, 38, 50, 111, 134, 140; and various countries, 45, 54–55, 65, 97, 141–42, 147, 165. *See also* Olympic movement
international political system, 89–90, 102, 153, 158
international relations, 131
international sport: characteristics of, xi, 92–95, 102, 106, 153; political significance of, 94, 100, 102, 105, 123–25, 128, 166
Iran, 17, 67, 72, 95, 102, 108–9, 132
Iraq, 2
Ireland, 61, 94, 101, 145
Islamic states, 64, 66–67, 69, 72, 92, 146
Israel, 93, 100–101, 141, 162
Italy, 52–54, 59, 61, 101, 107, 127, 145, 161
Izvestia, 156–57, 161–63

Japan: and boycott, 44–45, 64–65, 67, 92, 145–46; and Manchuria, 153; Olympic committee, 65, 154; Soviet perspective on, 164; and television, 76, 149; and tourism, 150
Jenner, Bruce, 29
Jones, David C., 26, 161
Jordan, 77
journalists, 79. *See also* media, televisior
Justice Department, 33

Kampuchea, 146

Kane, Robert: and alternate event, 30; and effects of boycott, 85, 124; and government policy, 18, 23, 25–26, 29, 42, 112, 133–34, 136; and IOC, 22, 24, 134

Kanin, David, 159

Kennan, George, 129–30

Kennedy, Edward, 95, 156

Kennedy, John F., 133

Kenya, 45–46, 68–69, 109, 147

Keohane, Robert, 131, 139, 152–53, 155, 158, 164–67

KGB, 79

Khrushchev, Nikita, 18, 67, 133

Killanin, Lord Michael: actions of, 140, 154; and Britain, 159; criticism of, 132; and Moscow Games, 4, 51, 101, 106, 140–41, 149–50, 152; and Olympic movement, 4–5, 7, 11–12, 100–101, 130, 132, 140–41, 152, 154–56; and Soviet Union, 149–50, 157, 162, 165; U.S. officials, 49–51, 105–6, 140, 156, 158–60, 164; and USOC, 50, 134, 155; and U.S. policy, 96, 135–36, 139–40, 156–57, 159–60; and West Germany, 143–44, 163–64. *See also* Olympic movement

Koch, Edward, 10, 30

Kremlin: and Afghanistan, 100; and boycott, 17, 19, 78–79; criticism of, 99, 120, 164–65; and Moscow Games, 13, 73, 75–78; and Olympic movement, 117; and sports, 117; strategy of, 70, 77, 108, 116–20, 165; and United States, 40, 118; and Western policy, 80, 120, 127. *See also* Soviet Union

Kuwait, 154

Labour Party: Australia, 148; Britain, 54

L'Aurore, 144

Lake Placid, 10, 13–14, 23–24, 49–50, 55, 66, 86, 107, 110

Laos, 146

Latin America, 48, 70, 72, 77, 147–48

leaders, 12, 14, 115, 119–21, 127–28. *See also* politicians, statesmen

Lebanon, 2

Ledsky, Nelson, 26, 39, 107

Le Figaro, 144

Le Matin, 144

Le Monde, 60, 144

Levin, Bernard, 28

Levi-Strauss, Claude, 41, 83, 151–52

Liberia, 46, 68, 92, 147

Liechtenstein, 62, 138, 142, 144, 154, 166–67

Lloyds of London, 82

Los Angeles, 51, 85–86, 88, 117, 148

Luxembourg, 53, 62

Malaysia, 146, 154

Manchuria, 153

Martin, Douglas, 55

Mathias, Bob, 11

Mayer, Albert, 130

Mecca, 146

medal count, 5, 12

media, 7, 13, 37, 41, 75, 77–78, 125, 128. *See also* television

Medina, 146

Melbourne, 2–3, 6–7, 9, 97, 103, 130, 157

Menghua, Li, 65–66

Mexico, 70, 154

Mexico City, 6, 141

Middle East, 110

Milburn, Rod, 163

Miller, Donald: and alternate event, 30; and effects of boycott, 33; and government policy, 22–26, 32, 35, 42, 120; and IOC, 22, 134

Moi, Daniel Arap, 68

Mollet, Raoul, 141–42

Mondale, Walter: and boycott, 19, 28, 39, 45, 84–85, 166; and Soviet Union, 8; and USOC, 26–28, 31, 44

Monoco, 62, 138, 142, 144, 166–67

Montreal, 2, 7, 62, 64, 69, 72, 75, 84, 92, 97, 132, 147–48, 150, 162

Morgenthau, Hans J., 132

Morocco, 68

Moscow Games: and Afghanistan invasion, 13, 45, 115–16; and Asia, 64–66, 147; cost of, 13, 76, 81; effects of boycott upon, 72, 75–76, 79, 84, 87–

Moscow games (*continued*)
88, 150, 152, 162; evaluation of, 43,
69, 75–77, 84, 87–88, 152; and inter-
rational federations, 155; and IOC, 44,
'+)–50, 101, 106–7, 111, 129, 132,
134, 140; and media, 13, 41–42, 76,
149–50; Muscovite opinion on, 163;
and protests at, 72, 148; and selected
NOCs, 53–54, 61, 93–94, 101; and
Soviet strategy, 17, 75, 77, 120; and
tourism, 81, 83–84, 87, 150; and
United States, x, 22, 27, 38, 40, 47–
49, 78, 110–13, 123, 139; and U.S.
business, 40–41, 81–83; and various
countries, 62, 68, 70–72, 147, 161–
62; and Western Europe, 45, 54–56,
60–61, 101, 107, 142, 144, 166–67.
See also boycott, Olympic Games
Moscow Olympic Organizing Committee,
24, 50, 82–83, 85, 106, 117–18, 150–
51, 165. *See also* Moscow Games,
Novikov
Moynihan, Daniel Patrick, 38
Mugabe, Robert, 147
Munich, 2, 7–8, 12, 100–101, 141, 149
Muskie, Edmund, 126, 150
Mussolini, Benito, 153
My Olympic Years, 160–61

National Citizens Coalition (Canada), 63
national federations, 94, 105, 142, 146,
155
National Olympic Committees (NOCs):
and boycott, 54, 72, 94, 165; characteristics of, 6, 22, 62, 73, 77, 93, 106,
108, 124, 154, 156; functioning of, 5,
11, 105; and governments, 22, 48, 73,
107–8, 154; officials of, 101, 108; and
Olympic movement, 3, 6, 94, 98, 108,
133, 142, 149, 152, 155; selected, 53,
57, 65–66, 71, 80, 93, 141–42. *See
also* boycott, Moscow Games
nationalism, 4–6, 12, 54, 86, 141–42,
162
national security, 26, 91. *See also* boycott
national security council, x
national sports festival, 29–30

national sports festival, 29–30
Nazi Germany, 3, 71, 97, 103, 127
NBC-TV, 41–42, 81–82, 84, 137, 149–
51
Netherlands, 2, 9, 53, 61, 94, 97, 101,
141, 144
New China News Agency, 65
New York, 10, 30, 100
New York Times, 37, 99–100, 148
New Zealand, 2, 97, 147, 154
Nigeria, 46, 68, 92, 109–10, 147, 154
NOCs. *See* National Olympic Committees
non-Olympic competition, 107
nonstate actor, 2, 130
North Atlantic Treaty Organization
(NATO), ix, 52, 56, 91, 127, 142,
145
Norway, 62, 138, 142, 144, 166–67
Novikov, Ignati T., 85, 162–3
Nye, Joseph, 131, 155, 158, 164–67
Nyerere, Julius, 46, 110

Oerter, Al, 11
Ohira, Masayoshi, 64–65
Okita, Saburo, 65
Olympic Boycott Recovery, 83
Olympic Charter, 61, 93–94, 155, 162,
164
Olympic committees. *See* national Olympic committees
Olympic movement: components of, 72–
73, 92–94, 106, 154–55; and boycott,
51, 84–86, 88, 156; future of, 49, 85,
88, 99, 101, 107, 134; ideals of, 66,
92, 125–26, 157; and IOC, 98, 100–
101, 152–53, 165; political significance of, 6–7, 85; reform of, 85–86;
threats to, 30, 47, 49, 71, 85, 111,
134; and United States, 2, 46, 50–51,
78, 84–86, 97, 99, 103, 105, 116,
152; and various countries, 45, 65, 69,
109, 117, 159
Olympic Solidarity, 149, 165
Olympic Trust (Canada), 63
Oman, 146
Onek, Joseph, 23–24, 26, 49, 107, 111
O'Neill, Thomas P., Jr. ("Tip"), 26, 35

Ordia, Abraham, 69. *See also* Supreme
   Council for Sport in Africa
ostpolitik, 57
Ovett, Steve, 56

Pakistan, 66–67, 146, 162, 164
Palestinian Liberation Organization
   (PLO), 2, 100–101
Palmer, Richard, 96
Pan American Sports Federation, 140
Paraguay, 162
Paris, 1
Parliament: Britain, 54, 56; Netherlands,
   61; West Germany, 58
patriotism, 11, 28–9, 36. *See also* na-
   tionalism
Pauls, Rolf, ix
Pepsi-Cola, 41, 83
Persian Gulf, 133–4
Peru, 70, 147
Philippines, 77, 146
politicians, 10
politics, 9, 98–99, 101, 153–54. *See
   also* sport
Portugal, 52, 61
Pound, Dick, 63
Pravda, 129, 143, 162–64
propaganda: and Olympic Games, 130,
   165; and Soviet Union, 21, 43, 75, 78,
   87, 116–19, 149, 162–63; Western
   perceptions of, 63, 127
"Prisoner's Dilemma," 152–53
public opinion: and Carter boycott, 22,
   25, 36–40, 42, 62, 80, 82, 114–15,
   138; influences upon, 37, 39–40, 136–
   37, 166; international character of, 98–
   102, 125–26; significance of, 11, 36–
   37, 62, 98, 114, 166; in various countries, 58–60, 62–64, 70–71, 143–44,
   146, 163; and 1980 Winter Olympics,
   131–32
Puerto Rico, 71–72, 101, 131–32, 154

Qatar, 146

Reagan, Ronald, 95–96
realist, 9, 113, 126, 131
"recognition day," 32

Republican National Committee, 38, 95
Rhodesia, 100, 132
Rodgers, Bill, 118
Roosevelt, Julian, 49, 96, 110
RTB Olympic Travel, 82–83, 151
Ruffini, Attilio, 52, 145
Rumania, 148
Russia. *See* Soviet Union

Sakharov, Andrei, 37, 52, 59, 144–45
Samaranch, Juan Antonio, 152
Saudi Arabia, 66–67, 146
Schmidt, Helmut, 57–60, 91, 143–44
Sears, Roebuck and Company, 35
Senate, 38–9. *See also* Congress
Senegal, 46, 68
Seoul, 88
Shagari, Alhaji Shehu, 46, 110, 147
Shcharansky, Anatoly, 129, 137
Shibata, Katsuiji, 65
Sierra Leone, 69
Singapore, 146
Smith, Red, 37
Smith, Tony, 153
Social Democratic party (West Germany),
   57, 59, 91
South Africa, 2, 46, 97, 103, 109, 132,
   139, 147, 159
South Korea, 162
South Vietnam, 161. *See also* Vietnam
Sovetskaya Rossia, 163
Sovetsky Sport, 85, 118, 142–3, 151,
   161–62, 164
Soviet bloc, 84–85, 96
Soviet Union (USSR): and Afghanistan,
   ix, 18, 22, 40, 45, 52, 58, 63, 109,
   111–15, 119, 146; and Asia, 64–67;
   and boycott deadline, 18, 112, 115–
   16, 120–21; and Canada, 62–64; and
   Carter, 39, 79, 113–14; Communist
   party handbook, 7, 76, 117, 149–50,
   162–63; constitution, 8; criticisms of
   United States, 96, 116–18, 156–57;
   and Cuba, 129, 133, 148; economic
   effects of boycott on, 41, 81, 83, 87,
   141; and hosting of Games, 4, 13, 37,
   75–76, 78–79, 84, 99–100, 132, 149;
   and Hungary, 97, 103; and IOC, 50,

Soviet Union (*continued*)
    107, 132, 137, 140–41, 149, 162; and
    media, 13, 77, 150; and NOCs, 73,
    120; and Olympic movement, 1–2,
    11–12, 76, 100, 117–18, 152; political
    effects of boycott on, 17, 76–79, 87;
    and propaganda, 21, 43, 72–73, 75,
    78, 87, 116–19, 149, 162–63; and
    public opinion, 78–79, 117–18, 162;
    response to boycott, 43, 70, 75, 77,
    108, 116, 147, 149, 164–65; and
    sport, 7–8, 12–13, 78, 84, 117–18;
    and Third World, 67, 70, 148–49; and
    United Nations, 148; and U.S. busi-
    ness, 40–41, 81–83, 150–52; and
    U.S. policy, 38, 43, 49, 77, 95, 110,
    114, 137–39; and Western Europe,
    52–54, 56, 59–60, 91, 144, 161, 163.
    See also Kremlin
Spain, 2, 61, 97, 145
spectators, x, 12, 38, 75, 79, 125
sport: common view of, xi; distinct from
    politics, 9; domestic uses of, 9–11,
    14–15; historical uses of, ix, 98; inter-
    national uses of, ix, xi, 4, 7–9, 11–
    14, 54, 132; and nationalism, 5, 9–11;
    obstacles to political use of, xi, 124–
    28, 167; organization of, 105, 123–25;
    perspectives on, 12, 100–101, 157,
    162; political appeal of, 9, 12, 14,
    123–25, 128; political characteristics
    of, 9, 12, 14, 38, 88, 123–24; and So-
    viet Union, 78, 118; and United States,
    135–36. *See also* Olympic movement
Sports Illustrated, 10, 37
State Department, 26, 40, 45, 47–48,
    72–73, 107–8, 127, 161
statesmen, 124–26, 127–28, 166–67
state system, 89–91, 127, 158. *See also*
    international political system
Strauss, Franz-Joseph, 57
Sudan, 154
superpowers, 67, 69, 85, 147, 152, 163
Supreme Council for Sport in Africa, 68–
    69, 147
Sweden, 61, 101, 145, 154
Switzerland, 2, 61, 97, 101, 130, 141,
    145
Syria, 146

Taiwan, 2, 65, 72, 108–9, 161
Tanzania, 46, 68, 92, 110
television, 22, 41, 48, 76, 80–82, 136–
    37, 150. *See also* media
Telling, Edward R., 35
terrorist, 7, 100. *See also* Munich
Thailand, 77, 146
Thatcher, Margaret, 45, 55–56, 124
Third World: and Canada, 63; character-
    istics of, 153; and China, 67; and Ja-
    pan, 67; and Olympic participation,
    152; and Pakistan, 66; and Soviet
    Union, 76, 120, 149, 165; and United
    States, 21, 44–46, 60, 90–91; and
    Western Europe, 148
Thompson, Kenneth W., 132
Time, 148
Tokyo, 152
tourists, 81–84, 87, 150–51
transnational relations, 90, 94, 101, 106,
    155, 158, 166
Trotter, Neville, 54
Trudeau, Pierre, 62–64, 92
Tucker, Robert, 139, 153
Turkey, 66, 133, 141–42

Uganda, 147
Unesco, 51
United Kingdom. *See* Britain
United Nations, 38, 49, 73, 77, 100,
    145, 148
United Press International, 162
United States: and Africa, 46, 67–69, 97,
    139; and alternate event, 29–30, 47–
    49, 139; and Asia, 64–67, 103, 132,
    156–57, 161; and Australia, 71; and
    boycott deadline, 18, 47, 111–21,
    164–65; and boycott strategy, 21, 40,
    43–44, 72–73, 91, 93, 108, 113, 115,
    120, 139; boycott impact upon, 19,
    79–84, 119–20, 161; and Britain, 53,
    56; and business, 40–41, 83; and Can-
    ada, 62, 64; criticism of, 73, 105,
    108–111, 116, 118–22; foreign influ-
    ence of, 36, 73, 79–80, 93, 127; and
    France, 60–61, 148; and IOC, 22–24,
    49–51, 106–7, 110–11, 139–40,
    158–60, 165; and Latin America, 70,
    133, 148; and Moscow Games, 22, 27,

39, 42, 76–77, 84, 112, 138, 140, 149; and Olympic movement, 2, 46, 50–51, 78, 84–86, 97, 99, 103, 105, 116, 152; problems of, 19, 91, 93, 95, 97–98, 101–3, 128, 139, 158–59; and public opinion, 38–39, 80, 114–15; and Puerto Rico, 71–72; Soviet view of, 43, 116–18, 161–62; and sport, 13, 37, 132, 135; and Third World, 21, 44–46, 60, 90–91; and United Nations, 100; and USOC, 22–26, 31–36, 124, 155; and various countries, 161–62; and West Germany, 56–59, 91; and Western Europe, 52–53, 62, 76, 80, 90–91, 108, 127. *See also* Carter

United States Olympic Committee (USOC): and alternate event, 30; and Amateur Athletic Act, 35, 135–36; and athletes, 23, 31–32, 124, 134; character of, 33, 124, 135–36; and government pressure, 22–23, 26–27, 32–35, 38, 40, 124, 134, 136, 161; impact of boycott upon, 31–33, 42; importance of, 21, 25, 34, 44; influences upon, 27–29, 31, 36, 38, 40, 42; and IOC, 22–24, 27, 33, 49–50, 134, 140, 155; and Pan American Sports Federation, 140; response to boycott, 22–27, 29, 34–36, 42, 134, 155; Soviet perspective on, 116–17, 161; vulnerabilities of, 32–36, 136. *See also* Carter

United States Olympic Council on Sports Medicine, 100

Upper Volta, 68

Van Agt, Andreas, 144

Vance, Cyrus: and boycott, 18, 23, 27, 39, 44, 99, 112, 114, 116, 119, 140; and IOC, 49–50, 110, 160; and per-

manent site, 86; and Soviet Union, 13, 49, 140; and USOC, 26, 33; and Western Europe, 53, 141

Vietnam, 17, 98, 103, 146. *See also* South Vietnam

Waldheim, Kurt, 77

Wales, Jane, 26

Wall Street Journal, 150–51

Washington. *See* Carter, United States

Wellbeloved, James, 54

Wells, Debbie, 163

Western Europe: and Afghanistan, 52; and boycott, 45, 52–54, 59, 61–62, 72, 127, 141, 163, 167; characteristics of, 51, 141; and national federations, 142; NOCs, 53–54, 61, 107, 119–20, 142, 156; and Sakharov, 52; and Soviet Union, 91, 163; and United States, 44, 48, 70, 80, 90–92, 96, 111

West Germany (FRG), 52, 57, 91, 143–44, 166–67; and boycott, ix, 45, 53, 56–59, 91, 111, 143, 145; and Killanin, 140; and media, 76, 149–50; and Munich Games, 8; NOC, 54, 57–59, 141, 143–44; and Olympic tourism, 150; significance of, 59, 141, 147; and Soviet Union, 91, 162

Western Olympic committees, 155–56

Western states, 125–26

Wexler, Ann, 35

Winter Games, 157

Yankelvich, Tatyana, 37

Yugoslavia, 11

Zaire, 147

Zimbabwe, 147